BREAKING THE LIMITS

The Sam Ermolenko Story

BREAKING THE LIMITS

The Sam Ermolenko Story

BRIAN BURFORD
AND
SAM ERMOLENKO

TEMPUS

First published 2003

Tempus Publishing Limited
The Mill, Brimscombe Port,
Stroud, Gloucestershire, GL5 2QG

British Library Cataloguing in Publication Data.
A catalogue record for this book is available from the British Library.

ISBN 0 7524 2585 4

Typesetting and origination by Tempus Publishing Limited
Printed in Great Britain by Midway Colour Print, Wiltshire

CONTENTS

ACKNOWLEDGEMENTS

I would like to express my thanks to Shirley Tillitson for all the long hours she put in when she was helping me with the revisions and editing of this book. I would also like to express my thanks to Keith Huewen for the foreword. A special thanks to my team, Warren, Steve, Barry and Jake, who were there from that first phone call and all the way through to the conclusion – we shared many a laugh talking about the old times. And, of course, Brian for all of his hard work and long hours he put into constructing the prose – it's a good job you knew my career so well!

This book wouldn't have been the book it is without the help of my sister Melody and my wife Shelley, for looking through all the photos and the family archive. I would like to express my gratitude to all the people who are mentioned in the book for their help throughout my career – but especially, Peter Adams and Chris Van Straaten. However, a very special mention must go to Trevor Harding for his help and kindness when I had my accident. I would like to dedicate the book to Trevor, my whole family and all of my friends who have supported me through the good times and the bad.

Sam Ermolenko

I would like to express my thanks to Nicholas Ermolenko for sending the fascinating chronology of the early life of the Ermolenko family, and to Peter Adams for his memories of that day at Herxhiem. Big thanks to James, Kate, Becky and Gina at Tempus Publishing.

Thanks also to Sam and the rest of his family and friends for making the writing of this book an enjoyable task. I would like to dedicate this book to my mother for her patience, support, and for generally putting up with me – thanks.

Brian Burford

FOREWORD

BY KEITH HUEWEN

Sam Ermolenko is one of speedway's enduring stars – a former World Champion who has raced at the top of his sport for longer than most competitors could find the energy, not to mention the talent to do so. He also bears the scars, and remembers the pain of serious injury with a unique matter-of-factness. He is an American, and proud of it, with the kind of personality you would expect from a West Coast racer: fiercely competitive, yet laid-back and extremely personable.

As speedway racing was largely a European sport, Sam was forced to move from California with his wife and young family to realise his ambition. Would he make an impression on the rest of the world? It would be a journey of unparalleled success, culminating in 'Sudden Sam' winning the ultimate prize in speedway – the World

Championship. Since that success, Sam has become one of the most recognised and popular speedway racers of his generation, and is also respected as a team manager, race tuner and engineer within the sport.

I have been privileged to know personally some of the biggest names in motorcycling and, since retiring as a competitor, have covered all the top two-wheeled sports as a television broadcaster. It was at Sky Sports, with the exciting all-new Speedway Grand Prix series scheduled alongside Moto GP and World Superbikes, that I was first introduced to Sam. Unlike the other two-bike disciplines, speedway was still raw and a little wild. Sam had some great stories – none of them broadcastable! It was immediately apparent that there was more to Sam Ermolenko than just a superb talent on a speedway bike … and you just couldn't help but like him either!

Since that Speedway Grand Prix, Sam has combined his talent on a 500cc methanol-burning bike-with-no-brake with a blossoming career in the UK as a television presenter, studio guest, and race commentator for Sky Sports and Channel 4. There is no doubt that Sam's star is ascending.

Like you, I look forward to reading of Sam's exploits over the years. His life has been one of excellence, and worthy of accurate documentation. If this book is half as eloquent as the man himself, then sit back and enjoy the ride.

INTRODUCTION

When I first followed up my initial approach to Sam about collaborating on a book, one of his mechanics, Steve Langdon, answered the telephone. When I introduced myself and mentioned what the call was about, he said of a book about Sam: 'You'll need a lot of pages!' I soon discovered what he meant, as Sam's story is one that befits a rider who has been battered and bruised in his pursuit to become the best.

It was on Tuesday 4 October 1983, a typical, cold autumn evening at Reading, that I first met Sam Ermolenko. He appeared in the Marcus Williams Benefit Meeting – which was a three-team tournament especially staged to raise funds for the seriously injured Williams – and he scored 4 points. Unbeknown to me at the time, a few days earlier he had already made his debut for Poole.

I must have been one of the few in the stadium that night who had heard about him, as I was a subscriber to the American publication *Speedway Magazine*. He had qualified for the US Nationals, and all the reports suggested that this was another talented Californian. After the meeting I had the opportunity to speak to Sam, and I discovered that he was very approachable and friendly. But that is Sam. It didn't matter how busy he was, he always had time to say hello, sign an autograph and ask after your well-being. And he didn't forget you. It was little things like this that would set Sam Ermolenko apart from the majority of the riders.

Speedway is a relatively simple form of motorcycle racing. It first began in Australia in 1923, and arrived in Britain in 1928. A race is usually of a four-lap duration, and an average speedway meeting lasts around 2 hours. There are usually four riders in a race, and in Britain and Europe the riders' bread and butter is club racing – when the riders are brought together to represent a team. A team encounter can last from 13 to 18 races – depending on what competition and country you are in at the time. A simple scoring format of 3,2,1,0 is used, but a rider can score bonus points when he finishes behind his team-mate for the benefit of his side. For example, if Sam finished behind his team-mate, he would score 2 points, but would get paid for 3 and also receive an extra point on his total. This would not count in the team's overall score, but this is where the term paid maximum/win applies. Therefore, it's a term used to describe a rider who hasn't been beaten by a member of the opposition.

The referee has control of the meeting and enforces the rules. A rider must be still at the start, and he is not permitted to touch the tapes – if he does, he will be excluded. A rider can also be placed on a two-minute time allowance at the referee's discretion, which means that the rider has two minutes to be at the start line or be excluded. This was introduced to prevent riders from holding up the show, and from playing psychological games with their opponents.

The bikes themselves are run on methanol fuel, they have no brakes, no gears and they are single cylinder 500cc machines that are capable of 0-70 in less than five seconds. When compared with Moto GP or Superbikes, this speed might not appear to be fast, but when you realise that the riders are racing on a shale-covered oval track and in a confined space with only a wire fence for safety, you soon realise the danger involved.

Sam's career is littered with stories of injuries which would have put the brakes on many riders' careers. A glance at the photographs will illustrate the horrors that he has endured to get to the top, but his determination, bravery and resolve make him one of the greatest riders of his era. If it hadn't have been for those crashes, he could well have won the World Championship more than once, but his list of honours reveals that there is very little that Sudden Sam hasn't achieved as a speedway racer – which shows that a winner never quits.

As well as racing, Sam has also begun to carve out a successful career as a commentator for Sky TV and Channel 4, and he also provides the viewers with his expert analysis. I am not at all surprised that he has become such a success at this, as he is both articulate and forthright with his opinions. He has always been a good ambassador for the sport, ready to provide the media with a picture or a quote. He is comfortable doing this, and it all helps lift the profile of the sport and also his own image.

I have followed his career from his early BL days right the way through to where he is now. He is without question one of the greatest riders I have ever seen, and yet for all of his success and 'star' status, he is still the same friendly man he was during that October night at Reading.

Brian Burford
March 2003

One

DOCTOR, DOCTOR

Sunday 16 July 1989: Herxheim, West Germany.

There was a sharp poke in my stomach as the drugs entered my body, and my senses dragged me back to consciousness. My ears were assaulted by the sound of sweeping helicopter blades which stifled the pop music that was blaring out of the public address system. I could see the blue sky above me; and then suddenly concerned and worried faces came out of the blue and were staring at me! I was aware of activity and people talking around me, but the drugs had transported me to a place where I felt mellow – I called it the comfort zone. I felt myself being lifted carefully onto a stretcher and then I was strapped in. There was a feeling of some urgency about what they were doing, and I realised that I had been on the ground and injured in some way. I was finding it difficult to breathe through my nose, but before I knew it, I was picked up and carried over to the waiting helicopter. The sweeping of the

13

blades grew louder as we got closer, and the rhythmic sounds they created became the soundtrack for my transportation. This noise only seemed to add to the drama of it all – here I go again.

When they slid me into the galley of the helicopter, I became stuck halfway in. The belts that were strapping me onto the trolley, or the stretcher, had got caught up on something inside the chopper. They were having problems pushing me all the way into the helicopter, and this caused a flurry of activity. A man behind me was trying to drag me in and another was pushing me. I looked down to try and manoeuvre the strap out of the way as this was a natural reaction to help out, but I wasn't really helping them, as all of sudden I felt myself slide the rest of the way inside. The door slammed shut … and we're off. I slipped away into unconsciousness again.

Sam Ermolenko was airlifted by helicopter from the track to a nearby hospital in Karlsruhe. He had been competing in the World Long-Track semi-final, when he was involved in a horrific crash. The red lights instantly came on, and the marshals on the infield frantically waved their red flags to signal to the remaining riders that the race had been stopped. Wolverhampton's team manager, Peter Adams, was in the pits as part of Sam's team, and he had been involved in speedway and long-track racing in one form or another for many years. Anytime now he was hoping to hear the applause from the crowd that greeted a rider when they wearily got to their feet following a heavy crash like this one – perhaps one of the most welcome sounds in racing.

But consternation descended upon the pits as the rest of the riders and mechanics began to realise that one of their own was hurt – and he wouldn't be getting up this time. Germany's three-time World Long-Track Champion, Egon Muller, underlined the serious nature of it all when he turned his back on the scene and walked away – he couldn't bear to look. Worried glances were exchanged among the various racing crews in the pit lane, as while they may be rivals, they are also a band of people who are brought together by the risks inherent in their sport.

Five minutes had passed but there had been no applause. Adams realised that he wasn't going to get up. He left the pits to make his way to the scene to check on his health. The pits were situated on the first turn at Herxheim, while Sam's crash happened on turn three, which was over the other side of the oval track. By the time Adams reached the starting gate, the helicopter had swooped in and settled on the centre green. As he closed in on the scene, the atmosphere was frantic and heavy. The noise of the helicopter dominated the area, and then he saw that Sam was already on the stretcher and the crew were hurriedly carrying him to the waiting air ambulance. After a moment or two, the door thumped shut, and the chopper left the ground.

Everyone in the stadium, spectators, riders, mechanics, and officials, all anxiously gazed skyward as this popular rider was taken away for emergency treatment. For Sam Ermolenko, and all who were associated with him, the drama would not unfold on a race track, but a hospital emergency room instead. The next few hours would be very long indeed.

I could feel myself being pulled out of the helicopter and being manoeuvred into the hospital – it felt like a very short helicopter ride. The trolley wheels chugged along, and they were clanking their way over the bumps and it was a bit uncomfortable. I was aware of people, medics around me, as I was pushed along on the trolley. Then we rushed into a long room and we came to a stop. Although I don't remember it, it must have been during this time that they took an X-ray.

As I was lying there, all I could see was the white of the room, the ceiling, and the lights. I was just looking around taking it all in and trying to figure out what was happening. A nurse came to my side and she began removing my necklace and whatever else I had on. I was still having problems breathing so I asked her for a tissue, but she didn't quite understand so I made a gesture at my nose and then she understood. She handed me a tissue and I began blowing but it wasn't clearing very well. As I removed the tissue I noticed that it was bright red, and this was why I was having so much trouble breathing – it was clogged up with blood! The nurse quickly removed it from my hand and replaced it with another one. I blew again, but it had been bleeding a lot. Therefore, I cleared out my nose as best as I could. The nurse remained by my side and every once in a while she wiped my face, and she was just taking care of me as I began to take in the location and the situation I found myself in.

It was a long room, with two doors at either end of the room. When I looked down through my feet, I could see through one of the doors, where there were two or three doctors, and I could also see the glare of the X-ray wall. They were all studying what they were going to do. I was a bit scared, and very concerned. It was clear that they were all discussing what they were going to do to me. With the delay, all I could do was think about what they had planned. There was no one who could speak proper English and all I could hear around me was German. What had happened, and what was wrong with me? No one was able, or willing, to tell me at this point. I hoped that there wasn't very much to worry about; perhaps it would be one of those things that would turn out to be just bad bruising or something. It happens, so why not to me this time? I hoped that it wouldn't be serious. But the way that they were studying the X-rays and talking to each other, it was making me feel very anxious. I wanted to know what the problem was.

Then a nurse came to me and asked me to sign a form. In broken English she said: 'Sign, sign please.'

'What's wrong with me?' I asked, 'I'm not signing anything until you tell me what's wrong with me.'

'You must sign. So we can operate,' she persisted.

I was aware of the fact that whatever I signed in hospital gave them the authority to do what they wanted to do, but nobody could tell me exactly what was wrong with me! I had been here before, I knew the procedure and I wasn't about to make that mistake. I wasn't going to consent to anything until I knew exactly what was wrong.

'I'm not signing anything until I can talk to somebody who can speak English.'

She disappeared and I was left there with my thoughts – and I was feeling quite apprehensive. I was left with just my imagination for company, and I wondered what they had planned for me. And, because of the communica-

tion problem, I feared the worst. This was not a good time to be waiting for news. I needed to talk to someone, anyone, who could speak English.

Finally, another person came in, a man this time, in a white coat, and he came from the direction of my feet. He looked like a doctor, not a nurse, because of the coat he was wearing, and he came up to me and said in broken English that I had to sign a form so they could operate on my leg.

I asked: 'How bad is my leg?'

The doctor replied: 'Very bad; very, very bad.'

And I panicked … The only thing I could think of at that point was unless I could speak to somebody who could speak English and could tell me what the heck was going on, I wasn't going to sign anything. Because of this man's broken English, I felt that I could wake up with my leg cut off! I needed more information.

So I said: 'No, no, man, come on, what's wrong with me? I'm not signing anything until I know how bad my leg is. You're not gonna amputate or cut my leg off or whatever.'

And the doctor shook his head, raised the palms of his hands in a calming gesture and said: 'No, no, no. Not so bad.'

At last he made it clear to me, after asking him, that I wasn't going to wake up with one leg and it wasn't that bad. So I signed the form, and they began preparing me to go through to surgery.

Peter Adams wasn't allowed into the emergency room, but he did get to speak to one of the doctors. This doctor was an experienced surgeon who had treated many accident victims from the Autobahn – Germany's notorious motorway – and he admitted that he had never seen a leg injury like it. He illustrated the injury to him by withdrawing a pencil from his pocket and, with the pencil in his hand, he rested on a table and broke it into several pieces. When he withdrew his hand, supported with an open-hand gesture, he remarked in his broken English, 'that is what the X-rays show.' Privately, the doctors thought that Sam would never walk properly again.

Sam underwent a six-hour operation, having broken his right leg, his wrist and also his nose. He had been riding particularly well that year, as he had just won the Overseas Championship at Coventry and the Coalite Classic at Bradford. A month before, he had won the American Final for the third successive year – thus establishing himself as the USA's undisputed number one rider. He was looked upon as the rider who was most likely to end the Danish domination of the World Speedway Championship that had been shared between Erik Gundersen and Hans Nielsen since 1984. But, at this point, the 1989 World Championship bid was most definitely over and, furthermore, there were some lingering doubts about another attempt in 1990.

I woke up in recovery, and found that I had broken a bone in my hand as well, but that wasn't a major problem – neither was my nose, which had been broken too. However, I was heartbroken to see all this metal work on my leg. I had an external fixation going right down the top of my femur, the big bone, right across the knee down to my shin bone – it was all fixed. I had broken my leg in over twelve places, and they were multiple fractures from the middle of my femur down to the middle of my shin. It wasn't a pretty sight. This external fix had to be put on because I had a big laceration on the inside of my knee. They had to take a skin graft from my thigh, and that had to heal before they could actually do any more surgery on my shin.

I admit there were a lot of tears, but I was more worried about the pain that my family were going through. There I was, in a foreign country, injured again, and my wife had to fly in and I had a young family too at that time. What must they have been thinking? What messages were they getting? Were they getting the same kind of messages that I was getting about cutting my leg off? I'm not sure who made the call to my family, whether it was Peter Collins or Carl Blomfeldt.

I was sat in the German hospital for two weeks. The wound was healing where they did the skin graft, but they were constantly treating it. However, they were not really worried about the bottom half of my shin at this stage, the tibia. They said that it was okay for the time being, but it needed to be operated on. But before they could operate, the wound had to heal.

The World Long-Track Championship is a discipline of racing that is particularly popular in Europe, and is basically a big-track version of conventional speedway. It was a lucrative form of racing for the top riders, especially as during this period the Polish and Swedish Leagues had yet to open their doors to foreign riders. There are fundamental differences in the bikes, but because the disciplines are so similar, the riders can slip between the two fields with relative ease.

At this stage, America's record in the Long-Track Championship is best described as reasonably successful, as only Shawn Moran had provided the country with their sole world title success in 1983. But Sam had won the 1987 and 1988 US Long-Track Championship, and he was considered to be the country's best hope of individual glory in both competitions. He was bidding to qualify for his second World Long-Track Final – he had made his debut in 1988 at Scheesel, Germany, where he finished in eleventh place with 13 points – when the crash occurred.

In 1989, I was trying to be competitive in long-track as well as speedway. At the time, we didn't have the luxury of riding in Poland. So in order to be as active as you could, you had to do long-track and grass-track for the extra income. The whole idea behind it was to earn extra money as well as being successful. I did one year in 1988 in the World Long-Track Championship and got to the final and finished eleventh. I analysed the reasons why I didn't do better, so with the help of my team we built on that for the following year. We built a good fleet of bikes and engines in order to be competitive, but above all I wanted to win the double World Championship – that was my goal.

The impact and the severity of the accident can be indicated by the fact that Sam has no memory of the actual crash. He can only recall that, as it was an afternoon meeting, there was dust coming off the track, so they watered the surface to keep the dust down. The television cameras were there, and the event had attracted a lot of media attention, so they were watering the surface heavily. As a result, the surface was quite wet. Sam went to the event with his team of mechanics and Peter Adams – who was the team manager of Ermolenko's British League club, Wolverhampton. He had already won a meeting at the venue earlier in the season, so he was feeling quite confident.

It was a warm day and I was just enjoying the sunshine. There was a big swimming pool at this track as there was a big athletics sports club there. I remember having a dip before the meeting. I was happy and was feeling really positive and confident about qualifying.

I was not dominating the meeting, but I was doing well enough to have a good chance of qualifying. I went out there for my third race, and I think I was in third position. Even now, I don't know for sure why I crashed. I only know what other people have told me: that my front wheel hydroplaned going into the corner, and I just lost my front end and I slid out. There was no fence at this track: it's a wide track, but it was surrounded by grass of the same width as the track itself before it met the fence. As I slid out, I probably thought that I wasn't going to be in anyone's way out there because I was way off line. But that wasn't the case at all; I was hit – and hard.

No one can tell me what actually happened. I met up with Egon Muller later in my career and he said: 'Oh hell, that was a bad one.' He said it was so bad that he didn't even want to look. He was stood in the pits, and I crashed in turn three and the pits are situated on the first turn, and as all this was happening he didn't want to know – he just walked away. I was told that it was Henka [Gustafsson of Sweden] who hit me; I heard that he had broken his thumb in the crash. But he didn't come to see how I was when I was in hospital, but with the schedule a speedway rider has, I can understand why. To this day, I don't know what happened; all I know is that I was hit – how, why, what, nobody can tell me. I've never seen any footage of the crash, even though the television cameras were there – nobody will show it.

The first reports of the crash that appeared in the British speedway press suggested that Sam had laid down his machine. However, information about the accident was not forthcoming, except that the opinion was that it was a bad crash. Even now, it seems that the organisers prefer to draw a veil over the incident.

It was 1976 World Champion Peter Collins – who was a spectator at the event – who told Sam that he was in third place when he slid off. He said that the other riders following him managed to avoid him, but the last rider was filled in from the wet shale and he ran over the fallen American. *Speedway Star* stated that it was Sweden's Henka Gustafsson who crashed into Sam, and another report had an unidentified mechanic of Sam's saying that there was a big gap in front and behind the American before he slid off.

Chris Van Straaten, who was the promoter of Wolverhampton which was Sam's British League team at the time, gave this reaction to the news of his number one rider's accident in the magazine *Speedway Mail*:

'The general opinion is that he was very fortunate to get out of it. Most of his injuries will mend in time, and we are thankful that he still has his mind. The problems of Wolverhampton Speedway are secondary to Sam's well-being.'

Wolverhampton was already hit by the injury to fellow American Ronnie Correy when the news came through that Sam was also injured. The club were chasing the league title, and covered the absence of their number one rider by utilising the guest facility. They maintained their challenge, but in the end the loss of their inspirational captain was too much and the Championship went to Oxford – other club honours also slipped from their grasp.

Sam's horrendous crash and resulting injuries had touched the hearts of speedway fans from all over the world – and other people from the world of motorcycle racing. The support he received over the coming months would be vital if he were to make a full recovery and race again in 1990.

While I was in Germany, Otto Schroeck and his family were great to me. Peter Schroeck [Otto's son] used to race and his brother Alex Schroeck used to be my mechanic in Germany and he was with me at the meeting. The Schroeck family were a great help as they made sure that the right people were around me. There was another guy named Rainer who lived quite close to the hospital, and he was my saviour. He spoke English and he gave up a lot of his time to be at my bedside. Every day he would come to visit and he made sure that all my requests were met – whatever it was, he was always there for me. I've lost contact with him since all that, but he was my saviour. Between this gentleman and the Schroeck family, I was well looked after and I had a lot of German fans at the time.

But the cards and the get well wishes were unbelievable, there were stacks of them, and I had a lot of time to read them. At that point I didn't really know if my career was over, or if I still had a chance of racing. To be fair, I didn't really think about if I would or I wouldn't race. All the get well wishes were saying stuff like 'can't wait to see you back' and 'get well soon', and Wolverhampton were right behind me too. Peter Adams was at my side when it all happened, and then Peter Collins came to see me in the hospital, and all this boosted my morale.

Then one day I had a phone call. I shared a room with two other people, but they were rarely in the room with me. The phone got passed around the ward until it eventually found me, and to my delight it was my buddy from Australia, Trevor Harding. I did a season racing for him in Australia in 1988/89, and he invited me back. He basically invited me over even though I was injured. The sunshine is the best healer in the world, and he suggested that I go over and take advantage of that. I found that very inspirational at the time, and it was a big boost to receive some support from him.

Between Trevor's invitation and all these good wishes, I thought 'well, what have I got to lose? I'm not going to get back on my feet right now and go back to work.' I had just bought a house in England and my kids were in school there, so I wasn't just going to pack up. I decided there and then that I was going to concentrate on getting back on a bike. What else was I going to do? And that's what I did. I turned my attention to getting fit again.

After spending two weeks in the German hospital, Sam took some advice from the medical staff and returned to Britain. He was escorted to the Manchester Royal Infirmary and underwent more surgery. The wound from the skin graft had healed sufficiently to be able to plate the lower part of his leg. Now they were able to remove the external fixation, but both the femur and tibia were now plated. This was done with two plates and twenty-seven screws, which held it all together. But once again, during his two weeks in the Manchester hospital, he was regularly visited by well-wishers.

Among the staff in the hospital in Manchester was a porter who was a Belle Vue fan and who is now working at Belle Vue Speedway. He came in and introduced himself and said, 'You don't know me but I'm a speedway fan' and that was really nice. During this time, the motorcycle racing Grand Prix was going on in this country, and Wayne Rainey's mechanic came in to see me and introduced himself, and said:

'How are you doing? I heard you were in a pretty bad crash, and I wanted to come and give you my support. I'm over here with Wayne Rainey, a fellow American, and I'm a good friend of Wayne's from Sealbeach, California, and we're in town and I just wanted to come and see you.'

I thought that was great, as Sealbeach was my local beach. But that was pretty good to receive that support, and we communicated a further two or three times after that. I know that Wayne had a bad accident in 1993 and he's now paralysed. A big bummer!

Carl Blomfeldt was a great help too and a great asset, because he helped me to sort out my equipment and generate some income – we sold everything. That supported me through the bad times, and that's how I was able to get through it. Carl was the best thing that ever happened to me at that point, and he really looked after me. Everything he did for me was spot on; he kept on top of things for me with check-ups on my progress. I also had great support from my family, and nobody discouraged me from wanting to race again. I met a lot of people; even the people in the gyms in my local town, everyone was very supportive.

By now he was free from the risk of any infection from the skin graft and he was released. He made his first public appearance at Bradford for the Inter-Continental Final – a meeting that he was due to race in – on 13 August. He was still very weak and managed to get around on crutches, but he had made good progress when one considers that only four weeks had passed since the crash. He was also seen in the Wolves pits, offering support to his team-mates in their quest for club honours.

But he needed the warm sunshine to aid the healing process, and he returned to California, where he sought the opinions and advice of other doctors. It was while he was in the USA that he heard about the horrific crash that left Denmark's triple World Champion, Erik Gundersen, with multiple injuries that almost cost him his life.

Earlier that season, a young rider, Paul Muchene, was killed at Hackney. Other injuries to top riders like Jan O. Pedersen, Armando Castagna and Tommy Knudsen and the high-profile accidents experienced by Sam and now Gundersen, meant that the sport came under the scrutiny of the media for its safety record. Gundersen's crash was described as the 'blackest day in British speedway', and it was second only to the tragic death of Peter Craven in 1963. It was unwelcome publicity, but highlighted the dangers that all the riders faced.

In the meantime, Sam's club, Wolverhampton, arranged a benefit meeting for him on 16 October 1989, called the Sam Ermolenko Gala Night. It was a match between a Rest of the World team and Ermolenko's USA Select – the latter won 49-41. Top scorer for Sam's team was Greg Hancock with 15 points, and the former Wolves number one and Sam's fellow countryman, Bobby Schwartz, also flew in from the States to ride in the meeting. It drew a big crowd and Sam was reported as saying that he was overwhelmed by the support of the public.

That was Chris's idea. There are some promoters who think of themselves, but that's not Chris Van Straaten. I didn't ask for that. He said, 'I'll do it for you.' He knew that I actually helped Wolverhampton out in the early days, and that was probably his way of paying me back. That was unexpected – very much unexpected.

Sam was having X-rays everywhere he went, in an attempt to get back on the race track as early as he could. But then a problem was discovered.

What I discovered was that the bone wasn't really healing. The plate that they put on my thigh left a big gap, and I had a bit of bone put in there that was donor bone to fill the gap from the original operation. But it wasn't knitting together very well. After about three months, there still wasn't any evi-

dence that the bone graft was filling the gap properly. It was knitting up on one side, but not the other. I was concerned because I was still on crutches and they told me not to put any pressure on my leg – and this was after three months, and I still wasn't getting anywhere!

My American doctor, Glen A. Almquist – he was a doctor who specialised in sport and regularly treated the LA Lakers and other speedway riders – thought that the metal work was keeping the bone apart, and it required stimulation to get the calcium to build up. The metal work was too stiff and it was keeping the bones apart. I was going through the normal process of healing, but when I was having my check-ups they were worried because the bone wasn't healing yet. And he asked me what my other doctors thought. I hadn't seen the German doctor since I left the hospital there. But the doctor in England said, 'Well it's a bit of a chance, why don't you think about giving up racing and calling it a day? That was a pretty bad break and if I was you, I wouldn't race again. Perhaps you should think about a new career.'

Well, I didn't accept that. I kept chasing doctors and went back to see Doctor Almquist. He believed that I should seriously think about having the metal work removed to help the bone to heal, but not yet – soon. And he asked me when I wanted to ride. I told him, 'Well, my focus has got to be the Overseas Final. Hopefully I can get through the American Final, but the Overseas is my goal.' And he said that the normal healing time for a femur break like I had was a minimum of a year. The crash happened in July, and the Overseas Final was scheduled for June. So that was my goal.

The 1990 Overseas Final was scheduled to take place in Coventry on 24 June. Before that, Sam would have to qualify from the American Final, which was set for 2 June. It was going to be a race against time for Sam to be fit enough to participate in the 1990 World Speedway Championship. Each week of rehabilitation was a vital cog in his wheel of progress.

I took up Trevor Harding's offer to go to Australia, and I went there to see another doctor. On the advice of the doctor in Manchester, he recommended a good doctor in Australia, who had trained in England and was practising over there. He said: 'Go see Myers; he's a good orthopaedic doctor.' I made contact with Doctor Peter Myers, and I made arrangements to see him when I got there. I hopped on the plane in November, and I found that Doctor Myers shared the same opinion as my doctor in America. I took all the photographs with me that showed that my leg wasn't healing, and he agreed that it was best that we removed the metal work. So I had the operation in Australia. After spending a month and a half out there, and taking full advantage of the warm sunshine, combined with a lot of training and rehabilitation, the bone was already showing calcium where it hadn't been showing before – the advice was right.

At last Sam Ermolenko had finally begun to show some progress on his long road to recovery. There was still a lot of work to do, but although he had plenty of help and encouragement around him, the one thing he didn't expect was the lack of support from his own federation – the American Motorcycle Association (AMA). Their indifference to the plight of their top rider was destined to throw a spanner in Sam's recovery plan, and wreck his chances of racing in the 1990 World Championship.

Two

HELL ON WHEELS

Sam was christened Guy Allen Ermolenko, and was born on 23 November 1960, in Maywood, California, USA. Maywood is in LA County, Los Angeles – the City of Angels. Guy, or Sam as he was soon to be called, was the second child born to Nicholas and Charlotte Ermolenko. He has a sister, Carolyn, who is two years older, and Sam was followed by Melody in 1964 and then his brother, Charles, in 1968.

Sam's grandparents had fled turbulent Russia, which was in a period of massive social and political upheaval following the revolution of 1917, and moved to Harbin, Manchuria, China. This is a much-disputed mountainous region that was once under Russian military control before Japan took over in 1932, and was finally handed back to China in 1950 – but even today it is an area that is still a source of political tension.

'My father, Victor, was born in Belarus, and my mother, Helen, was born in Siberia,' says Sam's father, Nicholas Ermolenko. 'Her father, Alexander, was Russian, but Antonina, her mother, was Korean and she was adopted by a Russian family and brought to Russia. Antonina was born in Seoul, Korea. Her mother was a concubine and her father was the Emperor Kojong of Korea [1864–1907]. She was given away for adoption because she had a slight deformity in one of her legs which meant that she walked with a slight limp.'

Nicholas Victor Ermolenko was born on 9 March 1933, and the whole family moved to Shanghai in 1940. He attended a French school, where most of the students were of Russian descent, and the school work was carried out in either French or Russian – and sometimes in English too. He also attended a school run by Jesuit fathers, where all the lessons were conducted in English. During the Second World War, Japan occupied Shanghai and as a result the port was bombed by the Americans.

'After the war, my parents got divorced,' says Nick, 'and my older brother and I lived with my father, and my one sister lived with my mother and grandparents. Shortly after the divorce, I ran away from my father and lived with my mother. In the evenings, I attended a privately-run school where I studied radio electronics, and in my spare time I used to make money by running behind rickshaws and pedicabs that were transporting US soldiers and sailors. As I ran, I used to yell: "No mama, no papa, no whiskey, no soda, give me a dime". That worked OK, but I got more money by showing the servicemen where all the brothels were located! Sometime in 1947, my father sent my brother to Russia without telling anyone. That was a big shock. Later, I heard that my brother had died. However, when my mother passed away a few years ago, my daughter, Melody, found some letters that indicated that my brother was still alive. She got in touch with the Russian Red Cross in Moscow, and they found my brother. With a little help from me on occasion, he is now doing okay.'

The turbulent political upheaval that the family had left behind in Russia then came to visit them during one night in 1949.

Communism sneaked into the city like a cloud in the night, and the Ermolenkos heard of its arrival through the frightening sound of gun fire. They awoke to find Chinese troops marching around the streets with the red star of Communist China emblazoned on their hats.

'We heard that some general sold out to the Communists,' Nick recalled. 'Soon after, there were many trucks full of people with shovels and picks heading to some unknown destination. I think we knew where they were heading. The foreigners in Shanghai were not harmed unless they had political backgrounds, but the Chinese wanted all the foreigners out.

'Later that year we went to live in a refugee camp. This was really a staging centre for evacuation under the auspices of International Refugee Organization (IRO). The Philippine Islands were accepting the majority of the refugees, but there were about three hundred people left in the camp when the repatriation stopped. I suppose the Philippine Islands took as many people as they could, but we were part of the people that were left behind. Therefore, we all had to try and make our own way out of China.

'We all sat around and waited for miracles. Then one day, late in 1951, Belgium granted ten blank visas. The requirements were that you had to be young, strong and able to work. I was a prime candidate. In February 1952, ten of us left for Belgium.

'We arrived in Brussels and spent the first few nights in a Catholic charity house,' says Nick. 'This was arranged by the Tolstoy Foundation, which is a Russian welfare organisation. In a few days, we were all working. The majority went to work in the coal mines, one in a Volkswagen garage, and one got a job in the fair challenging people to knock him out in two rounds. Another got a job out of town in Luxembourg, one got a job in a store and I started work as a typewriter mechanic – going to different offices and maintaining the typewriters.'

But he wasn't a typewriter mechanic for long. When he received his first letter from his mother, she informed him that a former schoolfriend was married to a colonel in the US Army. He was attached to the US Embassy in Brussels as a communications advisor.

'I met these people and the colonel introduced me to an electronics firm where I got hired as a radio mechanic,' Nick said. 'He also helped me in many ways. One of the most interesting things at work was participating in building the first television station in Brussels on top of the Palace of Justice building.'

In late 1952, he was able to sponsor his mother so that she could come to Brussels with his sister. In early 1953, the colonel informed Nick Ermolenko that there had been an act of congress which had been passed that allowed displaced persons to join the US Army and fight in the Korean War (1950-53). This act was the 'Lodge Act' – so named after Henry Cabot Lodge junior, who was the US representative to the United Nations – which was designed to allow stateless aliens the opportunity to enlist in the regular US Army. President Eisenhower proposed an army consisting of 250,000 anti-Communist young men from behind the Iron Curtain, and their reward for successful service in the army was American citizenship. His military and political advisors all supported the proposal because they had to enlist 'too many Negroes', according to General Collins. Another general coldly said that he was 'very much interested in any plan, in which other nationals do some of the dying instead of American boys.' The period of service was five years, and the colonel made arrangements for Nick to go to Germany and sign up for the US Army. But before this, Nick made arrangements to sponsor his grandparents so that they could join the family in Brussels – but he had already left for Germany by the time they had arrived.

'I was in the US Army in Germany for about a month and a half learning the rules and practiced marching, saluting, and the ways of the army before we were shipped on a boat to US for basic training. Meanwhile, the Korean conflict came to an end.

'We arrived in New York and got shipped to Fort Dix, New Jersey, for training. After sixteen weeks, I was transferred to Fort Benning, Georgia. I was honourably discharged at the end of my term in September 1958. While I was in Fort Benning, I attended a radio maintenance course for sixteen weeks, and I received top honours. I also met the famous Hollywood actor, Audi Murphy. I was assigned to Company B, 3rd Infantry Division, and this was his company when he distinguished himself in the Second World War.'

In 1956, Nick married Charlotte and they had their first child, Carol, in 1958. After his discharge from the Army, he stayed in Columbus, Georgia, where he opened a television repair shop. Furthermore, each school day he commuted approximately 30 miles to attend the Alabama Polytechnic Institute (API), later renamed Auburn University.

My father met a man called John Snider, and they opened up a shop together in Georgia repairing televisions. My mother's brother lived in California, and he told my parents how much better things were in California in relation to work and jobs, when compared to Georgia. Therefore, the decision was made to move to California in the mid-1960s ('Go West, my Son') where John and my father opened up another television repair shop in Los Angeles. It had a glass front, but both the Snider and Ermolenko families were able to live together in the shop as there was an apartment at the back.

I was born in Maywood Hospital, and when my proud parents brought me back from there, John Snider asked them what they had named me, and they replied: 'Guy Allen Ermolenko'. And straightaway John didn't think that it suited me, and he said: 'Nah, he looks like a Sam to me,' and it stuck. Therefore everyone, including my family and friends, has always called me Sam, ever since I was an infant.

The Ermolenkos were a working-class family, and while they were not poor, they did not live the popular image of the American Dream. They worked hard for what they had, and their father in particular, with his practical skills, was adept at being resourceful. In 1961, their parents both applied to work at North American Aviation Aerospace Group – later named Rockwell International, which is arguably one of America's most important development and scientific companies.

Its beginnings can be traced as far back as 1880, but it was the engineering specialist, William Rockwell, who founded the first

Rockwell Manufacturing Company in 1925. A look at the company's 'family tree' reveals that Rockwell has been associated with, and absorbed, some of the most innovative and inventive brains – and companies – during the twentieth century. These included the Collins Radio Company, which not only produced the first radio that was used by Admiral Byrd during his 1934 expedition to the South Pole, but also the first modem – which was the size of a refrigerator and weighed 700lb.

Nonetheless, it was in 1967 when Rockwell Standard and the North American Aviation joined forces to form North American Rockwell. This company was instrumental in the most significant moment in the history of mankind, when they produced the Apollo spacecraft that took three astronauts to the surface of the moon in 1969. Also during this year, Nicholas was able to sponsor his mother and his sister so that they could join him in America.

My father was an electronic engineer and he did a lot of work on the Apollo project, and my mother also worked there in the parts department as a parts expediter. He received a BSEE degree in 1964, so my father was a very clever man – too clever to be considered a normal person! For example, in our garage he had scopes and electronic machines, whereas in other people's garages you would find the normal stuff like tools, paint, and so on. That sort of thing went way over my head, but he was also good with his hands and he would fix things around the house. But as far as his skills went as an engineer, he was very clever. One of the giant hangers was situated next to the road that led to Sealbeach, and sometimes the doors were open and you could see a big section of the Apollo rocket – and that was quite exciting as a young boy to see this massive rocket that would eventually carry the first men to the moon.

In 1964, my family moved into a new five-bedroom house in a new development. There were a lot of young families in this neighbourhood, and there were plenty of things to do and a lot of mischief went on. My mother always said that I was the happy-go-lucky, adventurous type. Even as a young boy, I wanted to hang out with the older kids in the neighbourhood as I wanted to try and get a ride on their bikes. Most of them were older than me, but I used hang around, hoping I would get to ride one. Even then it seemed a cool thing to do and it was all I wanted really, so I used to ask them if I could try their bike. Most of the time they would tell me to get lost, but eventually one of them would say: 'OK get on.' The bikes were too big for me, but I would persevere with it and learn to ride them.

As we were a working-class family, I never experienced that all-American image of waking up on Christmas morning and finding a brand spanking new bicycle waiting for me. But as my dad was really good with his hands, he chose to restore an old bicycle; he gave it a paint job and, voila! I had a bike – pretty cool, really. That was my own bike, and now I was free to ride around with all the other kids in the area.

My mother's supervisor at work was a man called Bill Qualls. Our families used to meet up regularly, and they had kids that were the same age as us. So we used to go over to their neighbourhood and they used to come over to ours. As kids we used to tear up the area and have a lot of fun, while our parents used to play cards or whatever adults used to do at that time. During these discussions, my dad and Bill came up with an idea of opening a motorcycle business. My dad had an interest in motorcycles and he used to ride them, I guess, but it was Bill who had the vision for the business. He was the real motorcycle guy of the partnership, so I think it may have been my father's investment that married the partnership and, of course, his clever brain that brought them together on a business level.

This was 1970 and my dad continued to work at Rockwell, as they put an advertisement in the paper saying that they would buy any kind of motorcycle in any sort of condition. So my dad would bring these motorcycles home and store them in the garage. At the weekends, it turned into an adventure for all of us kids in the house, as he would open up the garage door and pull out these bikes. We would strip them down (I say we, but it was Dad until he found something that we could do) and clean them up, and this was a regular thing as every couple of weeks more motorcycles would arrive. Eventually he built a big shed in the back yard, and the bikes were stored in there. This made us quite popular with the other kids in the area because we had all these motorcycles and other cool things going on. However, we would often get in the way as unless we were doing something in there for him, we had to get out and leave him alone. That was what the *atmosphere was like around our house at that time: it was quite exciting and all the local kids in the area thought we were cool.*

This was my beginning with motorcycles. As all these bikes were being put in the sheds; well, this was heaven! Every day after school we would go and spend time in the sheds and dream about riding them. There was one bike, which I put my claim on as my bike, a Yamaha 80, an old-style box-frame bike from the '60s and it was a cool bike. I remember the other kids in the neighbourhood would come over and check out what was happening – including those older kids whose bikes I wanted to ride.

Then one day my father was building this huge trailer – it looked huge to me at the time. It was a wooden box trailer with drop-down doors on three sides of it, and I asked him what he was doing. 'Well, all these parts that we had been working on for the past month, I'm going to put them in here and tow them to a swap meet site and sell them,' he said. In the US we have drive-in movie theatres, and at the weekends they double as a swap meet – or car boot sales. It's an organised market place where you reserve your space for the day; you pay your fee, drive in and set up your display or spot, which was usually the size of two car spaces. People would come in and wander around and barter with you over the price to get what they wanted. As my dad still held his job with Rockwell, the weekend was dedicated to the partnership with Bill. They would display signs that said 'Machining available – and Parts for Sale'. They did the machining in Bill Qualls' garage, and they had a couple of machines to re-bore cylinders and so on. So my dad was trading at the swap meets and running advertisements in newspapers about servicing engines, while Bill was developing the engineering side. That's was how the business started, and they formed a small company called 'Q & E Cycle and Engineering'.

Eventually, the family decided that we were going to go out riding in the local deserts. We would pack what we could, sleeping bags and ice coolers, and put it all in a truck, and we would also pull a caravan behind. Some of the other neighbours used to go too. We didn't have many bikes then, but Bill had a couple of machines, one of which was a little Honda Q50, which was the first motorcycle I ever rode. It wasn't mine; it belonged to Bill's son, Vance. Vance and I were the same age, and we were always talking about getting all the bikes that were in my dad's shed up and running, so we could ride them in the desert. My dad, Bill and the older guys, used to go riding while we just played in the sands. We used to take turns to ride the Q50 and mess around, and my sister, Carol, used to ride it too. We shared this bike while all the time we were hoping that my dad would get the more powerful 80cc out of the shed and up and running, or even the Yamaha 100.

All the parents used to sleep in the campers, but we kids used to sleep in sleeping bags under the stars. We used to have a little fire going and there was a lot of mischief that used to go on. There was usually about eight of us, and there was no more than a couple of years between us. We didn't have proper motorcycle boots as such, but we had something like Army boots. Basically, whatever we could get our hands on we had, because we were bikers now. Vance's younger brothers, Curtis and Jeff, were running around in these boots, while Vance and I were dreaming under the stars. One of them was adventurous enough to walk through the fire with these boots on. It wasn't a big fire – it was just coals keeping us warm. Vance and I were watching them doing this and we start thinking mischievous thoughts – as you do at that age. We had these squirt guns, so we filled them up with gasoline, and as they walked through the fire we spurted the contents onto the fire and it would flare up! That caused a bit of a panic at first, but Vance and I was just rolled about with laughter. Looking back on it now, it was a bit dangerous but we didn't know that then – we were just kids.

Riding motorcycles in the deserts is commonplace in California. Vance was Sam's best friend, and in the mornings they would take the bike and head off into an area on their own and ride it. But Sam was already showing signs of attacking the track and being aggressive with the machine. Bill Qualls noticed that they would go off together and share the Q50, but he was getting concerned that they were coming back with the bike damaged in some way. He eventually worked it out that it was Sam's aggressive riding that was causing the damage and banned him from riding it! Undeterred, what they did was to go a little further away from the camp and then Vance would let his friend ride the bike when they were out of sight.

On one occasion, with Vance riding pillion, they were riding over bumps and fooling around. They were laughing and got out of control and crashed again. As they dusted themselves down, they looked at each other, and then the damaged bike, and wondered who would take the blame this time? They went back to the camp and, although Sam wasn't supposed to have been riding the bike, it seemed that Bill had worked it out that it was Sam who was riding when they crashed and not his son. Of course, it wasn't always Sam who crashed, but because he was the one who was always associated with aggressive riding, he would get the blame. Then one day, Bill Qualls got the Yamaha 100 going for Vance, and the cool machine was wheeled out for desert action.

Our parents and the older guys would go out into the hills and have hill-climbing contests. Bill always had the cool bike, and he would be the most aggressive of the older guys that were out there. He would always go the highest up the hill, and he was the daredevil of the adult riders.

On one occasion, we were all standing around watching them go up and down this big hill, and Vance decided that he was going to climb this smaller hill on the 100 – which was nearby to where we were watching the adults. As he was going up the hill, he lost his balance and fell over, and I ran over to help him. The way the battery was mounted on this bike, and with the bike lying on its side, there was petrol coming out of the carburettor. We were about to pick the bike up when the battery sparked and mixed with the petrol – it was flash, whoosh, fire! We backed off and wondered what the hell was going on, so we were vigorously trying to put the thing out and shouting: 'Help, help, Dad, the bike's on fire!' We were panicking and trying to put it out, but the oldies on the other hill were laughing at us! It didn't matter to them because it cost them nothing, but to us it was a disaster. They're telling us to get away from it, as we were trying to put it out with the sand. We stepped back about 20 feet and then whoosh, it's a blaze! It burnt down to a black mass of a shell. We thought that it was the coolest bike to ride and it was gone! That was the end of our summer riding. But at least I could say that it wasn't me this time, as they all saw that it was Vance who was riding it.

Sam's father was always making something and after the success of the trailer, he was then inspired to attempt a more ambitious plan.

It was a plan that unwittingly started off a chain of events that came to characterise the Ermolenko family.

The truck my father had at the time was a '59 Chevy, and he acquired a camper to slide onto the back of the truck. I remember him bringing it home and parking it up on the driveway. I originally thought that he had bought it so that we could go riding in the desert and we wouldn't have to use the trailer. But that wasn't his plan; his plan was to restore it and take the whole family back to Georgia to see our other relatives – which was a good 4,500-mile round trip. I remember him working inside of it, and he put in new panels, re-upholstered it and turned it into a nice camper.

In the house at this time there were my parents, us four kids and my grandmother lived with us as well. When you consider how far we had to travel, the camper was ideal. We made the trip to Georgia, but the return journey was a different story. Mom and Dad had some friends up in Maine, and they decided to leave us kids with my grandparents in Georgia while they travelled up to Maine to visit them. While they were there, my father bought a Ford because the Chevy was causing problems. He transferred the camper onto the new Ford but this was a tighter fit, so he drilled some holes in the floor and anchored the camper with some bolts and now the camper was in its place. It seemed perfectly solid – or so he thought.

On our return trip, we were about a hundred miles from home driving down the highway, and my parents were sat up the front, with my dad driving. The rest of the family were in the back sleeping. I was sleeping in the part of the camper that came over the top of the cab of the truck. Along this particular road, the area is vulnerable to strong cross winds, and we caught one of these strong blows. Even though the camper was wedged in the back and bolted, the wind was so strong that it literally ripped it out of the truck!

My father must have felt the force of it as he was driving, and I am sure he caught sight of the camper as it was flying out of the truck and crashing onto the road and down the embankment. It was utter carnage as the camper just broke up on impact. I found myself on the road, still in my sleeping bag, with a lorry heading toward me! Thankfully, it managed to stop within a few feet of me. My dad pulled up and told my mother to stay by the truck as, with a feeling of dread at what he might find, he made his way back down the road to see the outcome of the accident. At this time of the morning there wasn't a lot of traffic on the road, but people stopped to see if they could help because there was wreckage everywhere: glass, blankets, basically everything that was in the camper was spread across the side of the road. The rest of the family were strewn across the embankment, and they were in various states of shock and injury. There was a lot crying and screaming, and the sheer magnitude of what had happened was difficult to take in. Thank God everyone was still alive. I had a small cut on my back and face, but my sister broke her collar bone and there were a lot of cuts and bruises. My dad checked us all over to make sure there was nothing really serious, and then he salvaged what he could, and loaded it up along with us into the back of the truck. We were all huddled up with blankets and a rug as protection against the cold as we made our way to the hospital – which was still a distance away. That was start of it all. I don't think my father was too popular with my mother at that point.

Q & E Engineering increased its business to the point where they had to move to new premises, and, in 1971, they moved to a new location in Anaheim, which was one block away from Rockwell – this business is still thriving in 2003. Sam's father used to pass the business on his way to work, and he would drop by and repeat the process at the end of his shift. The amount of business had increased to such a degree that Qualls was able to leave Rockwell and run the engineering shop. Nicholas Ermolenko built the shop by putting in new electrical fittings, benches and other things, while Qualls saw to the motorcycles. At the weekends, Sam would also help his father in the shop, and was fascinated and thrilled to see all the bikes. As far as his friends were concerned, Sam was now associated with motorcycles, despite the fact that he still didn't possess one of his own.

Meanwhile, Qualls was able to provide his two sons with bikes, but because Nicholas Ermolenko was busy working at Rockwell and attending to all the requirements behind the scenes of the business, he wasn't in the same motorcycle circle at his business partner. Nonetheless, there were a lot of people in the area who had bikes, and they used to ride them in the fields surrounding the neighbourhood. The fields had jumps as well as a makeshift track, and every weekend there was someone out there riding a bike.

Just as Sam had to steal a ride on a bicycle when he was a young boy, he now found that he was doing the same thing with the more powerful motorcycles. However, it was easier this time because they all knew that his father was involved with a motorcycle repair shop. Sam was already displaying his natural talent, and to the casual observer it was clear that he was the best rider of the group. It was a fifteen-minute walk from his home, and on the way there they would pass a petrol station and a 'stop and go' supermarket. This became a meeting place for the young bikers and they would fill their bikes up with fuel, and then push the bikes across the road and into the field and ride them for the rest of the day.

Happily, there weren't a lot of houses in this area, but as this became a regular thing they did receive some complaints. It was in these fields where Sam developed his skills. He rode a Hodaca 125 that a neighbour had and, although it was big for him, he managed to master the bike and became a very skilful rider.

As with many boys of that age, Sam was doing a paper round to earn some money for himself. He was making good money by doing two rounds, and with assistance from his father he was able to reduce the amount of time it took to carry out the deliveries.

I had two rounds, which included my estate where I lived, and the town houses behind our estate, so I had a lot of houses to cover – 85 on my estate and around 100 town houses. After school the papers were dropped off for me, and I had to fold them and put rubber bands around them and put them in my bags. I would put the bags around the handlebars of my bike, do one side and then come back, load up and go out and deliver on the other side.

My dad could see that I needed some help carrying these papers, so he built me a three-wheel bicycle. He took the front end off an existing bicycle and bent the frame to a different angle. He bent up some tubes and welded it together, added two wheels and attached it to where the handle bars use to be. In the construction of the frame he placed a piece of plywood on the base of the front, so you could sit two people on there and give them a ride around if you wanted too. We made a frame box section that sat on the front of this and I could stack the papers in it. Now I was able to double the amount of papers that I could carry compared to my bags, and it was quicker. However, you had to be skilful to ride this bike, because if you turned too far one way then you would fall over, so you had to keep the balance just right.

Every once in a while, my brother and my sister used to sit in the front of it when I wasn't doing the paper rounds and I used to wheel them around. Charles thought that this was great fun. He always wanted to come with me and he would start crying if I wouldn't take him, and then one day my mom said: 'Go on, take him with you.' I had just returned to top up with more papers, she was having a coffee with one of the neighbours, so I agreed and Charles hopped on. I had to even up the load, so I had the papers on one side and my brother on the other side. As I distributed the papers I had to move Charles into the centre to maintain my balance – and he had to stay there otherwise I could lose it and fall over. This was especially so when I went from the road and onto the sidewalks. However, because of this, as I went up onto the sidewalk, I lost my balance and Charles slid to one side and we fell. The whole box shifted and his leg got trapped between the bar and the ground as we fell.

He started crying and screaming out in pain, but as I'm in the neighbourhood he was a little embarrassing for me. I tried to get him to get up, but he was still crying. I wanted to do some more deliveries, but he was making so much noise that I scooped him up and took him home. As I pulled up, my mom could hear him crying and she came to the screen door and said: 'What's wrong?' I told her that we fell, and she came out to see him. But as she picked him up, she felt his leg and said: 'Oh my God. Oh no, come on, hospital, now!' The neighbour that was with her helped us and it transpired that he had broken his leg. He was in traction for a couple of weeks. When he came out he was in a body cast from his chest down, and he was only around three and a half years old.

In 1975, Sam's parents separated and he discovered that he was the man of the house. All the children lived with his mother, and she relied on Sam and his sister, Carol, to take care of their younger sister and brother when she was at work. Unfortunately, because his father was always working, he wasn't the easiest of men to spend time with. However, Sam would make good use of the garage and the tools that were there to work on his bicycle, or perhaps someone's motorcycle. When his father came home at the weekend and wanted to know where his tools were – because they weren't in the correct place – he soon discovered that it was his oldest son who would know their whereabouts.

Charles Ermolenko, who would be known as 'Dukie', received a brand new bicycle one Christmas morning. One day he was out riding around with the rest of the children in the neighbourhood, and was watched by his elder brother from the front yard of their house.

He was about six years old at this time, and our house was situated on a long street with lots of other streets coming off of it. I could see him from our house, and he was being chased by some of the other kids for fun. There was a car parked by the road and he rode his bike off the kerb and rode straight out into the path of an on-coming car and bam! He was hit by the car and he was sent flying through the air thirty feet down the road, and his arms were flapping as he hit the ground. As his bike was swallowed up underneath the car, the vehicle screeched to a stop in the middle of the street. The driver got out and she was hysterical. Charles came to rest outside our neighbour's house, but I was already running towards him.

When I got to him, I couldn't even think, my mind was racing with different emotions. As I looked down at him I asked him if he was all right, and his eyes opened and looked up at me … and then they just rolled back. I thought he was dead. I turned around and walked over to the grass, and fell to my knees. I was devastated. I couldn't believe it. The driver was still screaming, and the neighbours were all rushing around and there was a lot of panic and concern in the atmosphere. And then through all this, I heard another yell. And boy was I pleased – it was Duke who was screaming! Thank God, he was alive after all. I ran over to him and by now the ambulance had arrived. Duke had broken his legs again and was in another body cast.

As far as his mother was concerned, she must have been wondering just what was happening in her life. After the camper accident, there had been a series of events that had hit the Ermolenko family very hard. Following the separation from her husband, life had not been easy, and the injuries sustained by her youngest son only seemed to drive home the difficulties. But she bravely battled on, and the family continued to rally round and help each other.

At the age of fifteen, Sam Ermolenko's interest in motorcycles became even stronger when he worked in his father's shop. He would come home from school, get on a bus and ride over to the shop and work there for a few hours – during the summer, he would work there full-time and he was placed on the pay roll. Then when his mother finished her shift, she would pick him up and they would go home together.

Vance Qualls also worked there in the evenings and they had light duties, such as sweeping the floors, moving the motorcycles around and generally keeping the place tidy. As time went by, they progressed to other jobs within the business. Sam would greet the customers and book in work, and he would also work on the internal parts of the engines. Meanwhile, Vance concentrated more on the machining side of the business. But in his spare time he would go out and ride motocross. All three of the Qualls boys had motocross bikes, and they would go off in the van and race in some meetings. As the Q&E van was visible at the race tracks, this brought in more work.

Unfortunately, Sam couldn't afford a bike of his own, and although he was working at Q&E, Qualls felt that it was Nicholas's responsibility to get his son a motorcycle. Therefore, perhaps with some persuasion from his mother, his dad bought Sam a two-year-old Yamaha 125 that enabled him to go with the Qualls to the meetings.

This was in 1976, and my father came with us to the track for the first time that I rode the Yamaha. He could see that I was safe to ride the bike on my own and he was happy with that. Therefore, all I had to do was get over to Bill's house at the weekends and I would travel with them to the motocross meetings. I did pretty well and managed to win a couple of trophies.

It was one of these early successes which prompted Sam to make a romantic gesture to a young lady who would eventually become his wife. He was appearing in a 250cc race in Escape County, and at this age he was still too small for his feet to reach the ground when he was aboard a 250cc motorcycle. Therefore, to maintain his balance at the start line, he had a milk crate placed next to him on which to rest his foot so he could keep in balance.

Shelley recalls: 'I kind of had two moms as I became very close to a lady called Lynda Curry, who I used to babysit for, and I became one of the family. I remember I drove up to watch the racing with my sister in a Monte Carlo car that I borrowed from her. I watched Sam racing and he passed one of the other riders for the lead. But as he passed the rider, he pulled a wheelie and the sun was shining on him. And then as he continued, he was still pulling wheelies and sunlight seemed to follow him. I thought that he was just made for the bike because he was so natural, and he would have been a World Champion in motocross, if things had worked out for him. After the race he gave me the trophy that he won, which was a nice gesture, and that was the start of our relationship. He was small and I thought that he looked about twelve! But all of sudden he grew after he had his accident. When I returned from the race meeting, I got into trouble because the car was filthy from all the dust and dirt.

'Later I worked in his father's motorcycle shop as a delivery driver. I used to pick up and deliver cylinder heads and all that sort of thing. So our relationship continued to grow and I've stood by him ever since.'

Vance and I became really good friends, as we were both doing what we always wanted to do. Bill could see that I was pretty good, and I was probably the best rider out of all of us — although Jeff was really good on the 80cc. Inspired by my success doing motocross, I had this dream that I wanted to take part in the Golden State Series, which was a winter series that started in January. I would be sixteen in November, so I could get a full licence and drive myself to the tracks. I was earning a wage at my dad's shop, and I wanted my dad to help me with the finance for buying a truck. Part of my plan was also to buy one brand new motorcycle for that season, so I was building myself up to ask my dad for his help.

It was something that I had to do for myself, as although I worked at Q&E, Bill wouldn't help me with this. He would buy his sons the bikes, but then it was up to them to produce the goods. But I knew the situation, and I realised that to make this plan happen, I had to make the decisions. I talked my mother into buying a van so that I could go back and forth to the races, so when I got my full licence at sixteen I could use the van to travel to the races.

I was really serious about doing this, and I prepared for it by getting myself fit. I used to go jogging on a regular basis, and at work we used to compare and talk about our training routines. One of my friends used to cruise in his van with the side door fully open and the stereo pumping out a good beat of music. I was really encouraged by everyone around me, as Bill and some of the others seemed to think that I had a lot of ability. With all this support, I felt that I could do well in the series, and I was determined to make a good impression as I felt that this was where my future was. I was confident about my own ability, and this was my dream.

During the summer of 1976, Sam had by now got a partial motorcycle licence so he could legally ride bikes on the road. In the USA, at the age of fifteen, a young rider can obtain a permit to ride a bike by filling out a form. There are restrictions on this, however, as the rider is not permitted to ride at night. To acquire a full licence, the rider is required to take a test. This allowed Sam to ride to and from his place of work, and therefore enabled his mother to change her shift from days to nights.

Most people in the neighbourhood knew that the Ermolenkos had a motorcycle business, and they were used to seeing Sam around. Therefore, he became the motorcycle guy in the area. However, one the employees in the 'Stop and Go' store knew that he could fix bikes, so he asked Sam if he could have a look at his Honda 125.

He couldn't get the bike to run that well – there was something amiss with the carburettor. I loaded the bike up into the back of the van and my mom drove me to the shop, and we unloaded the bike and she carried on to Rockwell. I worked on it and I got it running. This was 9 December, so I had my licence to ride at night now, as I was sixteen.

I had finished the bike and I was riding it on my way home. I hadn't got more than two blocks away from the business, when I came over the freeway, across a bridge and down to a set of traffic lights. A car was coming in the opposite direction to make a left-hand turn, and he didn't see me. He didn't give way to me at all, and I ran into the side of him. There was nothing I could do about it, and I was thrown from the bike and onto the vehicle. My head smashed into the roof line and the momentum carried me over the top of the car and I landed heavily on the other side.

The accident happened near where his parents were. Sam's father had made a flat in the building where the business was, while his mother was at work. His father recalled that when he arrived at the scene, his son was trying to get up. His mother was contacted at work by a friend, and she thought, given the accidents that had occurred of late, that it was some kind of cruel prank. This sort of thing couldn't happen again. But it was no prank; her eldest son had been hit by a car and he had been taken to hospital. She was given a lift to the hospital so that she could be at her son's side.

On arrival, all she wanted to do was see her son. It was her mother's instinct to be there to support him. While she waited in the emergency room, the doctors and nurses would only say that his condition was very serious, and they wouldn't allow her to see him. The police officer who had been at the scene, said that it was unbelievable that her son was still alive. This only made it worse for his parents, who were waiting for news while he was being examined. Finally, very much against procedure, one of nurses agreed to walk Charlotte Ermolenko through to see her son. Nick remained where he was and noticed the helmet. He leant down to pick it up as it was lying on the ground, and he nudged it with the tip of his fingers. To his horror, the helmet rolled and a pool of blood spilled forth from inside the helmet and out onto the floor. It was at that point that Nicholas Ermolenko's stomach turned and he never felt the same about motorcycles and racing ever again. Even though he wasn't behind Sam in quite the same way as Bill and other fathers, he had still given his son moral support for his interest in motorcycle racing. But after seeing the extent of the injuries that Sam had sustained, he didn't really want to see any of his children sat astride motorbikes again.

Nothing could have prepared Charlotte for the scene that she witnessed. Her son's face was bloody; part of the skin on his skull by the hair line was pulled back, and the red, raw under skin was exposed. The doctors heard the cry of shock and horror from his mother, and she was ushered out. There was no way that she should have witnessed such a sight, and the nurse who was responsible for showing Charlotte through to see Sam was severely reprimanded for her mistake, as the consequences of such a shock could have been very serious.

Sam had an operation that night, and his right leg and his left arm were put in traction. He had injuries to both his left elbow and shoulder, while his leg was crushed above the knee. He was placed in traction because this was the only thing they could do at this time. He sustained a lot of lacerations because of the glass, and his head was also bandaged because of the wound to his scalp.

I was in room 522 on the fifth floor, and I was in there for eight weeks – all through the Christmas and the New Year period. I was confined to my bed because I was in traction, but I took it all in my stride. I had my own room, my own TV because it was quite a modern hospital, and I could see out of my window and see the traffic on the freeway in the distance and the parking lot. Basically, that was my entertainment while I was in there.

I had to get over the shock of the accident before they could fix my elbow and shoulder. My shoulder and elbow were all strapped up while I was in traction, so I was scheduled to have an operation on my left arm and elbow both at the same time. They operated on my left shoulder, and it was dislocated as well, so they put it back in. But where the break was, they put two pins through but they left them exposed. That was because as I would be in traction it would be easier for them to remove them. The operation took longer than they thought, and unfortunately they couldn't do the elbow. This was because they couldn't keep me under the anaesthetic too long for health reasons. My left arm remained in traction until they could schedule another operation to fix it. A week later, I was in the surgery again. This time they put a long screw in the elbow, and also a piece of wire which was put in there to help find the screw when the time came to remove it.

I had also sustained injuries to my scalp, where I hit the roof line of the car and stitches were put in place to heal the wound. They took a picture of the injury because I think it was the law at the time. I had shoulder-length hair at the time and it was caked in blood, so they just bundled it up when they took the stitches out. The law stated that they were not permitted to cut my hair, so my father had to come in to do this.

They took the bandages off and I remember my father came in with a pair of scissors, and he used a trash can that was there, which he placed alongside my bed. My hair was not in good condition after the accident and it was coarse. It had been bundled up under the bandage and it still had dried blood in it. So as my father was pulling the hair, it gave off a crusty sound. As he chopped it as best he could, I could hear it cracking and breaking from where the dried blood had bound the strands together. He cut it as close as he could to my scalp, and when he dropped it into the can I could hear it colliding with the metal with a distinctive 'ting'. He was able to cut it enough to be able to give my hair a bit of a wash, and then he finished it by giving me a short back and sides. Then they were able to take the stitches out and I was left almost bald with a scar on my head, but eventually my hair grew back.

Any hopes that Sam had of riding in the Golden State Motocross Series were well and truly over for that year. His plans were in tatters. All his operations were over by Christmas, and this was the last way he had expected to be spending the festive season. Now he had to recover and rehabilitate. He was bored, frustrated, and fed-up with playing the waiting game. This would be an all-too-familiar pattern in his life, but his main goal now was to be fit enough to go home.

I had to spend the next five weeks recovering in hospital and twiddling my thumbs. I got to know the nurses quite well and they all looked after me very well. One of the worst things about it, especially to a sixteen year old, was that I had to use a bed pan. And at that age you don't want anyone to see you like that – especially not cute nurses! But I kept my spirits up, and I had regular visits from my mom, as the hospital wasn't far from where she worked. Also as my dad had his shop just down the road, he would rescue me with a pizza or a KFC so that I didn't have to bear hospital food 24/7 all the time. The rest of the family would come and see me, and that did a lot for my morale because I really wanted to get out after I had all of my operations.

I guess what I did discover was that I had a high level of resistance to pain. I didn't really need a lot of medication, and when the nurses used to offer me painkillers or whatever, I would pass on them! I don't know for sure why that was, but I'm sure my train of thought was still focused on my motocross and all that physical and mental training necessary to be a good racer. I would like to think, that before the accident, my level of fitness worked for me. I was what the nurses called 'a good patient'. I wasn't always pushing the button and I didn't complain or ask for much, I just got on with it and did my own thing.

However, on one occasion one of the nurses came in and said that they had another guy in the hospital that was about the same age as me. He was also on the fifth floor and he had broken his leg too. She remarked on how good I was compared with this other gentleman, as all he did was complain that he wanted more medication. They asked me to give him a call, just to talk to him. And I did; he was always telling me on the phone how it hurt all the time and how much pain he was in. He was really suffering, there was no doubt about it, and I felt sorry for him.

This was his idea, but I started taking the pills again. But I didn't swallow them, I would use that little paper cup (you know the one they used to carry the pills in) and stuff it in my mouth. Of course when the nurse wasn't looking, I dropped the pills in my mouth – or what they thought was my mouth – but really in the cup and take a drink and then say done. Then I would work out how to get them to him. I did this a couple of times because he was nearly screaming with agony, and he would say: 'They won't give anything, come on – help me out here.' So I shared my painkillers with him for a little while.

Eventually, Sam's right leg was released from traction and he thought that he would be able to go home. But the doctors told him that he had to build up his strength first, as not only was he weak from lying in bed for so long, but he couldn't put any pressure on his knee. He also lost a lot of weight and he had grown a little too, so all this meant that he wouldn't be leaving yet.

The doctors took a mould of his right leg and made a plastic strap-on brace. This took the pressure off his knee where the damage was and put it on his thigh. The brace supported the leg if he had a problem. The next stage was to help him to get out of bed and sit up. After spending nearly eight weeks on his back, it was expected that he would have lost some of his neck muscles, so he had to do this slowly while he regained his strength.

I didn't really believe them because I had this handle over the top of my bed, and I could grab that and pull myself up and manoeuvre around like that. Because of this, I thought that my neck muscles would be fine. However, when they did lift me up, and sit me upright, I just couldn't hold my neck up. I felt all dizzy and I was finding it difficult to get co-ordinated, and I realised then what they meant. It took me two days from the time I was taken out of traction and given the brace, to be able to sit upright and get my balance. I practised it a few times during the second day.

That second night, the night nurse that was on duty was a bit of a pushover. She wasn't so demanding as some of the others. What I really wanted to do was to sit down and use a proper toilet. It was only about five feet away from my bed, so when she came in I told her that I wanted to use the toilet.

'Oh,' she says, 'have you done that before?'

'Yeah, I've done that already.'

She said that she had to check the charts, and questioned me a few times. I pretended that I had already done this and it wasn't a problem, so she agreed to help me. She helped me to get from my bed to the toilet. Inside there were rails to hold on to, and she got me inside the door and I told her that I was okay from that point.

'If you need me, just ring the bell,' she said, and closed the door.

I was holding the rail and I had to turn myself around so that I could skip over to the toilet – but I slipped. I couldn't grab the rail with my left arm because it hadn't healed properly yet. I fell down with a thud on the opposite side to the toilet. I was lying there and trying to get up; but I couldn't. Fortunately I didn't hurt myself, but I had to think of a way of getting myself up. I couldn't tell the nurse what I had done, because she would have realised that I had lied to her and she could tell the doctor. I was doing everything I could to get up, when suddenly I heard a knock on the door ...

'Hello, how are you doing in there?' called the nurse, 'Are you all right?'

'Yeah, yeah, I'm not done yet.'

'Do you need some help in there?'

'No, no, I'm okay,' I said.

I managed to convince her that I was alright and then she left me to it. I must have been in there nearly an hour, but all I wanted to do was to go in there and sit on a toilet properly. I finally succeeded in getting myself up, and then she came in and helped me to get back into bed.

The doctor came to see him the next day, and Sam told him that he wanted to go home. He had been in there eight weeks and he was eager to go home. The doctor explained that the only way that he would be permitted to leave was if he could learn to walk again with crutches. It was agreed that if Sam could walk the whole of the fifth floor that he was on – he could go home. So that became his goal.

I was put into the pool on the third day, and the water maintained my balance as I walked in the pool and I was building up my muscles. That afternoon the nurse helped me out of bed, and I was able to walk around a couple of doorways. The nurse, who was there when the doctor said that I had to walk the floor before I could go home, came in for the evening shift. I told her that I had walked earlier that day, and I wanted to do some more exercise. This happened to be the same nurse who had asked me to help that other man who was feeling the pain from his injuries.

'Well, why don't you help me to walk over and visit him?' I suggested. And she agreed, because she knew of the relationship between us. I put my brace on, picked up my crutches and she walked with me to his room. I met

him for the first time, and realised that he was a bit of a complainer, but he was still cool and all right, I guess. When I finished with him, I walked over to his door and started towards the other way round to my room. The nurse had caught up to me by now and kept an eye on me. By doing that, I had walked the whole floor. I had manipulated her into helping me to achieve my goal of walking the floor. I said to her when I got back to my room:

'You know what I have just done, don't you? I walked the floor. That means I can go home now.'

And she said: 'Oh, OK. I guess you did, didn't you.'

The doctor was informed the next day and the arrangements were made.

Sam was released at last; his mother put a mattress in the back of the van and he was wheeled out and left for home. His family and friends organised a welcome home reception for him, and although he was wearing the brace and walking with the aid of crutches, it was good to be back. He was very popular in the neighbourhood and at school, so while he was recovering his weight and regaining his strength, he wasn't short of visitors.

The accident not only interrupted his motocross ambitions, but also his education. While he was in hospital, he still received some homework assignments, but as he was still not fit enough to attend class, he received some more homework from his tutor at Los Alamitos High School. Cathy Mullen was a neighbour who lived across the street from him, and she was not only very bright but also quite high up in the teachers' estimations. His tutor would therefore set Sam the assignments and Cathy would outline and explain to him what he had to do. On reflection, Sam believed that he probably received a better education this way, as he was able to benefit from the time he had to concentrate and the one-to-one explanations. Consequently, he was able to study at his own pace.

In spite of the accident, his standard of education was still good enough to sit for his diploma, but with his interests elsewhere, he chose not to do it. Later he was advised to attend night school for six weeks as a refresher, so that he could sit again for his diploma. However, by this time he was able to work full-time in his father's shop and he was still dreaming of a motorcycle career, so the diploma was put on the backburner.

Speedway in the USA was, and to a large extent still is, confined to the state of California. The sport was enjoying something of a mini-explosion after being reintroduced in 1969 – after lying dormant for most of the 1960s. But, by 1977, mainly through the efforts of promoter Harry Oxley and the Kiwi duo of World Champions, Ivan Mauger and Barry Briggs, America was enjoying a vibrant scene in California.

Scott Autrey became America's first World Finalist for twenty-five years when he qualified for 1976 Final. There was enough talent emerging in the USA to suggest that they had the potential to repeat the success of the pre-war years, when their riders filled the top three places in the 1937 World Championship with Jack Milne crowned as America's first World Champion. It was while Sam was recovering from his accident that he saw speedway racing for the first time.

My mother was dating a guy called Gino and he was a speedway fan. I didn't know anything about speedway at that time, but I went along with him as my mom said that it would be good for me to get out and do something.

We went to Irwindale in April, and I was still limping around from my leg injury. We sat about mid-way up in the stands in front of the start line. To me it seemed like, a little bit chaotic as the bikes came out of the pits and onto the track, then they went different ways, the pit gate was shut and they went up to the start line. There was a race of four-lap duration, and then a bit more chaos as everyone was going in different directions. Those riders returned to the pits, and then some more came out and there was another race. It was a bit weird because I didn't really know Gino that well, and I was still far from fit. I was pretty fragile. But that was my first memory of speedway. Even then, I didn't really take a lot of interest in it – I could say that I had seen it and that was about it. I remember Bruce Penhall, Danny Becker and Mike Bast, but I never followed it. I liked any motorcycles, so it obviously interested me, but it didn't give me the same kind excitement as motocross did.

But speedway was to make another innocuous appearance in his life at this time. However, on this occasion he would also get to ride a bike, and have an insight into what it was like to slide a brake-less motorcycle. Before the accident, he had been impressed by the work carried out on a truck by one of his friends, Dave Wooten. Wooten was a desert biker, and along with his stepfather, he would go off and ride in the deserts on motocross bikes.

Dave was about a year older than me, so he got his licence before me. In my father's shop, we sold CZ motocross bikes, and they also included the Jawa emblem on them. His stepfather, Jim, was a veteran desert racer, and Dave also used CZ motocross bikes in the desert. On one occasion, I went into his garage to check out what was going on as he only lived next door to us, and I noticed he had a speedway bike on his work bench, which was painted the same colour as his truck — and it looked real cool. This surprised me because he kept this a secret and he hadn't told any of the kids from the neighbourhood. I asked him: 'What's that thing?'

'It's a speedway bike.'

'I know — do you race it?'

'Well, yeah.'

'Where?'

'Costa Mesa.'

He didn't brag about it, and to this day I don't know why he wanted to keep it a secret. But he had the leathers and all the gear to go racing at Costa Mesa. I was slowly regaining my fitness, and I really wanted to ride again. Although still not totally fit, I tagged along with Dave one weekend out to the desert where he was scheduled to race. A race in the desert would go on for half the day from start to finish. To get a view of the race, you would either have to ride a bike or have a good four-wheel drive truck, and head up to the high ground. I was offered a ride in the back of a truck that a couple of girlfriends of Dave's fellow riders were using to hit the high ground for the start of the race. So I jumped in the back and there was a roll bar fitted that I could use to hold on to as we headed off. Dave made his way to the start line as we made our way to our spot. The truck was bouncing around through this rough desert ground, and I'm sure they had no idea what I had just been through and the injuries I had. I was trying to hold on to the roll bar for my dear life, while at the same time I was concerned about my strength and ability to do this. We finally got to the place where we stopped. Boy, talk about feeling pretty stupid – the girls had no clue as we watched the start and I regained myself and built up the courage to let them know my feelings. That was the first major fitness test I had – and what an ordeal! On the way home, I told Dave of my little adventure and all we could do was laugh about it. We talked about when the time came, and I was ready to have a go at riding again, he would help me out. Time went on and one day we decided to go out to Lake Elsinore, where they had both a speedway track and a motocross track. I took my motocross bike, while Dave took his speedway bike because he planned to do some practising there.

This was my first real taste of speedway and encountering the riders. When I was with Gino, it was a bit of a blur. While Dave was taking part in an organised practice event, I decided to go off into the back side of the park on my motocross bike. While I was out there, I came across another rider wearing black leathers with flames on them, and he had long hair sticking out of the back of his helmet. We had a little bit of a battle racing around the turns. Later in my career, I discovered that the guy in the black leathers with the flames on them was Shawn Moran – the 1983 World Long-Track Champion!

When I returned to the pits, Dave gave me the opportunity to ride his speedway bike. I did four or five laps and I actually broke a slide – I did okay. That was the first time that I had been on a speedway machine. John Foster, a First Division rider, was with us at this practice session, and during the journey home he said that I looked pretty good on a speedway bike. It was my first time riding since my accident, so I didn't really think too much about that. Speedway hadn't really entered my mind – I just wanted to ride.

Sam's recovery continued and, in fact, he rode a motorcycle as often as he could as another way of recovering from his injuries. Of course, doing this also allowed him to exercise the muscles that he would use while riding a bike that, perhaps, he wouldn't normally exercise. Furthermore, as his family and friends continued to be involved in one form or another with motorcycles, his opportunities to get on a bike were plentiful.

Out of the Vance brothers, Jeff was probably the most natural on a bike. He was racing at a place called Saddleback Park – where as well as a motocross track they also had a track for speedway too, but I didn't know that at the time. I went along to watch them, and Jeff had a crash in the first race and hurt himself. He had to withdraw from the second race, which meant in my mind I was thinking that there was an opportunity to ride.

I came up with the idea of taking his place. I tried on his protective clothing and snuck up to the staging area and joined the rest of the field at the start line as Jeff! This was the intermediate class, which was one grade down before you were considered an expert. So I took his place and I was in the top three during the first two laps, but there was a problem with the bike as I went over a couple of the jumps. The exhaust was spring-loaded, so as I came down from the jumps, the exhaust would pop out of the manifold and it lost its power. While I was in third place, I pulled off the track, and I literally kicked the pipe back into place and got back on.

I managed to claw my way back up into sixth place, but the pipe came out again, so I had to retire from the race. Bill Qualls and the rest were there, and they couldn't believe how well I was performing following the accident. This gave me the incentive to get a bike and enter the Golden State Series again.

I entered the series at the end of January 1978, and I took part in a meeting in northern California. The conditions were not good, the track was muddy and wet, and I didn't get a good result. The first local race was held at the Indian Dunes, and my future wife, Shelley, and I went up in my truck while the bikes were transported in Bill's van.

The track was sandy, and I felt really good in practice and I was flying. However, because of the sandy surface, the suspension was bottoming out through the corners, so I asked Bill to set the suspension a lot stiffer. The suspension wasn't a spring, it was air suspension, so he had to fill them up with gas to make the shocks stiffer. As well as the motocross track, there were other tracks and areas in this park where you could ride. I took advantage of this to test the settings by doing some jumps. It had rained a little and there were a few puddles around. I went high around the turns and aimed at the jump, but as I hit the jump I was going too fast and ended up partially landing on one of the other jumps. My front wheel hit it and I was flipped over the handlebars. As I hit the ground, the bike also flipped and the seat part of the machine landed on my stomach as the bike rolled over me. The reason why I crashed was because my right leg could hyper-extend, and it caused me to stretch over too far and I lost my balance.

There was so much pain in my ribs that I thought that I must have broken them. As I was lying there, I thought to myself: 'Oh no, man, what have I done?' Jeff came up to me and asked me if I was okay, and I told him that I thought that I had hurt my ribs, so he should get some help. Bill came walking up, and as he already thought that I was radical and crashed bikes, he said with an air of resignation: 'What did you do?'

Bill helped me back to the pits, which was about a distance of 300 metres. But when I was sat down, I wasn't feeling very well. Shelley was with me, and the ambulance driver came up and looked me over. He agreed that I had probably broken my ribs, and he advised me to get to the hospital and have an X-ray. So that was my racing over with for that day, and I was hurt again!

Shelley drove me to the hospital, which was only about twenty minutes away. When I arrived, I told the nurse that I had been riding motocross and I fell off my bike and I thought that I may have broken some ribs. The hospital was pretty busy, so she told me to take a seat. But I really wasn't feeling very well at all, and my stomach area was really uncomfortable. We had been waiting there for around forty minutes and I was tired of waiting – especially as I was feeling so uncomfortable – so we decided to drive home.

My home was about an hour away, and during the journey back every bump in the road was causing me pain. It was so tight and uncomfortable that I was telling Shelley to watch where she was going, and yet they weren't big bumps at all. I was really having some problems. Finally, we arrived home and Shelley helped me up the stairs, as all I wanted to do was to lie down on a bed. I was still wearing my racing gear and boots.

I closed my eyes to relax when all of sudden my stomach area jerked with pain, and it really hurt. It happened again; my stomach tightened, and the pain galloped through my stomach in a sharp spasm. My mom had come home from work, and she came up to my room and took one look at me at me and said: 'What d'you do?'

'Oh, I crashed and I've hurt my ribs.'

'Right, come on we're going to the hospital.'

'No, Mom, I'm all right,' and then I got another really painful spasm. There was no arguing with her when she saw me in that sort of pain. She helped me get my boots and trousers off and change, then get down the stairs and into the car. Three hours had passed since I crashed, and when I arrived at the hospital, my shoulder was starting to hurt too. I was not feeling well at all. A nurse asked me what was wrong.

'Oh I crashed earlier, I don't know, maybe I've hurt my ribs,' I replied, while I was clutching my stomach and chest. She disappeared and then a doctor came and examined me. He carried out his examination and then he left, saying: 'Hold on a second.'

When he came back, he asked: 'Your shoulder hurts – your left shoulder?'

'Yeah.'

Within a minute there was a bed alongside me and there were three people in the room and the doctor said that he was going to do some tests. It was all happening so fast that I hardly had time to think about what was going on, and I said:

'Okay, what are you gonna do? Do you think I've got broken ribs?'

Then I was wheeled down the hall, the doors opened up and I was in theatre. A doctor was called in and he introduced himself and he said:

'I'm going to put a needle in your stomach, and I'm going to inject some fluid in there as I think you might have some internal bleeding. Because your shoulder is hurting, and the main artery goes through your shoulder, we're going to put this needle in with some fluid and we think it will show blood.'

It hurt so bad at that point, that I just wanted them to figure out what was wrong. There was a little shot where he numbed my stomach, and then he stuck the needle in. I could feel a double movement as he hit my stomach. As he did that, I suddenly saw the doctor pull back and he went, 'Whoa!' and blood shot right out of my stomach and spurted out of the tube and hit the ceiling! Immediately, the pain was gone; he was right, I had internal bleeding and I was filling up. Seconds later, I heard 'prep', and there were doctors all around me and they were scrubbing my stomach and putting me under. I had ruptured my spleen ...

The doctor said later that he would have given me an hour, and then I would have been dead. If I had fallen asleep, I would have died. The spasms and jerks of pain were what was keeping me awake – my body was telling me.

Sam was in hospital for a week as they carried out the necessary surgery to his stomach. He wasn't able to work for a month, and during this time he evaluated the situation with his leg. At that point, he was still covered by the medical insurance from his mother's work place. Therefore, as he was still under nineteen and living under his mother's roof, he was still covered by her policy, but he had to make a decision within a month about whether or not to have the corrective surgery before the policy ran out.

He decided to have the surgery, and he spent another three months recovering before he could return to work. His leg was re-broken and reset, but the legacy of this was that his right leg was almost two inches shorter than his left. It was during this time that Sam Ermolenko made some life-changing decisions. He started a company as a 'struggling mechanic' and he specialised in Volkswagens. However, he would turn his hand to almost anything that had an engine, from cars to forklifts. For now at least, motocross and bike racing were put aside as he channelled his energies into developing his business and making it a success. But, once a racer …

It would be fair to say that speedway as a motorcycle sport had gently shown its hand to a young Sam, without actually prodding him for attention. But the sport had attracted a lot of attention among the locals because of its base in California, and it wasn't long before this particular discipline of motorcycle racing would enter his life again.

Dave was racing speedway regularly at Costa Mesa with John Foster. We went to watch him at Costa Mesa – he didn't invite us, we just went along to see it. Shelley's sister lived in a flat with a guy which was about one mile away from the track, so we decided to go along one Friday night. It was entertainment really; we were just having a beer and enjoying the atmosphere, but Shelley and her sister, Lorie, used to go to school with one of the riders. He still races today and that was Eddie Castro. After the racing, we went to see him in the pits and said hello, and I got to know him.

We had a party after the speedway at Lorie's ground-floor flat, and they had a car port with a light. We would have a beer or two, play some table tennis and have the music going, and this was where we used to hang out after the races. Ed Castro came over one night with his bikes, and he pulled up in the car port. I remember looking at the bikes in the back of his truck and they had Jawa written on them. And I thought, 'Jawa? Where had I seen that before?' I recognised this from the CZ-Jawa that my dad distributed, and because of this connection, I decided there and then that I was going to look into it.

As a spectator, I think I saw two or three more meetings. But when I got around to asking my father about the CZ-Jawa, he gave me the telephone number of the distributor, and I spoke to a man called Burtis. He was based in La Puente in LA County, and I went to see him. He showed me some of the bikes in the showroom, and I bought the bike there and then and took it with me.

I took the bike back to my dad's shop. It was late in the day, the working day was over and the guys in the workshop were having a beer and winding down. We were all studying this bike, and no one in the workshop knew anything about it. 'Speedway? What's speedway?' They all thought it was a bit comical, because to them it looked like a bicycle with an engine. It wasn't anything like the bikes they had been working on: it had thin tyres when compared with other motorcycles, a small fuel tank, and a skinny frame and, to top it all, it leaked oil! Costa Mesa was only twenty minutes away from the shop, but no one knew about speedway. They all laughed.

The bike sat there for two months, and one of the mechanics in the shop had a friend who came to see him. My father used to let the mechanics do their own projects there, and this particular guy would build land speed bikes. I rode a Kawasaki and I reached a speed of 161mph. I was testing the bike at El Mirage, and I got a plaque saying that I did that speed. He knew about engines that ran on methanol because his bikes ran on methanol too, and he was very knowledgeable about high compressions. His friend saw the bike and he knew all about speedway, and he told me:

'Speedway? Yeah, I know what that is. I know Briggo.'

'Who?'

'Barry Briggs. He's a good friend of mine and I've known him a long time. He's the guy to tell you all about this, Sam – he's a World Champion.'

It didn't really mean anything to me, but I remembered the name of Briggo. I rode the bike a couple of times at Saddleback Park, as I remembered that they had a track there. Over the rise, there was another track which was bigger and it was used for flat-track racing. It was mid-week and the park was pretty empty; you could hear the odd motocrosser in the distance, but then I heard the sound of a speedway bike. So I walked up the bank, and when I got up there and looked down, there was this speedway guy racing around. I thought that was weird, as I was on the small speedway track and here he was on the flat track.

I went down there to see what was happening. All he was doing was a practice start, first turn, practice start, first turn and so on. I had never seen this before; it was usually get in a line and then dump the thing. This rider had a mechanic with him who was hobbling around on crutches. I asked them what they were doing and he said: 'Practising starts.'

'For what? Shouldn't you be riding on the other track, that's the speedway track?'

'No, we're practising for tracks in Europe, because that's where we ride.'

I didn't have the gearing for the big track, so I stuck to the small one, but they walked over and watched me ride. He saw me skidding and he said: 'You're not doing too bad – it's your first time you say?'

And I said: 'Well, yeah.'

'My old man's coming out here tomorrow – he's the man you should talk to.'

'Who's your old man?'

'Briggo.'

The rider was Briggo's son, Tony Briggs, and his mechanic was Chris Martin. I recognised the name and he said that he would take a look at me and he knew all the promoters in the US. I went back there the next day, and I was introduced to Barry Briggs and he watched me do some laps. He said that he could see that I had the talent to ride the bike, but I just needed to get in more laps. Then he asked me what my name was, and I said: 'Sam Ermolenko.'

'*Ermolenko?*' he says, '*That's a Russian name isn't it?*'

'*Well, yeah, it's a Russian name.*'

'*There you go! If you want to get on old Oxley's programme [Harry Oxley, the Costa Mesa promoter], you've got to have some kind of gimmick. You either got to sign on and earn your way, or you've got to have a gimmick. You should get a set of red leathers made up, and we'll just call you "The Mad Russian",*' he suggested. '*You'll get rides for sure, and you'll get good rides too as you won't be in the Third Division getting hurt, you'll be able to go in at the top.*'

I've never forgotten that day when Barry labelled me 'The Mad Russian'. That wasn't for me, but later I discovered what he meant.

Sam was all set to marry Shelley the following week. Given the serious accidents that he had already experienced while riding motorcycles, one could have forgiven Shelley for not wanting her future husband to pursue a career in speedway racing. Shelley was well aware of Sam's interest in bikes, and if she was secretly hoping that the responsibilities that come with marriage might make her husband re-evaluate his motorcycle interests, they were soon shattered. Even on their wedding day, wearing his wedding suit, Sam managed to find time to celebrate on a motorcycle!

The very next week, Sam was practising again and he was gaining in confidence and feeling more positive. As he was now mixing with the speedway crowd, he discovered that Bill Cody was the speedway distributor for Jawa and other accessories for the sport. It was Cody who told him that regular racing took place at Costa Mesa, San Bernardino and Ventura, and that they practised at Saddleback Park, Indian Dunes and Maely's Ranch. Ken Maely has been associated with American dirt-track racing for all of his life. He was once a racer himself but, latterly, his skills in the workshop and his training facilities have become invaluable to Californian racers. Furthermore, he developed his own speedway engine during the mid-1980s, but it was only moderately successful. However, the ranch has continued to be a place where riders of all levels are able to go and practise.

Cody told me roughly what ratios I needed to use for the different tracks: 16/72 for Costa Mesa, Maely's ranch was a 16/74, and the Indian Dunes was 16/69, so he suggested that if I had a 16/70, I could do all of them. So I bought the sprockets from him, and I went to Indian Dunes to practise. There were only about half-a-dozen speedway riders there, but there were hundreds of motocross riders. Some of the riders that were there included Rick Miller and Lance King, and I recognised them because they were wearing cool leathers.

I didn't know the sport that well, I didn't realise you were expected to dress up in all the colourful leathers. At this point I just wanted to ride and work on the bike; I wasn't that keen that I wanted to spend a lot of money. If I had a pair of Levis and a pair of boots then I would be fine, but I ended up acquiring a steel shoe and a helmet. One of the mechanics that worked in my dad's shop knew someone who had a set of leathers that I could use. This suit was suede looking – a bit like the inside of a leather suit – and one side was red and the other side was blue, and it was the opposite way round on my legs. It was a funky-looking suit.

When I got to the Dunes, my suit attracted a lot of attention from some of the other riders as it wasn't as cool as theirs. They were smirking a bit, but I didn't care as all I wanted to do was get out there and ride. I remember Rick Miller and me having a real go when we staged a race – we were banging handlebars and everything. But he crashed out and went straight into the barbed wire fence and hurt his shoulder.

As I was working at my own business, I could arrange my own time to go riding. I wanted to go riding one day at the Dunes, but I didn't have a vehicle that was reliable. Mike Reubal had just bought a new truck, and it was a Ford pick-up truck. The Dunes was a good hour and a half from where we lived, and he agreed to go with me. I said that I would buy the beer and along with Paul Burton – who was my best man at my wedding – we went to the Dunes. When we got there, we were the only people at the track – although there were one or two motocross guys on the other track.

I was spinning laps, and my buddies were sat on the back of the truck drinking beer. When I came in, I said: 'Okay guys, your job is to put the oil in and yours is to put fuel in it.' I would cool off while they were doing this, and then I'd go out and do it again. As I was riding around, a big truck pulled in, a big Chevy dual cab truck, and there were two speedway bikes in the back. Mother and father, brother and sister, speedway rider and girl-friend all got out of it, and I saw them and thought 'Oh great, someone to race against.' So I came in to get fuelled up.

I was telling the guys to hurry up, because this other rider was firing the bike up. But because they had been on the beer all day, by this time they were half-pissed, and it was taking longer than it should – which was frus-trating me because I wanted to get out there and ride with this guy. 'Hurry up, man, come on I wanna get out there, let's go,' I said to them. The other rider was already out there, and I was watching him ride and he was fast.

When I got out there, he was just finishing and then he did a practice start. As I'm doing my laps, I looked up and he was already loading up to go. I pulled off and took off my helmet and strolled over there with my two buddies following me with their cans of beer.

'What's going on guys, where are you going? I was hoping to ride with you.' I said.

'Oh we just stopped off to test the bike. We're going racing at Taft.'

I had never heard of Taft, but it was over the grapevine and it was a min-ing town in northern California. He said that he'd take a look at me and I completed a few laps, and he said that I was pretty good. His name was Chris Hedge, and his father was a famous drag racer in the 1960s. All of his cars used to be a dark metallic brown and he was known as 'root beer'. Chris used to race at Ventura and was very fast round there, but he seldom went to Costa Mesa or San Bernardino.

'Have you ever raced?' he said.

'No, this is only my fourth time on a bike.'

'You're good enough to ride where I'm going for sure,' he said. 'You should come along, and they need riders there anyway. Are you from Southern California? Heck, South Cal. guys always get rides there. You'll get a ride there – no problem.'

'Don't I need a licence or something?'

'Oh no, this is a club thing, you just pay your entry fee and you're in. You're good enough – you should go.'

I looked at my buddies and we all agreed that I should go, so I decided that I had better call my wife. There were no mobile phones in those days, *so I had to go and find a pay phone, and we found a trailer park in the hills and pulled in there. The door to the truck was open, and there was Mike Reubal with a beer in his hand and eager to go to Taft, while I was on the phone to Shelley.*

'I'm just calling to let you know that I have met these guys and I'm gonna go up to Taft, so I won't be home until later.'

She was at home on her own, and she replied: 'Well, that's not the plan …'

'Look, no big deal I'm just gonna go up there and race …'

'What? You say you're going to race?'

The conversation on the phone was getting a little bit tense, when Reubal made the situation worse, by adding his advice in the background by shouting something like, 'Tell her to get lost, man, we're going anyway.' I was trying to get him to shut up, but he was tanked up by all the beer he'd been drinking. Paul also added his support, and I was trying to get them to be quiet. With all this going in the background I was trying to explain the situation to Shelley, but my buddies were not helping the situation at all.

'I met this guy and he says that I'll fit right in up there, and maybe I'll win some money as they pay prize money.'

Chris and the rest of the family were waiting for us, and Mike was still shouting his advice as I was talking on the phone. Of course, Shelley remembered the accident and I'd just got married and all that stuff and she said: 'You're not racing. You're not going.'

'Look, I'm going, don't worry about it. I'll be all right.'

'Oh right, whatever, I'm here with the kids …'

It wasn't a major argument, but she clearly wasn't pleased. But as I put the phone down, the rest of the boys were saying: 'All right, yeah, we're going!'

When we got there it was like a rodeo arena, it was a bit smaller than Costa Mesa, but they had pig stalls so speedway was one of the few entertainments they had up there. I did okay, and I enjoyed it. It was here that I first met Tim McCasland and Bob Bechtold, and we went a few more times and I managed to make a bit of cash.

This was in 1981 and Sam continued to make progress with regular practices at the Indian Dunes, and appearances at Taft. However, he required a licence to race at Costa Mesa, San Bernardino and Ventura because they were AMA-sanctioned venues. Therefore, in order to be able to participate at these tracks, he had to take a test – and unknown to him at the time, his inexperience would have an effect on the result. It is a requirement that all riders are able to lay down their machine safely before they can race as a professional. It is a simple enough test: while the rider is circulating, an official who is situated on the infield drops a flag, and at that point the rider has to drop the bike to his satisfaction.

I did my test at Ventura, and when the official dropped the flag I laid it down but kept the engine running and I was able to pick it back up. But the official said that I had failed because I had to drop the bike, stop it, get off and get out of the way. So that was it – I failed. In the US, when you arrive at the race track you have to sign up to be on the programme for the following week – unless of course you have already raced, or have done well in the meeting and then you're automatically on the programme. As I was new to all this, on the day I took my test, when I entered to go in, there was a board there to sign up for next week's programme. I thought to myself that I wanted to race, so I paid my fee and signed up for the following week's programme. I did the test and failed it, so then I had to reschedule the test for the following week.

This time I went out there and passed the test. I had already paid the fees and all I needed to race was the licence. Now that I had that licence, I could race in the event. I went out there and smoked the opposition and won the Third Division. The referee came up to me after I'd won and said:

'You just took your test today, how did you get on the programme?'

'I signed up last week.'

'You're not supposed to do that.'

'Too late, I won,' I replied.

While Sam was racing speedway he met Bill Hartke. Hartke was a mechanic to Dave Wendlant who was a Second/Third Division rider. Bill was interested in helping Sam for the following season because he could see that he was going places. Wendlant was just out enjoying himself and was not too serious about the long term as his youth had passed him by. It was during this conversation that they talked about what they did off the track as well.

I discovered that Bill worked in a Porsche shop as a mechanic, and also did side jobs out of his garage at home specialising in Porsche vehicles. That was unreal as I was doing the same out of my garage but with VW bugs. After we talked for a while, we both realised that we ought to get our heads together and talk about the future. Up until this point, I had been working on my own and graduated out of my garage to renting a unit. I had taken out a lease for one year, and I was working away at paving a future for myself. At one of the supply houses I used, the owner asked if I was interested in working on fork-lift trucks – he had a friend that owned a paint manufacturing company with a couple lifts that needed attention. I said sure. They were delivered to my unit and I rebuilt three lifts for this company. When I had finished my work, and arrangements were made for them to be picked up, I went along to visit the factory and pick up my payment. I had a meeting with the owner and he was real pleased with the job that I had done, and asked if I would be interested in keeping all of his lifts serviced on a regular basis. He also knew of a couple other factories that could put work my way. Well, I had to think fast; as I was starting to see a bit of a future with regard to my racing, and merging both of Bill's and my skills together. So I declined and said that I was going racing instead! I know that it sounds a little harsh, but it would have meant that I would've had to set up a mobile service van to maintain these lifts on site. All this would take a good investment and commitment, and I wasn't sure that was what I wanted.

I was getting to the end of my lease on the unit, and I used to visit The Frame Shop. This was owned by Gary Fuca and he was a speedway fan. He used to work for my father's shop Q&E. The Frame Shop was on the way to my unit from where I lived, so I would stop by and shoot the breeze with Gary. His interest in speedway made him pretty handy because he could straighten my frames when I bent them. All this was going on around the same time. Gary said that a unit in his complex was coming up for rent and that I should take it on. It was much cheaper, so both Bill and I looked into it and we went for it and formed a business together called E&H Autowerks.

It was an appointment-only business so we could plan our day as long as we saw to our customers' needs. This unit was in Stanton, California.

Gary's business was checking motorcycle frames of all sorts of makes, as they used to come from the insurance companies. He used to acquire them after they had been crashed. If the insurance company decided that the machines were not worth repairing, he would make an offer to buy them. He would then restore them and he would often stop by our shop and we would step out and check out the bike. Consequently, I had a lot of opportunities to ride these different machines.

I was known in the area for my ability on a motorcycle, and I was known for being able to pull wheelies on any type of machine. This wasn't a problem for me — I had a lot of confidence in my ability to do this. It didn't matter to me what the speed was, whether it was 30mph or 90mph. Gary stopped by on this occasion with a Honda 750, which was a big bulky motorcycle and he rode it into my shop — as he had done so many times before. We checked it out, and I said: 'Looks good, Gary, just leave it there and I'll have a ride on it in a minute.' 'Don't crash it,' he said, as he walked back towards his shop.

Many of the bikes that came to him didn't have any ignition keys, so he would modify the ignition system and you could start it with a screw driver. This Honda was like that, but I hopped onto it and rode it out of the estate and was doing some good old big wheel stands. I wasn't wearing a crash helmet and was just wearing a t-shirt and jeans. This was a powerful machine, but while I had the bike on its back wheel, the ignition locked the steering! Without the key to keep the tumblers and levers in place, the gravity and the angle I had the bike at — straight up with the handle bars locked for my balance — meant that this let the pin in the locking system fall into place. Oh shit! And it locked it!

I was coming down the street and it was an L-shaped road, and I had to make a decision whether to flip it backwards or to let the front wheel come down and get off it that way. The decision was made for me as the front wheel was already coming down, and when I hit the ground I was thrown away from the bike. That was probably a good thing because if I had come off the back I would have had a big frame, engine and fuel tank land on top of me.

I went straight for the water hose and placed it over my head. Gary came out and took a look, and I could see from his expression that he wanted to say something; but he just shook his head and turned and walked back into his shop. I told Bill to get Shelley to come and pick me up, and I spent the next three hours in the tub picking gravel and stone chips out of my body. About three days afterwards, I was due to race at Ventura.

But my wheelie displays were not popular with everyone in the neighbourhood of the shop. Quite often, we had to bump start some of the motorcycles, and on this particular occasion I pointed the bike down the drive and it started; I drove down the street for about 100 metres or so, then turned around and headed back. As I was crossing the entry to the drive, I popped a wheelie. I didn't realise that a policeman was watching from his patrol vehicle. I rode into my shop and stopped. The phone was ringing, so I answered it. I saw the front end of the patrol car pull up, and the policeman came rushing in and was looking all around. He didn't really acknowledge me or anything, and I asked the caller to hold on and said:

'Can I help you?'

'Where's that motorcycle guy with the yellow shirt?'

I attended to the call and then asked him: 'What guy? Yellow shirt?' I had a white shirt. 'It was me on the bike, what's the problem?'

Apparently I had violated the law.

He was a bit hot under the collar, and he said: 'Look, you got two choices here: I will have to charge you with either reckless driving or exceeding the speed on the rear wheel, and you don't want the reckless driving, 'cos that's straight to jail.'

'But I wasn't exceeding the speed!'

'Sorry, but it's one or the other!'

Well, I tried my charm on the guy, but he was well past that point, and I took the speeding ticket. I contested it in court, as I pleaded my case to the judge, he asked if I had done a wheelie and I said yes, but …

'There is no but – guilty!' And the hammer went down! I was fined.

I was doing Third Division at San Bernardino when I blew up my engine. I left the start and the con rod broke in the engine and it blew a hole in the engine casing. It filled up with dirt and stopped me right out of the start. As I had made the Third Division Track Championship at Ventura, I bought a brand new bike from Bill Cody.

In my very first race in the Track Championships, a rider from Colorado made the start on me but he fell off going into the corner. I hit his back wheel and went flying over the top of him and straight through the fence. I had disappeared from view and couldn't be seen for a moment, then I emerged from the fence with my arms waving for another bike as mine was all bent – my brand new bike! I ran back to the pits to try and borrow another bike as it wasn't my fault, but everyone turned their back on me. But I did manage to borrow a Weslake bike from a rider called Keith Larsen, who was known as the 'Snakeman', and I won the race.

Little did Sam know that he was running the wrong gear, which he discovered during a discussion with Chris Hedge about what gear he used at Indian Dunes.

I told him that Bill Cody told me to run a 68. We were leaning over the truck looking at my bike while were discussing this, and he asked me what engine sprocket I had on. I answered that it was a 15, and he said that it was an odd size. He thought that it was small, and he asked me if I was sure, and I replied that I had counted it myself. I pointed to the sprocket behind the clutch. He looked at it and said that I was running a 19, and he pointed out the numbers through the little holes where the chain guard goes. I counted the wrong gear as I didn't know what I was doing at this stage. Therefore, I had been running an equivalent to nine teeth smaller, and because the bike was geared too tall, I failed the test because it was still driving when I put it down slow. But I didn't know that at that stage. I had done all these races with the wrong gearing – but that was how I learned to ride.

Before Chris noticed the gearing, Sam made his first appearance at Costa Mesa, and was leading his first race by a long way when he was excluded because his rear mudguard – or fender, as it is called in the US – came adrift. He negotiated the small oval with this tall-gear ratio. Once Sam had sorted out the gear ratio, he progressed in leaps and bounds, and found it much easier to ride the bike. He was really pushing the likes of Chris Hedge around the practice track at the Indian Dunes. I believe it taught him how to handle the power in a different way. Consequently, once he got the gearing right, he found the bike was much more controllable.

By now he had bought a pair of leathers that Barry Briggs had imported, and they were known as the 'Briggo leathers'. Although he was on a tight budget, he was starting to look like a professional rider. A Ventura Speedway programme revealed that during his brief season in 1981, he won ten main events at both second and Third Division level.

You may believe that Sam had been unlucky to suffer all these accidents, but on the other hand, Lady Luck had not totally deserted him – any of these accidents could quite conceivably have cost Sam his life.

Sam was now beginning to make a name for himself, but not the one that he had expected. Although everyone knew him as Sam, when he got his licence, he had to sign up with his legal name of Guy Ermolenko. However, success would give him both the credibility and the freedom to change to his preferred first name.

Three

LET'S GO RACING

Twenty-one was, and still is, considered to be a late age to commence a career as a speedway rider. England's Michael Lee, who would be a future team-mate of Sam's, had already won the World Championship in 1980 before he was twenty-two. At twenty-one, Sam had a lot of catching up to do.

All motor sport, whether it is on two wheels or four, is an expensive undertaking. Sponsorship is vital to be able to compete against the more established riders. The early years for a rider, who is starting out and has yet to make a name for himself, are usually very hard from a financial standpoint. For Sam, it was more difficult than it was for many of his rivals, because he had a wife and a child to support. Not only did he have to make his racing break even, but he also had to support his family – that was his number one priority.

However, his appearance at the end of the 1981 season at Costa Mesa may have ended with his mudguard coming adrift, but he displayed enough ability to capture the interest of a businessman who was watching from the comfort of one of the corporate boxes.

I rode at Costa Mesa at the end of '81 and I was pretty determined to make an impression there because of the reputation of the place – it was the centre of speedway in America. My mudguard came loose, and it was swinging on the push bar and around the back wheel to the ground and then back up again. The referee deemed that to be dangerous, and probably thought that I would crash, so I was black-flagged and excluded.

That night, when they opened the pits gate to let the fans come in, a man called Al Gaston came up to me and introduced himself. He said that I was surely the best rider in that race, and it was a shame that my bike had problems. He was a big John Wayne type of guy, and he possessed a lot of presence. He was well known within speedway as he was the owner of a company in Chino, California, called 'Gaston and Dillon'. At Costa Mesa, he had one of these corporate boxes which are situated about two feet away from the fence. So when we would rev up at the start line, they could view it at first hand. What he proposed was, because he owned a business, he was interested in sponsoring me. He gave me his card, and said: 'You won't have problems like you had tonight with your bike falling apart. If you join me, I'll help you and you'll go places. Give me a call and let's talk about it.'

I called him the next day, and I made an appointment to meet with him at his business in Chino. It was about a forty-minute drive from where I lived. It was a big building, and I felt pretty special as he was the owner of the business, and here I was sat in his office listening to a sponsorship proposal. His idea was to form a two-rider team using Danny Becker and myself. I was the young protégé coming up through the different levels, while Becker was meant to be the leading rider and the showman of the team. We would all work together in the team during 1982.

Danny Becker was the kind of rider who would turn up at the race track and just get on the bike and ride it. He wasn't interested in doing the maintenance on his bikes. Therefore, Al suggested that he would buy a couple of bikes, acquire a van, and gave me a credit card to cover the fuel expenses. It was also agreed, as part of the arrangement, and because we were forty-five minutes away from each other across two counties, that I would maintain the bikes for Danny. I had the business, E&H Autowerks with Bill – who was also my mechanic at the races as well – and we both agreed to do this as part of the package. We got two new bikes as part of the team and we could switch between them at the races, plus I still had my other bike as well.

We started off slowly. To begin with, I used my new bike that I had bought at the end of the previous season with Gaston's colours on it. I went along to see the new bike, and he explained to me what he had done to the cam timing and all these other things. But I couldn't really see Al Gaston as this hands-on type of guy working on a motorcycle engine. From my own experience at that time of working on motorcycle engines, I felt that he wouldn't want to be in a suit working on speedway bikes when he owned a corporation. It didn't make me feel comfortable having my bike based at this location as I felt that I had more experience than he did. This was when it was agreed during the off-season of 1981/82, that I would have the bikes based at my workshop and I would work on them there. It was a mutual agreement.

Gaston wanted us to be in the same leathers, and the company's colours were orange and yellow – which were the colours I wore. Danny wore the same design but in yellow and the bikes were co-ordinated in the same colours too.

Danny Becker was known as 'Berzerko Becker' because of his wild man image both on and off the track. Legend has it that during his first appearance at Costa Mesa as a raw rookie, he completed his first lap around the track on his back wheel. There was no doubt that he had the ability to ride a speedway bike, but his party animal lifestyle meant that he never made any impression in the US Nationals or the California State Championships.

However, he did make a handful of appearances in the USA teams during the mid-Seventies, when matches were staged against a Rest of the World team that was part of the Ivan Mauger/Barry Briggs-inspired Champions' Troupe tours. It was Gaston who brought the unpredictable Becker out of retirement to join the young charger, Ermolenko.

Danny was hard work. It didn't work out as Al Gaston thought it would because of Danny's lifestyle. He still had that party animal attitude, and he wanted everything as easy as possible and hopefully handed to him on a silver platter. As far as Bill and I were concerned, it wasn't our responsibility to make sure he got to the race tracks. But we did make sure that the bikes were there for him to race when he did turn up at the track. At that point, Al was trying to be the leader of our little Gaston and Dillon team, and he would throw his weight around a bit. He didn't really know all the things he needed to know about speedway to be able to run a successful team, and we didn't either. But heck, he ran a GD business so he tried to organise it all from behind his desk with just a telephone. Therefore, he relied a lot on me and Bill to make sure that the bikes and the van were there and so forth.

When Sam arrived at the tracks to race as a Gaston & Dillon rider, all his hard work during the final third of the 1981 season seemed to count for nothing. He had done well enough to be pushing the door open to First Division level, but to his surprise he was programmed to start back in the Third Division! When he questioned it, the authorities brushed it aside and he was told that he had to start among the rookies – but not for long. For Guy, as he was called then, went out and totally outclassed and annihilated the rest of his Third Division rivals. No matter where he went, whether it was Ventura, Costa Mesa or San Bernardino, the authorities soon realised that they had made a mistake and he was far too good to be in the Third Division.

By June 1982, Sam, who was wearing number 257 on his back, had won four main events and made First Division status at both Ventura and Costa Mesa. At Ventura, he won the handicap main three times during a five-week period, and was now regularly starting from the 30-yard line in the handicap races at both tracks. He was regularly finishing top of the Second Division and he was starting to make his presence felt at First Division level at all of the southern Californian tracks.

Journalist Bill Locey, who was the person who nicknamed him 'Sudden' Sam Ermolenko, because of his rapid and sudden way of carving through the field, had this to say of him in a feature that appeared in one of the Ventura programmes:

'You can notice him by his style – he seems to be part of the motorcycle, gliding around the track like an electric train.'

1982 was also a milestone year in the history of American speedway because they staged the World Individual Final at the Los Angeles Coliseum – which was later the venue for the 1984 Olympics. Bruce Penhall was there to defend his world title that he had won in such exciting style at Wembley the previous year, and he was joined in the 16-rider line-up by his fellow Americans, Dennis Sigalos and Kelly Moran.

The majority of the field for this one-off night of action consisted of riders who regularly raced in the British League. With America currently holding all of the major world championships, British League scouts took the opportunity to travel over to LA and take a look at some of the prospects currently racing in California. There were several who went to Costa Mesa and, although he didn't know at the time, there were one or two scouts who made a mental note of Ermolenko.

I went to watch the World Final at the Coliseum, and I was sat high up in turn one. I wasn't very familiar with speedway on an international scale, so I didn't really know who the other riders were. Of course I knew of Penhall, Sigalos and Kelly Moran because they were Americans. I remember there were 90,000 seats and there were about 40,000 inside, so there was plenty of room for our little group to sit. We were looking through the speedway programme and we were messing around and joking, and we nominated Phil Crump as the ugliest speedway rider! But when I went to England, I realised that it could have easily have been Steve Regeling and not Crumpie! Still, just joking, guys!

While it could be described as an apprentice year for Ermolenko, it was also a learning year for Al Gaston. He had first-hand experience of the politics of speedway racing in California, which led to their boss flying his two riders out of the region.

On a regular basis we were having trouble getting on the programme at Costa Mesa and San Bernardino due to the politics. He wanted to showcase us to his clients and so forth, but the politics prevented us from getting these rides. So Al had this idea of going to Visalia, which is about 35 miles south of Fresno – they staged about half-a-dozen meetings a year. He loaded up the van and Danny drove there, while I flew up with Al Gaston in his private plane, and we all stayed in a really nice hotel. We were the star attraction, but neither Becker nor I did that well.

Unfortunately, Al Gaston was not very happy with the off-track antics employed by Becker. He went a bit extreme with his drinking and partying – he had a hard night at the hotel and enjoyed himself. We had our vans parked next to a chain-link fence, and the spectators would pass by on the other side as they made their way to the entrance to the track. I remember on the day of the meeting, Danny was standing there and all of sudden he said: 'Oh no, I gotta take a shit – quick!' He had the runs from all the drinking he did the night before. He ran around the back of the van and he was peeling off his suit as he was running, and then he squatted down. I couldn't believe it, he was facing us in the pits while he was doing his business, but all the time the fans were walking by on the other side! But he didn't care.

I don't think Al was too pleased about that little episode. He went to all the trouble of getting him out of retirement, and he just wasn't getting the co-operation out of him. He knew all the problems that Becker had with his lifestyle, but Al thought that he could handle him … he couldn't. Nobody could handle Becker.

Gaston & Dillon did not continue with the sponsorship in 1983. I believe that was due to a number of reasons. He was very frustrated that I had to start in the Third Division after I had already made my way into the Second at the end of 1981 – that got things off to a shaky start. The politics in speedway also irritated him, as Harry Oxley had his rules and they were his rules. And then the problems with Becker – all this combined together and burnt him out. We had a big party at the end of the season and celebrated our learning curve, and that was the end of it. You never want to lose a sponsor, but I have to say that I was ready to do my own thing in 1983.

I was beaten to the 'Rookie of the Year' title by Rick Miller. But there were two distinct riders here: Miller had the Penhall look, the cool leathers, the stars and stripes and I believe he was a protégé of Penhall's. Everything looked good. I was the opposite side of it, as I was a Gaston & Dillon rider, and we had our own team, but it wasn't a big fancy Bruce Penhall World Championship-type of team like Miller's.

At the end of the season, we had a dinner which was organised by Harry Oxley and his promotion. My sister, Carol, embarrassed me while I was sat there talking to Bobby Schwartz. She came up and said: 'Hi, Bobby, I've seen you ride. Sam Ermolenko, remember that name, because he will be beating you one day.' Bobby didn't really know me that well because he wasn't a California-based rider as he was racing in Britain at the time, and he just looked at her and said, 'What?' That was embarrassing; but she did it and all I could say to her was, 'What are you doing, shut up.'

In 1983, he was finally able to revert to his preferred first name of Sam. He was also able to choose a double-figure number, and the number he chose was 13. Former Belle Vue star, Larry Kosta, was the holder of that number, but he had retired and no one wanted it. As he was not superstitious, he took the number and was all set for his second full season of racing on the Californian circuits.

He was riding a Weslake now, and he began the new season with encouraging results. At the Spring Classic at Ventura, he finished in fourth place with 12 points, and he faced Schwartz and Steve Lucero in a run-off for the minor places, but trailed them – his sister's words to 'Boogaloo' Schwartz had not yet come true. The meeting was won by Robert Pfetzing, with 13 points. He also appeared at Hemet, where he scored 10 points to finish in fourth place. This was not an AMA-sanctioned event, and the meeting was won by Mike Curoso.

This was no fluke, as his early season promise continued throughout the year. In an interview he gave to the American *Speedway Magazine,* he stated that his ambition was to make the National Championships. He duly achieved this by scoring 43 points. Furthermore, to underline his undoubted First Division status, he won his first scratch main at San Bernardino on 13 July, by sweeping around the outside of Gene Woods, while Mike Bast and John Cook squabbled at the back. He finished third in the Ventura Track Championship, with 13 points, behind the winner Mike Faria and Bobby Schwartz.

But his best achievement of the season was his victory with Robert Pfetzing in the Californian Best Pairs Championship. In a meeting that was marred by controversy and problems on and off the track, this duo scored 25 points (Sam 12 and Pfetzing 13) to finish ahead of their nearest challengers – Dubb Ferrell and John Cook – by four points. Incidentally, Ferrell was the last winner of this competition when it was previously staged in 1976, when he won with Jeff Sexton.

In the USA, the season was beginning to wind down in September. Sam had eight main events to his name racing at Ventura, and was now handicapped 50 yards at the track they called 'the commotion by the ocean'. But he also won a handicap event at Costa Mesa too and, just as he was at San Bernardino, he was now handicapped 40 yards at America's two premier tracks. He was now a First Division regular. It was around this time, when he was beginning his preparations for the Nationals, that he received a long-distance telephone call.

I received a call from a man who introduced himself as Brian Maidment of Poole, Dorset, England, and he was calling with regard to see if I would be interested in riding for them in the British League. At that point I had no ambitions to ride in England. I had a business with Bill and it was an appointment-only type of business, so we could come and go as we pleased as long as we kept our customers happy. We were happy with the arrangement, and we were making a bit of money out of it, so I wasn't really that interested in riding in England. After he told me who he was, he asked me if I had a manager he could talk to about it. This surprised me that he asked for a manager.

I had to think on my feet, and the person I thought of was Paul Heffernan. He was from Western Australia, and he really looked the part as if he had taken a page out of NASCAR or Indy Car racing, as he wore this shirt with STP and Kal-Gard logos on it. I saw a lot of him, especially around Ventura, and he represented these companies within the sport. He also acquired sponsorship for some of the riders. After the races, I would constantly approach him by saying stuff like: 'Hey Paul, I'm better rider than some of your guys, how about getting me some sponsorship?' And he would shrug it off and tease me by saying maybe he could and maybe he couldn't. I would talk to him as a racer to a professional, and we used to get along quite well. But he was the only person I could think of that knew anything about racing in England. So I told Brian: 'Yeah, I'm managed' (even though I wasn't) and I told him to call back tomorrow – that was how I left it.

I knew I probably couldn't go to England because of my family commitments, but I gave Paul a call and I asked him what I should do. I told him that I didn't think he could afford me because I had a business to run and a family to support, I couldn't really see it working out. And he said: 'Well, what do you want to do. Tell him no? Then tell him no.'

'I don't really want to tell him 'no', I just want to hear what he's got to say.'

We put something together on paper and then when Brian called the next day, I passed on Paul's number and told him to call us in the evening on that number and said we'd all talk together.

That evening, when I finished work, I called Paul and he told me to stop by and get some donuts from a donut shop on the way. The idea was that we would eat these with a cup of coffee while we waited for Brian to call. It was a warm pleasant evening and I was wearing my shorts, flip-flop shoes, and a t-shirt when I pulled in at this donut shop. As I opened my car door, I looked across and there was this car next to me and the door was open and I could see this girl lying across the seat with her head on the driver's lap. Then all of sudden she sat up and she was hysterical and screaming, and saying 'help me'. This woke me up! When I asked what the hell was going on, the driver grabbed her hair and pulled her down and said: 'Yeah, fuck off! Mind your own business.' I closed my door and walked toward the shop, but I asked her again before I went in if she was okay, and he told me to get lost – or words to that effect – and to get away from the car. I couldn't handle this. I noticed a phone box inside the shop, and I decided – as there were only two girls serving behind the counter – to call the police.

As I was dialling the number, I had my back towards the door, and where the car was parked, this guy must have seen me going for the phone. All of a sudden the door came crashing open just as I turned, and I jumped back and started running for the door at the other end of the counter. What must the two girls behind the counter have been thinking, as this guy was in hot pursuit and yelling that he was going to kill me! He had just about grabbed me, when I burst out of that door and I went crashing into a newspaper stand. I went straight over the top of it onto the street. He was on the other side, still saying that he was going to kill me, so for a little while we were chasing each other in circles around the stand as I was trying to dodge him. Then I bolted down the sidewalk, and it was a road that had four lanes of traffic. But I was heading away from the intersection and it was getting darker. I realised that was a bad idea, so I ran across the street and back in the other direction. I was barefoot by now as I had lost my flip-flops, but I passed the donut shop and headed toward the traffic lights as there were cars there and I was hoping that someone would help me. This guy was bigger than me, but he was still pursuing me and I was scared. I ran around the cars that were stopped at the red lights, but no one wanted to know. The lights turned green and everyone pulled away. The chase continued around the bushes until more traffic stopped at the lights.

This time I was running around a truck, but I was getting tired now. But my adversary was still saying that he was going to get me and kill me. He was right behind me, so I bent over and threw an elbow into his stomach and then we were both on the ground. He was on top of me and was trying to punch me, but I had a hold of his hair and twisted his head so he couldn't see where exactly he was punching. We were in the middle of the road when a car pulled up and the driver said: 'Hey come on guys, what are you doing? Take this off the road.'

I took the opportunity to tell him what was happening, and I said: 'I don't know who this guy is, he just started attacking me, and he's threatened to kill me. Can you get him off me?'

He jumped out of his car and broke us up. I took about ten steps back from him, and the other guy ran off. The cops arrived and I told them all about it. But when we went back to the donut shop, the car was still there, but the two people were nowhere to be seen. So they couldn't do anything.

I got the donuts and carried on to Paul's place. I couldn't find my other shoe, so I was sat there with just one shoe and when he came out with the coffee, I said: 'You wouldn't believe what had just happened to me.' It's kind of funny when I look back at it – it could only happen in the USA.

Sam and Paul drew up some terms that he would need to be able to ride during the last six weeks of the British season and maintain his family. The draft included a van, a bike, points money and a guarantee, plus with the Nationals and the State Championships coming up, he would have to fly back to the USA to fulfil those commitments. They thought that there would be no way that the promoter could afford these terms.

When Maidment called, he explained that he wanted Sam to race in the last few weeks of the season so that they could have a look at him and maybe do a deal to race a full season in 1984. Heffernan passed on his terms and Sam thought that would be the last that they would hear about it. But, to their surprise, Maidment said that the terms were acceptable. They put the final decision off for a day, and Sam decided that he could afford to go and Bill could look after the business while he was over in England for six weeks. All that remained was to tell his family.

We were at my mom's place, and I sat them down and told them what had happened. They already knew that I had had a phone call, but they didn't know what would develop from that. I explained what had happened, and that he wanted me to go over and race in England for six weeks. The first reaction I got from my wife was 'No way. What about us? You can't do that, you have two kids and me – I don't think you should go.' I thought it was a good deal, but she didn't agree. It continued like this back and forth, and even my mom was saying that she didn't think it was a good idea, as I had a family to think about and they had to come first. I said:

'Look, the money ain't bad. I could earn quite good money at this, and there are only two meetings left here and he's going to fly me back for the National and State Championships.' But the more I talked about it, the more she disagreed and said that I shouldn't do it.

By now, I was getting a bit more forceful and more aggressive. I was still defending the idea by saying that the money was good, and don't be so negative and look on the positive side. I was still going on about the benefits of it when she agreed. But I was still defending the idea, and was going on and on and on, when she said; 'Yeah, OK.'

'What? Oh.'

'I just wanted to make sure that you really wanted to do it,' Shelley said. 'If I said "Do it" and you didn't want to do it, then it would have been a waste of time. If you are sure you want to do it – then do it.'

She was behind me one hundred per cent. I told Brian that I would do it, and I had to rush down and get a passport and Brian had to organise a work permit. I asked some of the riders that were here who had raced in Britain, like Kelly Moran, what it was like, and he told me a little bit about it, and I knew Rick Miller was already over there.

Then I got onto a plane and Brian Maidment met me at the airport. I remember wondering what it was all about, because we were driving on the opposite side of the road to where we drive in America and everything was so green. I remember travelling the whole way to Poole and I didn't know where we were going or what was going on. I stayed at Brian's house and he had a very warm family, he had three children – two girls and a boy – that were younger than me.

I had to get a bike, and the only person I knew was Bobby Schwartz. Brian had already made contact with him to tell him that I was coming over. After my sister had told him to watch out for me because I would be there one day, now he knew I was there. I asked him where I could get a bike and he told me to call Trackstar Equipment, and I ordered a complete bike. All the stuff was shipped to Bobby's house.

During the first couple of days, we went to Weymouth to watch some racing, and I drove there to make sure I was okay to drive in England. I watched the meeting and it was quite a culture shock because the racing was totally different – it was more professional and it was a lot colder! I didn't feel intimidated by it; I was just taking it all in. The next day, a Swedish rider, Leif Wahlmann and I were at the Poole track having a trial. I can't remember whose bike I rode, it may have been one of Neil Middleditch's or Andy Campbell's, but Wahlmann was going really fast with the throttle wide

*open. I was just cruising, pulling wheelies and testing the track and trying
to figure it out. They were all watching from the offices and Reg Fearman,
who was the co-promoter, came down and introduced himself. Later that
evening, we were all sat around having dinner when Brian remarked that
Leif looked really good, and he was a little concerned about me because I
wasn't out there putting the laps in like Leif was. He asked me if I was okay
and did I feel comfortable?*

*Brian Maidment gave me his keys and I made arrangements to drive all
the way to Bobby's house in Sutton Coldfield to get my bike. When I
arrived, Bobby let me use his workshop to put all the bits together, and that's
when I began riding in England.*

Sam Ermolenko made his British League debut for the Poole Pirates
on 28 September 1983. He appeared in a challenge fixture against
Reading – Schwartz raced for Reading – that ended in a 39-39
draw, and he scored one point by relegating Stanislav Urban to
fourth. In the USA, all the racing is on an individual basis, whereas
in Britain it is a predominately a team structure – although there are
individual tournaments that take place throughout the season. If a
rider is serious about making his mark on the international stage,
then it is considered to be most important that a rider races in
the BL to acquire the necessary skills that regular team racing
can provide.

*It was quite an experience riding for Poole. When I stepped on the plane to
come over to England, I was trying to get used to the idea that I would be
racing for a team. The only things I could compare it with were American
football, ice hockey or basketball teams. I thought that we would all train
together and race together, but it wasn't like that. Basically we were all indi-
viduals who came together that night and raced for Poole. The rest of the
time, the riders would go off and do what they did: some had jobs, and some
raced abroad.*

*I used to have my bikes at the Bailie House, which was owned by the
Middleditch family, who were really nice people. It was an unofficial hotel for
speedway riders. I couldn't maintain my bike at Brian's because the shed he*

had there was full of tyres. Apparently he bought all these tyres because he expected that this particular make of tyre would be the one they would have to use during the season, but they changed the rules and he got stuck with them. Therefore, I did all my work at Bailie's, and that's where I met all the boys. They had little garage units there and I had a little propane heater to keep the autumn chill off, and that was where I worked on my bikes.

I remember I was paired with Michael Lee in the opening race. I was preparing for my first race when he was pushed off, did a practice start and roared into the third bend. I didn't know what to do – it was my first time racing in England, so I thought that was what I was supposed to do. So off I went sliding into the bend, but when I looked up Michael had parked it and was getting ready to do another practice start. And I thought, 'Oh no.' Just as he released his clutch, I was already starting to lay my bike down as my engine cases bumped his back wheel. He must have thought 'Man, this bike is working good from the start!'

The other riders used to say to me, 'Sam, when you go to start line, look at the tapes and when the tapes go up – go!' They used to call me 'the 1-2-3 go guy', because I had no idea what the technique was of getting out of start in England when compared with America. What I used to do was, wait for the tapes to rise, 1-2-3 and I guess it seemed that I didn't respond fast enough, as the rest of the field were already gone by the time I dropped the clutch. All I knew was how to ride my bike, as in America the start wasn't as important as it was here.

Predictably, Sam took a bit of time to get adjusted to racing in the BL, but he received an early confidence boost when he replaced the injured Mitch Shirra at Reading. He finished ahead of Erik Gundersen, who was one of the top five riders in the league. His scores improved with each meeting, including an encouraging 6 points at home to Wimbledon, and then he added a paid 9 score in a challenge match at home to Cradley Heath.

However, his showmanship attracted immediate attention from the long-serving Wimbledon rider, Roger Johns, who was staging a testimonial meeting. Although the American had only been in England for a few weeks, Johns asked him if he would ride in his testimonial. Somewhat surprised to be offered such an invitation so early in his BL career, he asked the Wimbledon rider why. 'I want you to come and do some of your wheelies,' he replied.

Sam raced in only four official fixtures for the Pirates, but he appeared in other challenge matches. Therefore, as the challenge fixtures do not count in the official statistics, his 4.25 finishing average would not be a problem when it came to getting a work permit for 1984. Poole were happy with his performances and he was set to return for a full season of British League racing.

Meanwhile, Sam scored only 2 points in the US National Championships which were won by Kelly Moran, but he did much better in the California State Championship, when he scored 8 points – Mike Bast won that title. When he returned to the States, they closed the business and kept one unit where Sam stored his possessions. Speedway was more of a hobby until he went to Poole, but from that moment on he became really serious about racing speedway. His partner in the business came over with him, and his wife and children all stayed in a rented house in Bournemouth.

Poole Speedway, despite having some great riders in their teams over the years that included the Americans Ron Preston and Scott Autrey, had not enjoyed a lot of success since they had won the League Championship in 1969. Ermolenko was joined in the team by the 1980 World Champion, Michael Lee – who had returned to some of his best form for the Pirates in 1983 – Australian Stan Bear, Neil Middleditch and Kevin Smith, Leif Wahlmann, and Brian Jakobsen from Denmark. They might not have been the strongest team in the league, but they did possess a lot of potential.

I had travelled over with a deal on paper ready to sign, but the promotion was a little reluctant to honour the deal we made, but after the opening meeting they responded with open arms ...

Sam had the whole stadium buzzing when he scored an 11-point paid maximum as the Pirates defeated a Phil Crump Select side 45-

32. His first race win in England came over Bo Petersen, Frank Andersen and Andy Fines. He continued to score well until – ironically, given how his career developed – he made his first trip to Wolverhampton and crashed heavily into the fence with Steve Schofield and his team-mate Wahlmann, sustaining severe bruising to his back.

Nonetheless, he was back in time to make his first appearance for the USA Test team in the first match between England and the USA at Swindon on 14 April 1984. He was paired with Shawn Moran, and scored 4 points in America's 58-50 victory. Sam appeared in all five matches in the series, which the Americans won 4-1. His best performance came in the Third Test at Cradley, where he scored 7 points.

Poole's season was wrecked when the tempestuous Lee was handed a five-year ban by the sport's authorities – a successful appeal reduced the ban to 12 months. He had been in all sorts of trouble: he failed to arrive at Wolverhampton, walked out of the England *v.* USA Test at Ipswich following a disagreement with referee Frank Ebdon over a starting offence, and another incident at King's Lynn meant that Lee was in hot water with the authorities. For Sam, this would mean that more would be expected of him.

I had a small workshop in my house in Bournemouth, but I would rely on Neil Middleditch and Michael Lee during my apprenticeship year. Michael helped me a lot. I remember that he was often working on other people's engines as well as his own, and because of this he was very tired. On one occasion, he just made it in time to race in a Golden Helmet match race. He only just had time to put his gear on and get on his bike.

1984 was the first year when you weren't allowed to touch the tapes. Michael was very good at anticipating the start, and someone like referee Frank Ebdon hated it, because he said that he wasn't still and he excluded him. Erik Gundersen was another rider who found it difficult to adjust to this rule. I was still learning, so it didn't have the same effect on me.

Sam entered the World Championship for the first time when he appeared in the American Final at the Veterans Stadium, Long

Beach. He scored 6 points and failed to qualify – which was not surprising, when one takes into consideration his lack of experience at that level, and the fact that there were only four qualifying places available for a quality field to fight over.

Nevertheless, he had returned home with a more professional approach to his racing, and one could see that this professionalism came from his character. This was no longer a hobby to the likeable American; he was serious about climbing up the ladder of success. This was illustrated to the US public when an interview appeared in the US publication, *Speedway Magazine*, when he was speaking to journalist John Chaplin about racing in England:

'The best thing about it is that everyone is really professional. Everyone is serious and everyone wants to win. You know any guy can beat anybody here, and I just find that the competition is so high,' he said. 'You gotta be on top of it by keeping your bikes maintained and organised, and it's real good experience.'

Poole continued to struggle with the absence of their number one, Lee, and even the signing of former World Finalist, Finn Thomsen, did little to prevent the Pirates from finishing in the lower reaches of the league table. Towards the end of the season, however, he was joined by another American, Bobby Ott, who had a few meetings for the team.

But the biggest tragedy to hit the club was the death of Leif Wahlmann in a crash at King's Lynn. He was competing in the European Under-21 Championship when his engine seized while he was leading Andy Smith, and 'Smudger' was unable to avoid him. He died the following afternoon from head injuries. Poole felt the loss deeply, as in 1979 the club had suffered the loss of another Swedish rider, Christer Sjosten, who was killed in a track crash in Brisbane.

One of the few bright spots was provided by the performances of Ermolenko. In the absence of Lee, the role of the club's number one rider passed over to him. He did very well; his best performance was a 14-point score in their fixture at fellow strugglers, Newcastle. He was the darling of the Dorset public – his natural ability meant that he could pick the right lines to pull off some magnificent and breathtaking passing manoeuvres. His smooth but entertaining style, combined with his showmanship, made him very popular with the Pirates' supporters, and he was their representative in the British League Riders' Championship.

This event is one of the toughest in the world, and the line-up was stronger than the World Final itself. It was staged at Belle Vue's Hyde Road circuit, and it was Aces rider Chris Morton who won the event, with 13 points. Sam was assisted in the pits by Lee and scored 6 points. However, he brought the crowd to their feet when he defeated the new World Champion, Erik Gundersen, in heat 11 – the Danish rider's first defeat of the evening.

His first full season of British racing had been very encouraging. He had an average which was close to 7 points a match and, subsequently, he was automatically guaranteed a work permit for 1985. It seemed likely that he would return for another season, and he began making more solid preparations. But such a hard season had taken its toll on the Pirates' promotion, and clouds of doubt began to gather over the Pirates' unsteady ship.

I was interested in buying a property in England. I had viewed a place and even got to the stage of talking to solicitors about it, when Brian advised me not commit to anything as he was unsure of the financial situation with Poole Speedway. So I held off buying the property and went home. I took all my equipment with me, some of which I acquired from Michael Lee, and because I could use Bobby Schwartz's frequent flyer connections, I was allowed to have extra baggage. Michael was selling all of this stuff, so I took full advantage of the situation.

Poole withdrew from the British League, and the nearby Weymouth promotion moved their National League Wildcats team to Wimborne Road. It proved to be a big success; but this meant that Sam was without a team for 1985, as the National League was only open to British and Commonwealth riders. Despite one of the best debut seasons in recent years by an American, Sam was not contacted by any prospective British League promoters about a team place. Therefore, he began his preparations for a season at home in California.

In those days, it was quite a big expense to bring my family over to race in England, especially when you compared it with someone like Rick Miller, who was a single rider. I was the only American in the British League that had a young family, and I wouldn't like to think that was the reason why Poole had financial problems – but you never know.

I went to San Bernardino to practise before the new season began, and through my dad's motorcycle shop I was able to practise what I had learned in 1984 about setting up engines. I used the experience I had gained from listening to the advice of Michael Lee, Neil Middleditch and Phil Pratt, and I started on a shoestring. England paid its way, but it wasn't anything to brag about. I couldn't plough a lot of money into my racing because I had to feed my family – they came first.

In 1985, as well as Costa Mesa, San Bernardino (IMS) and Ventura, two more tracks were added to the programme in southern California, and they were Ascot and Carlsbad. This would represent a peak in the boom in speedway racing in the USA, which began in 1982 when Bruce Penhall won the second of his two World Championships.

Sam finished in third place overall in the traditional season open-er, the Spring Classic series. But he soon got into the winning habit at the Inland Motorcycle Speedway, bringing all the experience he gained in Europe to the fore to win the first three meetings at the track. They introduced a short competition for the riders, called the IMS/Cycle Rider Inc. Trophy Series. However, such was the success that Sam was having that, by the time the third round had been completed, *Speedway Magazine* described it as the 'Sam Ermolenko/IMS/Cycle Rider, Inc. Benefit series.' During a hot period that began in mid-April and ran through to mid-May, Sam won at Ascot, Costa Mesa, Carlsbad, and Ventura, and strengthened his grip on the series at San Bernardino with another scratch main success. His success at San Bernardino attracted an old fan and a new fan all rolled into one.

When I signed up for my licence, I had to go with my legal name, which was Guy Allen Ermolenko. I told them that everybody called me Sam, but they said that I couldn't do that. It was only later in my career, after I had made a name for myself, that I was able to change my name to Sam because I was now one of the boys.

Then, after I had a good night at San Bernardino, I was in the pits packing up, when this guy came up to me and congratulated me after I had won all my races, and he said: 'Jeez, man, you're going good, tell me, whatever happened to your brother Guy?'!

Sam established himself as *the* in-form rider at a time when the reigning National Champion, Kelly Moran, started off his season with a hot winning streak at Ventura, when Lance King was showing US fans why he was once ranked number three in the world, and when Flyin' Mike Faria had kicked off his campaign by winning the Spring Classic. Therefore, there was no shortage of top-class competition. Unlike some of his rivals, he was achieving these results without a major sponsorship package behind him, and he knew that to maintain that kind of form and achieve his goal of making the World Final, this was something that he had to address.

There was a rider called Randy Blevins who had an injury at Ventura in 1984, and he wasn't able to ride the following year. Therefore, he turned his hand to doing some journalism, and he used to tape interviews with the riders before the racing and then they would be played in between the races. It was an opportunity for me to ask for sponsorship. So when he asked me to comment on how well things were going, I took the opportunity to explain that as long as I was winning, I would be able to keep my equipment in first-class condition. But I wouldn't be able to maintain my equipment at such a high level for long once my winning streak had come to an end. So I was looking for sponsors, and if anyone was interested then come and see me.

One of the spectators came down to the chain-link fence that separated the public from the pits, and he called me over. He said that he had a brother-in-law who owned a company based in Irwindale who was a speedway fan, and he was quite sure that he would like to help me out. He asked me what sort of figure I was looking for, and I told him $10,000 off the top of my head.

'Oh yeah, he can afford that – no problem,' he said. 'I'll bring him down after the races and introduce him to you.'

I won again that night, and this man came down to see me. He gave me his card, and he told me to call him so we could talk business. His brother-in-law gave me the thumbs up, as if to say 'no problem, he'll sponsor you'. His name was Gary Gugelamo, and as they walked out of the pits, I was telling my mechanic that it looked as though we would be getting some help – which was exactly what we needed because we were having a good run, and we needed the support to keep the momentum going. As I was watching these people leave, I saw a yellow Ferrari leaving the parking lot with Gary inside. I knew then that he was serious about sponsoring me, so I didn't waste any time and I called him the next day and arranged to meet him.

He told me that he was a fan, and he ran a company called PC Laminated, and he asked me how he could help. So I explained what I had done, and that my goal that year was to make the 1985 World Final. He gave me a cheque for $10,000. That was a turning point in my fortunes for that campaign, and it inspired me.

I put together a little sponsorship package on my computer that I had at the time. It was an old DOS machine and not the fancy Windows we have now. I was motivated to get some more sponsorship. A friend I went to school with, his father ran a company called Pick Your Part. This was basically a group of vehicle salvage venues where someone could go and get the parts they needed. They are really big in Southern California now, but at the time he had three sites where you could go in and get the parts you needed with your own tools. It was suggested that he could be a good person to approach because his company was doing well, and I had this tenuous link with his son.

I called the company and managed to get through all the red tape by saying that I was a friend of the family. His name was Glenn, and I said to him: 'You don't know me, but I used to go to school with your son. I have an advertising proposal which I would like to present to you, and I wondered if I could make an appointment.' He agreed to see me the next day.

When I arrived, the man was casually addressed and he was ordering his lunch. Just as I sat down, the phone rang and he excused himself to deal with the call. Then I had my opportunity to put forward my proposal. This was the first time that I had done anything like this, but I outlined what I did, how I perceived that it would work with the five tracks that were operating in the area at the time, and the benefits that his company would get in relation to the number of fans. And he said: 'Sure, how much money do you want?'

Those were the only words he said, and it caught me off-guard. A lady came in and she was his marketing person, and she thought it was a good idea. He told me to work out what budget I wanted and to come back. I came back with a figure of $20,000, and he agreed, as long as I didn't want it all in one go. So we worked out a schedule to spread the deal over the course of the season.

These two sponsorship deals arrived just in time for Sam to compete in the World Championship. They would be vital in the final analysis of how his world title hopes would work out.

The first round was the American Final at Long Beach. This time the number of qualifying places was increased from four to five – but it was still a very tough round to negotiate with the top US riders from the British League returning to join the field. There was no stopping John Cook, who won the event with an immaculate 15-point maximum, but Sam was second with 13, and they were joined in the next round by Shawn Moran, Lance King and Rick Miller. Sam's determination in the meeting was illustrated when he swapped the lead and traded elbows with Bobby Schwartz in heat 15. The 10,000 crowd went nuts when 'Sudden' Sam sealed victory by passing Schwartz on the last lap. It was a win that all but ended Schwartz's Championship hopes, and his sister's prophecy was fulfilled.

The next round was the Overseas Final at Bradford. It was another American, Shawn Moran, who won this round, but Sam was puzzled by the way he struggled to make the all-important top 10 with just 7 points. He had a bright start with 5 points from two rides, but then only added a further 2 points from his remaining rides. In heat 12, he was surprised to lose the lead and was relegated to last, when he was passed by Lance King, John Davis and Phil Collins. However, a third place ahead of Neil Collins in heat 17 eventually made sure of his passage to the next round. He was looked upon as a surprise qualifier, but told the press that he had no intention of racing in Britain.

'I cannot see it doing me much good,' he told *Speedway Star*. 'I just want to get to the World Final. I've got good sponsorship in the States, and I'm not going to sacrifice what I have at home to come and race here.'

The Inter-Continental Final took place on a rain-soaked track at Vetlanda, Sweden. Moran won again, but this time Sam was more consistent and scored 9 points to book his place in his first World Final. But in the wet conditions, Sam had to battle for his points, and his brave riding made sure that he scored at least a point in each of his races.

I had a good practice at Vetlanda – I was posting some fast times, just as I did at the Bradford practice. We had a lot of rain, and the meeting was held up when Kenny Carter had a crash and injured the leg he had broken a month or so earlier. Extra shale was put down, and that delayed the meeting for half an hour or so. Despite the conditions, they continued with the event, as they said that it would have been very difficult to reschedule it because of all of the international meetings that were going on at that time.

One of those was the World Team Cup Final, which was staged for the first time in the USA. As hosts, the Americans were favourites to win their second team title. They faced the holders, Denmark, together with Sweden and England, and the format was a four-team tournament. It was held at Long Beach, and it was a track that Denmark's Erik Gundersen described as one of the best he had ever raced on.

Sam was selected to ride at reserve, and he was joined in the team by Bobby Schwartz (the captain), John Cook, Shawn Moran and Lance King. Bruce Penhall was the team manager, along with the Americans' usual manager, John Scott.

Everything was geared toward an American success, but Denmark were in no mood to let the title slip from their grasp. Sweden and England were left to scrap over the bronze medal, while the Yanks and the Danes went head to head in a gold rush on the track.

However, Cookie was off the pace, and a fall in his second outing meant that 'Sudden Sam' emerged into an electric atmosphere to face Denmark's Preben Eriksen, Jimmy Nilsen of Sweden and England's Richard Knight in heat 11. In front of a capacity crowd, the USA held a slender 1-point lead over the Danes, as Sam began his preparations. Eriksen made the start and was away, while Sam slipped by the other two riders to make sure that the two countries were level on points as they entered heat 12.

By the time Sam rolled out for his second race of the evening in heat 14, the Danes had established a 4-point lead and had provided all the race winners. Shawn Moran was the last American to win a race in heat 10. Sam faced Gundersen, Kelvin Tatum and Tommy Nilsson of Sweden. He was last from the gate, and while he swept by Nilsson, he soon discovered that you couldn't let a couple of fast starters like Erik and Tatum get away from you at that level.

The destiny of the World Team Cup was decided in heat 15 – the penultimate race – with a classic speedway struggle between Denmark's unbeaten Tommy Knudsen and 'Captain America' Bobby Schwartz. The American led for two laps, but he left the slightest of gaps and Knudsen took the lead. Despite a magnificent effort, Schwartz was unable to overhaul Knudsen and the title remained in Denmark.

Although America lost the trophy, they won the praise and support of the speedway world by providing the most competitive final in the history of the competition. The presentation, the racing and the atmosphere were the best ever for a World Team Cup Final. Sam finished with 3 points from his two rides, while the top scorers for the Americans were Shawn Moran and Schwartz with 11 points – both only lost to the unbeaten Knudsen.

'We had everything going for us, but I don't think we were as strong in depth as we needed to be,' admitted Schwartz.

All this was good experience for Ermolenko, and it was the kind of knowledge that would only help his performance for his next big meeting of the year – the 1985 World Individual Championship Final. His preparations for the final at Long Beach were hampered by a lack of practice. Along with King, he had only ridden on a similar sized track on a handful of occasions that year, so they both needed the practice to experiment with their set-ups. He warmed up for the World Final by making sure of his place in the US Nationals, and he posted main event victories at Ascot, Carlsbad, Ventura and San Bernardino.

Terry Clanton was an announcer, and he was keen to follow in the footsteps of Bruce Flanders and Larry Huffman – although he liked Flanders' style. He used to be a rider himself, so he was keen to draw on his experience as a rider and combine it with his announcing. There was a weekly television programme that was going out on ESPN, and he was keen to be a part of that.

He said that if I qualified for the World Final, then he would like to come over with me. Terry was a very enthusiastic man, and because of his experience as an ex-rider, I thought that it would be a good idea. We collected my bikes from the Baillie House, as they were stored in one of the sheds there, and we were on quite a tight schedule, as we were due at Bobby Schwartz's house in Sutton Coldfield. As well as Terry, my wife was with me, but I believe it was Terry's first time in England. He was taking everything in and he was amazed at how different it was compared with America. At this point I was feeling pretty tired, and we were all jet-lagged from the flight. But I was having problems staying awake and, as I was driving the van to Bobby's, I needed a rest. I could barely keep my eyes open, but I knew that my wife wasn't comfortable driving in England at that time, so as Terry was there to help, I asked him to take over the driving so that I could grab a few minutes' sleep. But he said 'No way', as he was worried about driving on the left-hand side instead of the right. I was giving him a bit of grief over this because he talked the talk, but he didn't feel confident enough to help me, so I wondered what he was going to do.

We were just cruising down the motorway and I was really tired and I was desperate for some rest. As we were on a tight schedule, I knew we couldn't afford to stop travelling. Shelley was sat in between Terry and me so I said to her: 'Just steer it for a minute and I'll wedge my foot up against the accelerator pedal so that it holds a consistent speed, and you can steer the van.'

'How are we going to do that?' she asked.

'Well, just bump me and I'll wake up, and I'll lift the accelerator a bit or put it back on. I just need a few minutes' sleep to give me that extra bit of energy to stay awake.'

That's what we did; and Terry couldn't believe it! I think we did that two or three times during the journey. I would drive for twenty minutes or half an hour, and then I would get tired and then I would have my five minutes' sleep. It worked out and we got there on time.

I discovered that Terry had great enthusiasm but didn't know how to do anything much. When we were at Bobby's house preparing for the practice, he was going on and talking like he does about nothing much, so we gave him a job. His job was to cut the sipes in the tyres a little bit deeper – which was a standard thing that we used to do, it just helped the tyre spread a little bit better so that you could get the maximum amount of grip from it – that was Terry's job, and it kept him busy so that we could concentrate on what we had to do.

I was doing really well in the practice sessions, and I was consistently among the fastest times. But what I discovered was that my engines would be fast in practice, but not during the meeting itself, because the tracks had more grip and my engines were too soft when it came to race day.

When it came to the World Final, I asked Bobby Schwartz if I could borrow his bike. He loaned me his bike and his mechanic, Billy Sutton, and I practised at the World Final on my bike to begin with. As had happened before, I was going well in practice. Then I rode Bobby's bike and it was spin-

ning and vibrating and it wasn't hooking up so well. Therefore, I believed that it was going to be better than mine on race day when the track would have more grip. I explained this to Bobby and he agreed with me, and Billy pulled out the engine and put it into my frame. We had 24 hours to get everything ready, and Bobby told me to go to bed as they would take care of it all. 'Go on, Sam, get some sleep,' he said, 'we can take care of this for you. You don't want to be doing this before a World Final; you need to get some rest for tomorrow.' He told me to go back to my hotel in Bradford, and that Billy and himself would be with me in the pits at the final. So that's what I did, and Bobby and Billy were a great help to me – they were my saviours.

The pre-meeting favourites were the reigning World Champion, Erik Gundersen, his fellow countryman and runner-up from 1984, Hans Nielsen, and Shawn Moran, who had won the last two rounds and was enjoying the best season of his career. As well as Sam, there were two other Americans in the final, Lance King and John Cook. It was the first time that the nation had provided four World Finalists.

The pressure was off Ermolenko, with no one expecting him to make a serious challenge for the title. Ivan Mauger, in his World Final preview in *Speedway Star,* said that he didn't expect him to finish any further than halfway up the field. *Speedway Mail* described him as 'an unexpected qualifier'; although no one denied he had the ability, it was his lack of experience that turned the spotlight away from him. Only the ever-patriotic American *Speedway Magazine* gave him a hope of figuring among the front-runners.

I am not superstitious, but I was drawn to race at number 13 for the final, the room I was staying in at the hotel was 13, and when I went down to breakfast in the morning, the table was number 13 as well. From my point of view, I was pretty excited about the whole thing as everything seemed to be falling into place.

We talked about a game plan for the meeting, and it was decided that second places would be my aim. Basically if I was in third, then I would try really hard to get up into second, but if I was second I would defend and consolidate that position unless I really felt that I could take first. If I was fourth, then I planned to really go for it and fight my way up the field.

My first race was against Erik Gundersen and Hans Nielsen. There was such a rivalry between them after they had such a battle in the 1984 Championships, that Bobby felt that they would be so worried about each other that they could take each other out. Therefore, I could pick up some useful points if I let them go in the first bend.

I arrived at the track and Bobby was there with his mechanic and my mechanic, and everything was in place – it was all organised. Bobby and I took a look at the track together, and he gave me a little speech to gee me up for the event. When I was sat in the pits, and the bikes were warming up for the racing, I suddenly realised that I didn't have my goggles or my tear-offs! It was a bit of panic – I didn't know what I was going to do as I had left them at my hotel.

There was no way that I wanted to use anyone else's because you don't want anything to upset your routine. There were no mobile phones in those days, so what we did was to get someone to put out a message over the PA system for Brian Maidment: 'Would Brian Maidment please go to the pits please. Brian Maidment to the pits please – thank you.' Brian came in, and the start time was fast approaching, and he said: 'What's the matter?'

'I've forgotten my Jones goggles and tear-offs and left them at the hotel. Can you go and get them for me, please?'

He readily agreed to do this and, of course, with maybe only about twenty minutes to go before the parade – if that – the traffic outside was horrendous at this time, as everyone was queuing to get into the stadium. So he had to battle through that to get to my hotel, find my goggles, and then be able to get back in time. Luckily, my first race wasn't until heat 4, so that gave us a bit of extra time.

There were around 40,000 people there, and all the riders were called down to go on parade. I couldn't really take in the atmosphere because I was more concerned about not having my goggles. Therefore, I didn't get wrapped in the pressure of it all, because I was thinking, 'Oh man, where

*are my goggles?' I was more excited about the fact that I was in a World
Final, and I had my game plan. But when I got off the parade, there was
Brian standing there with my equipment. I was really happy to see him, so
I sat down in my pit and prepared my tear-offs and so on as the event
began to get underway.*

England's sole representative was Kelvin Tatum, and he set the Odsal
crowd buzzing when he won the opening heat. Pre-meeting
favourite and Yorkshire's adopted son, Shawn Moran, won his first
race too, while another rider making his first World Final appearance, Jan O. Pedersen, made light work of winning heat 3 over
another expected contender, Tommy Knudsen.

The crowd were ready for the big showdown between the two
main Danes in heat 4 – Erik Gundersen and Hans Nielsen. Sam
Ermolenko and Hungary's Zoltan Adorjan were looked upon as
extras for the two leading men, who would surely carry out the
drama of heat 4. Sam was off the outside gate, with Adorjan alongside, while Gundersen was in gate two, right next to Nielsen on the
inside berth.

Gundersen nudged the tapes twice as the tension grew, but it was
Nielsen who nosed ahead. Eager to keep in touch, the defending
Champion locked slightly coming off the turn and this was the
opportunity that Sam had been looking for, and he roared through
into second place. Suddenly – no pun intended – the American
had split the warring Danes, and he held on to a comfortable second place.

*It worked out just as we thought it would. They were so concerned about
each other that I was able to split them and get a second. When I returned
to the pits, Bobby congratulated me and said: 'Good job, Sam, I told you
they would be looking for each other.' That race gave me the confidence for
the rest of the meeting.*

Sam was out again in heat 5, and he hardly had time to consider his
achievement in his opening race before he faced Moran, Knudsen

and Tatum. Starting from the inside berth, he was unaware of the clash that sent Knudsen into the dirt, but he chased Tatum for first and moved him over on the back straight and went into the lead – only for the diminutive Moran to go outside both of them … but the red lights came on and the race was stopped.

The referee, Torre Kittilsen, allowed all four riders back in the race and it was re-run. There were no mistakes this time, and Sam emerged in the lead coming out of the second bend. He was able to pull away for his first race win, as Moran and Knudsen squabbled over second behind him.

He then had to wait for seven races to pass before he emerged from the pits for his third race – the final race before the interval. Once again, he started from the inside, and he won an emphatic victory with a tapes-to-flag win from Armando Castagna, Pedersen and Karl Maier. After all the riders had completed three rides, only Nielsen was unbeaten on 9, Sam was second with 8, and Gundersen had put in two determined rides to be joint third, with Finland's Kai Niemi, on 7 points. The challenges from pre-meeting favourites Moran and Knudsen were over.

Gundersen set a new track record in heat 13 of 59.3 seconds, as he won his fourth race to remain in touch at the top of the score chart. Sam took up gate two with Championship rival Niemi alongside him in gate three. Fellow American, Lance King, was on the outside, while the lone Soviet Union rider, Viktor Kuznetsov, was on the favoured inside. Kuznetsov wheelied off the start line, but it was Niemi who led, with the American in hot pursuit. The Finn blocked Sam's attempts to go round him at the end of the second lap, and although he continued to pressure Niemi, he finished in second place.

Niemi squeezed me a little bit, and at that point I thought that I could be a bit vulnerable, so I backed off. I didn't want to lose second as that was what I went there to do. So I settled for second, but that was the moment that cost me the World Championship.

Heat 16 saw the points leader Nielsen come off worst in a first-bend clash. Luckily he was not excluded, but he dropped his first points of the afternoon in the re-run, as he finished third behind John Cook and Knudsen. With the final round of races to come, the destiny of the 1985 World Championship was wide open, with Sam, Gundersen, Nielsen and Niemi all locked at the top with 10 points each. The next four races would decide the outcome.

Nielsen made no mistakes in heat 17 and won the race, but Kai Niemi was out of contention as he finished at the back – the best he could hope for was a place on the podium. But Nielsen had finished with a total of 13 points, so his rivals had to win their last races to face him in a run-off for the world title.

Sam was off gate three for his final programmed ride, with John Cook alongside him in gate four and Jan Anderson and Egon Muller inside him. With the prospect of at least a rostrum place in his sights, and a crack at winning the title, he wasn't short of motivation. It was the Swede Anderson who emerged in the lead, and he took Ermolenko wide on the first turn. Not be denied of his chance of glory, Sam raced after him, but then he came under pressure from Cook as they sped along the back straight. He fended off the attentions of 'Cowboy Cookie', and then with a ruthless piece of cornering, he passed Anderson around the outside of the second lap. As he took the chequered flag, he knew that he would face Nielsen in a run-off for the World Championship.

When I got back to my pit, suddenly all these people started peering round the curtains at me: people like the Briggos and the Maugers were saying things like 'Well done, Sam, you're doing well – you can do it.' At the beginning of the meeting, I was sat on my own in my cubicle they have there, but now that I was having success, all these people were coming to see me to give me support and encouragement. There was one race left, and Erik had to win this one to be in the run-off with me and Hans. We were watching the race and Shawn Moran and Lance King were beating Erik Gundersen, then before you knew it, Erik pulled off a big swoop around the outside of them and took the lead and won the race. It was felt that

King didn't try that hard to prevent him from doing this as they used to be team-mates at Cradley Heath. Before that I was in second place, but now it was a three man run-off.

At that point, Bobby put his serious cap on and said: 'Look, Sam, whatever happens at the start – it's green light, go!' I asked him what he meant and he explained: 'Well, when you see that green light go on, drop that clutch because the referee is going to be pretty quick.' That was something that I had never really practised, and I wasn't sure if I could get away with it. I was over the moon with my result, and before the last race I was second, and at the very least I was going to be the third-best rider in the world.

I was really pumped up for the run-off. All three of us were at the start line, and I was leaning the bike over on the footrest, while Erik and Hans were having their mental games. I was on the inside, with Nielsen next to me and Erik off the outside gate. I was thinking that it was perfect that I was on the inside, as I knew that I could get a good start there. I was revving up and getting ready to go, and then the green light came on. As I looked down, the tapes were already gone ... Bobby was right. I should have just revved it up and dumped that clutch, but I didn't do it. I was going into the corner and both of them went straight for the dirt line, but Erik was there first and he hit the dirt and left me for third.

Gundersen did all the hard work within the first 30 yards, and pressed down on Nielsen to make a successful defence of his world crown. For Sam, he had achieved more than he had expected. It was the closest an American had come to winning the World Final since Bruce Penhall's victory in 1982. It was almost lucky 13 for him as he finished with that total to add to the riding number, the table number and the room number.

In an interview in *Speedway Star*, Schwartz said: 'I geed Sam up, told him where to ride and he followed it to the letter. I couldn't believe it; he did far better than I could.'

Terry Clanton was not backward in coming forward either when it came to his contribution to Sam's success.

The first thing that Terry said was that because he cut the tyres correctly, he also helped in my success that day. Even when I see him, to this day, he always reminds me that he cut the tyres for me in that final, and it's his claim to fame.

While everyone was singing the praises of Gundersen's success, the sport's press were now praising Sam's performance and describing him as a 'shock merchant'. But there was no doubt that they now saw him as a future contender, and rumours immediately began to circulate of a return to the British League, with Coventry earmarked as his likely destination.

His performance meant that he was in demand, and he went to Vojens, Denmark, to race in the World Final revenge. He also raced for the USA in the Test series against England that saw them whitewash the hosts 3-0. Sam's best performance was 10 points at Ipswich, but he also made significant contributions in the other two Test matches too. He won his first international race for his country in the first Test at Belle Vue, when in dreadfully wet conditions he finished ahead of Kelvin Tatum, Lance King and Neil Collins. As he flew back to California as the number three rider in the world, his thoughts began to concentrate on his programme at home.

When I got back home, my sister Carol had organised a big hotel reception for my sponsors, family and friends. They showed some footage from the World Final, and we had a sit-down meal and I made a little speech. It was really nice, and I was made to feel very special. 'Pick Your Part' used their sponsorship of me to publicise their business, and I was featured on their posters and billboards on the sides of bus shelters and other advertising hoardings. It read something like: 'Pick Your Part – sponsors of Sam Ermolenko, third in the World Speedway Championships'. We both got a lot of publicity out of it.

Special he certainly was, as his good form continued when he returned to a hero's welcome at San Bernardino and won the scratch main. Two days later, he won at Costa Mesa, before he finished third in the Ventura Track Championships behind the winner Mike Faria and Lance King – the latter defeated him for second in a run-off. He returned to IMS and won another scratch main. This meant that he had clinched his eighth Cycle Inc-Riders'Trophy and won the overall series. He had justified the sport's claim in the US that he was the 'winningest rider on the scene'.

However, Steve Lucero won the California State Championship, while Sam defeated Faria in a run-off to secure the runners-up spot. As if to underline that this was a temporary blip, he won the US Masters at Carlsbad, another scratch main at Costa Mesa, a handicap main at Ascot and then a scratch the following week, before he lifted the track championship title there as well.

Therefore, he entered the US Nationals as one of the favourites for the title. He won his first race with a victory over Alan Christian, Keith Chrisco and John Cook, but he finished third behind Schwartz and Brad Oxley in his second outing. That meant that nothing less than a win in his third race would do to keep his title challenge alive. However, Faria won the race, while Ermolenko took second. His hopes of winning his first US National title were over for another year.

Nonetheless, as his best season so far was drawing to a close, he was named as *Speedway Magazine*'s Rider of the Year and also won 'the most popular rider' category too. 'Sam had a brilliant year, and was by far the most popular rider with the fans,' wrote their contributor, Paul Heffernan. He had an amazing season, which was also very lucrative, and it helped him to launch and maintain his ambitious career path.

As the magazine's Rider of the Year, they also devoted a page to his race statistics for that season. It was an astonishing record that revealed that hardly a week passed when he didn't claim a main event victory somewhere within the Californian circuits. Most of the time, he was racing in Europe when he didn't win a main event, and it was a record that stood tall alongside the greats of US racing like Bast, Moran and Faria.

As he began making plans for the 1986 season, one only had to refer to an interview he gave to a journalist after he stepped off the World Final rostrum to gauge how serious he was about his racing, when he said: 'I haven't peaked out yet, the best is yet to come.'

Four

BAD LUCK KNOWS NO BOUNDARIES

1985 had been without question Sam's best season so far. But although he admitted he realised that he had to race in England to win the World Championship, when he flipped the calendar page over to announce the arrival of 1986, he had no plans to pack his bags and fly over the Atlantic Ocean. However, being third in the world is a performance that is certain to attract attention from ambitious British speedway managers.

His plans at this stage were to remain in America and build his programme around the success he had achieved. The British League is notorious for leaving their plans for the new campaign until the last moment – this is something they still do, even though they now have increased competition from the European leagues. 1985 was a hard year for British clubs, which was not helped by a very wet summer – even by British standards.

There were very real concerns about the alarming rate at which crowds had decreased, and many promoters were looking around for riders who could bring the public back. Therefore, British promoters gazed across the ocean at the flamboyant, entertaining and colourful Californians. Their style of racing had always been popular with the British public, and they were all showmen – some more than others.

I received a phone call from Peter Adams, who wanted me to come over and race for the Wolverhampton Wolves. I wasn't that interested to begin with, because I had good sponsors in the US and I was convinced that I could do it again. When he said he wanted me to race for him in England, I asked him why.

The more he talked about it, the more it made sense to me. When I was with Poole, all the other Americans that were racing in England were based in the Midlands, whereas I was stuck down on the South Coast – I was a loner in a geographical sense.

Furthermore, I had a family to support, so I couldn't really go off with some of the other boys and enjoy the off-track antics with them – I had responsibilities. The centre of speedway was in the Midlands, as the top people like Eddie Bull, Joe Hughes and GTS products, all these people were based here.

Therefore, Peter Adams talked to me about the fact that I would be based in the Midlands, and he had experience of helping Ole Olsen, Bruce Penhall and Erik Gundersen during their World Championship days. And now he wanted to help me. It made sense to be a part of that, as the ingredients were there: I would be based in the Midlands, where it was all happening, and I would be racing for Peter Adams who, in my eyes, was one of the most successful managers, so it appeared that everything was there to have a secure future.

I agreed to join Wolverhampton and pursue what I thought were good odds of becoming World Champion – I had already come close as it was. I left the house I had recently bought and renovated, and also the sponsors I had got, so that I could resume my career in England.

Wolverhampton Speedway had been through some tough years when Sam arrived at Monmore Green. They had not won a major trophy since the British League was launched in 1965, and the club was closed in 1982 and 1983. This disappointing record is all the more surprising when you consider that riders of the quality of Ole Olsen and Hans Nielsen were among the riders who had led the team. Adams was the manager of Black Country rivals Cradley when, after guiding the Heathens to another League Championship success in 1983, he quit to re-open Wolves.

His first season in charge was ruined by the career-ending injury to his number one, Dennis Sigalos. Siggy was chasing Sam in the 1984 American Final of the World Championship, when he crashed and badly broke his ankle. He made a brief return at the end of 1985, but it was clear that his career was over. Bobby Schwartz did a sterling job at the top of the score charts in 1985, but he fought a lone battle, as the Wolves finished in tenth place out of eleven clubs. Therefore, Sam was the third American to pull on the number one race jacket in as many years – it was a move that would establish Sam as arguably the best ever Wolverhampton rider.

He was the only American in a side that resembled a Danish national team. His team-mates were Preben Eriksen, John Eskildsen, Peter Ravn, Jan Staechman, Sam Nikolajsen – all Danes – and the only Englishman in the team, Andy Phillips.

He also discovered that there had been some changes made since he had last raced for Poole in 1984. The number of clubs in the league had been reduced from 16 to just 11 in 1986. In an attempt to reduce riders' costs, the British Speedway Promoters' Association (BSPA) decreed that riders could only use Barum tyres while racing in the BL, and were forbidden from being able to use any other make.

I came over with my mechanic at the time, Stuart Monger – known as 'The Reverend' – and we based ourselves at Peter Adams' house. He had a small farm at Kidderminster, and we prepared my bikes there. We did this for up to six weeks, and then my wife and children came over to join me.

The Rev. and I were picked up from Heathrow Airport, and I probably had ten big bags with me. Colin, the man who Pete Adams asked to pick us up, met us as we came strolling out of the customs gate. He introduced himself, and behind us there was a porter with this huge trolley and all the bags were on it. Colin looked; and then looked again, and said: 'I think we might have problems getting all this stuff in my Ford Cortina estate!' I can tell you that the Rev. is no small man; well, we started to pack all the bags into the estate, and Colin still talks about this venture today. We ended up getting the bags in, with the Rev. sitting up front as this was the only place he would fit! I ended up sliding up into this little gap on top of the bags, and just slept the whole way back to the track. It was really no problem as I needed the sleep because I was due to race that night.

I had no bike, but Pete had arranged for Jan Steachmann to lend me one. Jan was happy until I picked out all the things that I thought needed attention, and he wasn't happy about that. He thought how ungrateful this American was. We still laugh about it, because Jan and I are really good friends.

Sam made his debut for Wolves on Monday 17 March 1986, in a challenge match against the Belle Vue Aces of Manchester. He scored 4 points, as the home side struggled in the greasy, wet conditions and lost the match 45-33. Adams promised the fans that he would run a meeting at reduced admission costs later in the season, because the surface was so bad he didn't believe that they had received value for their money.

It wasn't the start that either Wolves or Sam had hoped for, but the wet weather meant that March slipped by without the club completing another match. It was 4 April before the side raced again, and their lack of meetings saw them lose a League Cup match to Sheffield 42-36 – Sam scored 7 points. The following day, they were heavily defeated at Bradford 52-26, but Sam won his first race for the club in heat 10 to top score with 9 points. Rain continued to disrupt their programme, but Sam scored 10 points in their narrow 41-37 defeat at Sheffield – a score that included a victory over

Shawn Moran – which was no mean feat around Owlerton. He then went to Belle Vue and showed the critics why he was the world number three. A quality field had been assembled for the Peter Craven Memorial meeting, and the American finished second with 13 points behind Chris Morton, and he also established the fastest time of the night. It seemed that all he needed to hit top form was regular racing.

He took a guest booking for Sheffield and scored a paid maximum as the Tigers won at King's Lynn, but the Wolves fans were eager to see him display this sort of form for their team. They didn't have to wait very long. On 28 April, he sped to an unbeaten 15-point maximum, but he couldn't prevent the team from losing to Bradford.

Nonetheless, 'Sudden' Sam had shown the form that the weather had previously prevented him from displaying to his new fans. Less than a week went by before Wolves thrashed Belle Vue 53-25, and Sam scored another paid maximum. He was able to display his team-riding skills as he shadowed his riding partners round for *5-1s* in each of his races.

By May, he was regularly scoring double figures, and he began to be compared with Bruce Penhall – especially as the latter raced for local rivals, Cradley Heath. 'If people are comparing me with Penhall, they must regard me as a future champion – which is a good thing,' he said. With an average hovering around 10 points a match, and the club also beginning to register some good results, the 1986 season was shaping up to be a promising year.

The USA had qualified for the World Pairs Final through the efforts of the Shawn Moran and Bobby Schwartz. But Schwartz was dropped in favour of the in-form Kelly Moran – the brothers had been displaying some excellent team-riding skills at Sheffield together. Then just four days before the final that was scheduled to be staged at Pocking, Germany, Shawn broke his ankle in a crash at his bogey track, Oxford. The US team manager felt that Sam was the obvious choice to replace the younger of the brothers and ride with the charismatic Kelly. Shawn's bikes and equipment had already been shipped over to Germany, and it was agreed that Ermolenko would use his machines.

It was a World Final, and some of the world's top riders were present, including the Danish pairing of Erik Gundersen and Hans Nielsen, and England's Jeremy Doncaster and Simon Wigg. But it was the Danes who were the favourites for the title. However, if the Danes wanted to bring the bacon home again, they would have to contend with an American duo that planned to make them sweat in the heat.

The Americans emerged for their opening heat, and as they glanced across the start line, they found the Danish pairing of Gundersen and Nielsen alongside them, with the Czechoslovakian duo of Roman Matousek and Tony Kasper. This was the first World Pairs Final to feature six riders in a race – a format which was greeted with dismay by most of the riders.

In the mêlée of what was a highly competitive first bend, Matousek clattered into Gundersen and the Dane retired from the race, as he had sustained an injury to his left ankle. Nielsen won the race, but the Americans slotted in behind him and they collected 7 points to Denmark's 5 – which gave them an immediate advantage. Gundersen was able to continue, but when Sam and Kelly scored maximum points in heat 4 over New Zealand and Sweden, it seemed the title was theirs for the taking, especially when England's Simon Wigg finished at the back in heat 3.

Denmark bravely battled on, but when Gundersen withdrew from his third outing, it seemed that it could be the Americans' day. However, Sweden's Jan Andersson won heat 9, which was a race win that would have a significant bearing on the outcome of the event. Sam and Kelly restored the status quo with another first and second in the following race, only for the Danes to do the same as they entered the second round. With a scoreline that read USA 32, Denmark 28, it appeared that the Americans just had to race safely to carry off the gold medals.

Advised by Germany's former World Champion, Egon Muller, the Americans responded to another maximum heat win from the

Danes in heat 13 with one of their own in the following race. Still holding a 4-point lead over the Danish pairing, they entered the final round of races, knowing that they only had to split the Danes to win the Championship. But for the Gundersen/Nielsen pairing, nothing less than a first and a second would do to force a run-off.

The slick-starting Danish duo were away like lightning from the tapes, leaving Kelly and Sam in third and fourth. All afternoon the Americans had thrilled the crowd by battling their way from the back, but this time there was no way through. It was enough to force a run-off.

It was a surprise to Sam and Kelly that they were in this position, as they had fought the heat, the mechanical gremlins, and their unfamiliarity with each other as a team-riding pair, to race in the Final. As Sam was riding borrowed machinery, which he wasn't comfortable with, it was decided that Kelly would face Nielsen in the run-off. Nielsen had not dropped a point to an opposing rider, and he made a super gate and swept to victory to retain the World Pairs title for Denmark.

Czechoslovakia took third, but England lay a lowly seventh, and Jeremy Doncaster in particular couldn't believe how badly they had done when he saw what was happening in the American pits.

'You have to admire their ability,' he conceded. 'But we try to be thoroughly professional. They don't seem to give a stuff, and yet they very nearly win it and we don't get anywhere.'

Speedway Star described the Americans' laidback approach as 'have a nice day, any-old-bike-will-do mentality'. At the end of the day, you cannot argue with natural ability, and this is something that both Sam and Kelly possessed in bags. But this wasn't the way Sam approached his racing. The circumstances were not of his making, but he made the best of it. He was riding borrowed equipment, which wasn't suited to him because it was a late arrangement, but he got on with the job. Kelly was notorious for his 'Oh well, never mind, let's have a beer' outlook on life, and yet as a pair, they very nearly won, in spite of their less than satisfactory preparations.

The pits are situated in turn two at Pocking, but the dressing rooms are at the other side of the stadium. But there is a lake situated with dressing rooms and toilets between turns two and three, and you just entered through a gate. It was so hot at Pocking that I decided to take a dip because it looked refreshing. I was splashing around when I saw one of the officials at the gate.

'Sam, Sam, come', he was shouting.

'What?'

'Come quick.'

I climbed out of the lake, and was getting myself dressed as I made my way back into the pits. When I got there, the riders were already on the horse and carriages they had for the parade, and they were baking under the hot Bavarian sun. I arrived all refreshed from my dip in the lake, and I just stepped onto the carriage and sat down when the parade started – I had just made it. I didn't know about the horses because the riders entered the complex a different way.

The only problem I had with Shawn's bikes was the clutch. He had a Jawa clutch fitted to his bike, and it dragged as I left the start. After that, his engines were fine and they were really quick. But it was just a case of the fact that I wasn't used to his machinery, and because Shooey was smaller and lighter than I am, that's why his clutch settings didn't suit me. It was because of this that Kelly went into the run-off with Hans as he was on his own bikes and equipment. But we did well, considering it was a late arrangement and neither of us had been there before at that stage.

Sam then flew off to America to race in the American qualifying round of the World Championship, where he had to finish in the top five to qualify. He put in an effective and solid display to finish in third place with 13 points. Just weeks after a breaking his ankle, Shawn Moran won the meeting, with Lance King defeating Sam in a run-off for second.

A fortnight later, the five qualifiers from the American Final assembled on a hot sunny afternoon at Coventry's Brandon Stadium to contest the Overseas Final. This time there were nine qualifying places available for the Inter-Continental Final at Bradford, and they were joined by riders from England, Australia and New Zealand.

If there was anyone who had doubts about Sam's performance in the World Final, then the Overseas Final put those reservations to rest. He began by winning his first race in the fastest time of the afternoon – 63 seconds exactly – and looked to be in a class of his own throughout the meeting. Riding engines tuned by Eddie Bull – who had worked his magic on engines ridden to glory by Champions Penhall and Gundersen – he was also joined in the pits by Adams. He won his first four races in convincing style, and was not troubled by anyone.

As Sam entered his last race, he knew that just a third place would be sufficient to claim overall victory. Rick Miller made the start and led the race. But Sam exercised his maturity by settling for second and claiming the top prize – even though he looked the faster of the two riders. This impressive performance meant that there was no denying his claim to be one of the world's best riders.

With the Inter-Continental Final at Bradford – the scene of Sam's sensational World Final debut – he was confident of qualifying for his second World Final. The sun was shining again as the riders took the track and competed for the eleven qualifying places. But by the interval stage, Sam had just 4 points to his name. There was no room for error in his remaining two rides. He defeated Swedes Jimmy Nilsen and Tommy Nilsson and England's Chris Morton in heat 14, to put himself on 7 points, and was looking far more certain to get through. A third place behind Gundersen and Jan Andersson proved to be enough to ensure he made it safely through to the Final that was to be staged at Katowice, Poland.

But unbeknown to outsiders, there were storm clouds gathering at Wolverhampton, and they were affecting the performances of Sam Ermolenko on the track. It was a week after the Inter-Continental Final when Adams announced that he was quitting Wolverhampton due to 'health and personal reasons'. Then the shocking news came through that the riders hadn't been paid for four weeks, and that they were owed thousands of pounds.

Chris Van Straaten had been running things while Adams had been absent, and he revealed in the sport's press that there was a group of businessmen interested in taking over the speedway rights. Van Straaten had been the right-hand man to Dan McCormick, the legendary promoter of Cradley, who was responsible for bringing over the Americans Penhall, Schwartz and King to Britain.

Peter Adams was having marital problems and, basically, he vanished from the scene. We knew what was going on because we were living with the family, and his wife had left him. It put on a strain on our relationship, and we weren't getting paid.

Therefore, all of a sudden, my big push to build on what I achieved in 1985 was fizzling out. Peter Adams wasn't around any more, he was keeping a low profile because of the problems he was having. I wasn't earning the money, and it significantly affected my racing programme. I learned a lot about speedway in Britain at that time, as I was spending a lot of time trying to find out what was going on. It was very disappointing.

We had to find new accommodation and 'Cookie' – John Cook – came to the rescue, and we rented a place from him in Milton Keynes. This was already on the cards before all this blew up, but it just so happened that it was finalised and the move took place around the same time as Peter was experiencing his difficulties.

Fortunately, Chris Van Straaten, Tony Mole and a few other business men got together to rescue the club. They re-negotiated all the riders' contracts, and I took a considerable pay cut to keep the club alive. I would like to think that Chris and Tony would thank me for that, because they now have a very successful club. And that was all down to the fact that the riders stuck it out and didn't walk out on the club – and we had every right too. But Chris is a nice guy and he has helped me a lot during my career, and I guess that the benefit meeting I had when I was injured was his way of paying me back. So we finished the season in 1986 without Peter Adams.

The Reverend had come over to help me out, but his skills as a mechanic were not up to scratch for racing. Peter Ravn had a crash and he was ruled out for the rest of the season. His mechanic was a Danish man called Henrik Envolsen, but he couldn't speak English that well, so he suddenly said in his broken English:

'That's it, I'm fired – gone.'

'What? What are you talking about?'

'No job. Peter can't race no more – I go home now.'

So I suggested that he come and work for me. He agreed, and he was just the kind of mechanic that I needed at that stage, because Stuart had come over to help out and he eventually went to work with Lance King. Reverend is an educated man, and he is very knowledgeable about history, and he is a bit of a fanatic. They called him The Reverend because of that big bushy beard he had. So he would say things to Henrik, and because he was learning English, he would pick up all these sayings from him.

I remember on one occasion we were travelling home and Stuart said, *'We're happy campers now'*. And Henrik instantly picked up this phrase and he would always be saying *'We're happy campers now'*.

Sam appeared for the USA in a Test series against England, and also in the new World Team Championship – which was run over three finals at different tracks. The Americans struggled to stay in touch with Denmark in all three rounds of the Team Championships. Sam top-scored with 11 points at the second round in Vojens, Denmark, but the Yanks managed to hold on to second place overall. In the Test series, they were whitewashed 3-0 by England, and Sam scored 11 in the third Test at Ipswich. The sport's press blamed the lacklustre performances of team skipper Schwartz for their downfall.

On the eve of the World Final, Sam revealed that only two of his American sponsors had stayed by him when he returned to race in England, and he also made it known that the Wolverhampton crisis had cost him £6,000. It was his first trip to Poland, and he didn't make the impression he would have liked.

I went to an open meeting at Poole and I saw a family looking over my bikes and so on. When I arrived, all the kids were like, 'Oh here's Sam.' I signed all their autographs and posed for photos and then I got talking to their father, who was Mo Baker. I told him that I had to go to Poland and it was a long drive and I only had a van at that point. And he said that he might be able to help me out, and Mo rented a bigger van that you could sleep in. We have been good friends ever since – probably one of the best friends I have in England.

Brian Maidment and his son wanted to come to the World Final, so they packed up their Citroën and travelled with us. Henrik was up front driving the van with Richard Childs – who is now the US team manager – while I slept in the back. My wife and Richard's wife, Sherry, had decided to join Brian and his son James in the comfort of his car. After we crossed the checkpoint in Berlin, the girls left their passports in the van with us and moved to the Citroën to continue the journey in more comfort. There was no problem, and we carried on into Poland. We were travelling along this road, which was the main road that we had to follow to get where we were going. There was a heavy rain storm, and the Citroën was having a few problems with the excess water and was hydroplaning and it lost touch with us. Eventually, Henrik pulled into a lay-by to wait for the others to catch up. When they pulled in, Sherry got out of the car and walked up to Richard and started yelling at him: 'What d'you think you were doing, going off and leaving us like that?'

'What if we had an accident, you got our passports and no one would know who we are or anything about us.'

She was going on and on about this, and Richard was sat next to Henrik just taking all this in, when he suddenly said: 'Shut up, asshole!'

That brought an end to it, but Henrik picked up this phrase. As we continued this journey, all I could hear was Henrik saying 'Shut up, you asshole.' When I meet up with him in Denmark now, we still laugh about that.

In the much-anticipated heat 2, that brought Ermolenko, Gundersen, and Nielsen together again, it was Gundersen who pulled away, with Nielsen in second and Sam in third. He was sandwiched between the Danes on the first bend, but this time he was squeezed out of the equation. In his second outing, he battled hard with another Danish rider, Tommy Knudsen, but Knudsen was the victor and Sam was left with 3 points and a podium finish was his best hope. That hope evaporated when he locked up on the first turn in heat 9, which left him trailing the field. Chris Morton made a mistake and Sam slipped through to take third place and 1 point.

His victory over Poland's Ryszard Dolomisiewicz, Neil Evitts and Tony Kasper pushed him up the leader board. Then a second behind Kelvin Tatum meant that he had finished in seventh place with 9 points.

I had very little confidence in the motors I had, and I borrowed an engine from Don Godden. The thing that I had learnt from racing in England was that you had to have a good combination in order to be successful in the World Championship – and I didn't have it. My world had been turned upside down when Peter Adams had his problems. I just didn't have the money available to be able to reinvest for a meeting like that.

Hans Nielsen won his first World title after his rival, Tommy Knudsen, was excluded after a coming together between the two riders. To all except the Nielsen camp, it looked as though he had taken Knudsen's front wheel away and dumped him onto the track. But the referee saw it differently, and it was Nielsen who was controversially crowned the Champion for the first time. Seven years later, and Sam would find himself in a similar situation – more about that later.

He missed out on riding in the British League Riders' Championship, because he returned to America to race in the California State Championship and the US National Championship. Unfortunately, he could only finish fifth in the Nationals, and he lost a run-off for third to Keith Chrisco in the State Championship. However, he returned to Wolverhampton in devastating form by setting a new track record of 58.9 seconds and scoring a paid maximum. But the icing on the cake was a superb from-the-back victory over Nielsen in the process. The next day, he made a return for Poole in a challenge match against a Young Czechoslovakia team, and swept to an 18-point maximum.

In spite of a mid-season crisis, Wolverhampton's third-place finish in the league was their best since the formation of the British League in 1965. Sam finished with an average of 9.72, and established himself as one of the top riders in the league as well as one of the most entertaining. But when he looked back on his campaign, it was one that was ruined by the club crisis that put paid to his ambitions. He wished for better luck in 1987, but another unlucky broadside would severely rock his title aspirations.

The only way you can build on something like that is to make sure it doesn't happen again. What you do is you go out there and find good tuners that you can rely on, so that you don't have to go and ask the Don Goddens and fellow riders if they have something special and can you borrow it. What you need is something that your own team is developing, so I made a commitment in 1987 to work with a tuner from London, Alex McFazdean, who used to work with Kenny Carter and Bo Petersen. He wasn't involved in speedway at that time, but he decided that he would like to get back into it. This happened through Ivan Henry. I met up with Ivan one night at his place, and he came to Ipswich with me and I met Alex. We had a meal together, and that was how it all came about. Bo Petersen used to live at Ivan's house, and I was hoping that Ivan would get more involved financially, but he was committed to helping Brian Karger.

It turned out that Alex and myself both knew the same people in America and we hit it off straightaway. He basically did some engine building for me and all I paid for was the parts. He donated his time and we used his workshop in South Ockington, and we built our engines from there. Otto Lattenhammer supplied the engines and we did the rest.

In 1987 the World Final was held over two meetings in two days, and was scheduled to be staged in Amsterdam's Olympic Stadium. It was the first and only time that a two-day World Final had been staged.

At Wolverhampton, Sam was joined by a young up-and-coming rider from California, Ronnie Correy. Correy was a product of the junior system in the US, and he was the first of the new generation of riders to try his luck in England. Danes Preben Eriksen, Jan Staechmann, and John Eskildsen were retained, along with Andy Phillips and a rider who had impressed the promotion in their junior team, Chris Cobby. The club was eager to build on their best league position, and they were looking to the potential of Correy, and the expected progress of Staechmann, to do this.

Sam started off the season with a maximum, and he was leading the side at the top of the averages. He came to the rescue again when Kelly found himself without his brother in the World Pairs Final. The brothers had qualified comfortably for the Final, but Shawn withdrew as he wasn't happy with his own form.

Therefore, it was the same pairing that almost won in 1986 who would take the fight to Denmark again. But this time they didn't fare so well. The contest took place on the big Pardubice track in Czechoslovakia, but they finished in third place on 36 points, 16 points adrift of the dominant Danes, Gundersen and Nielsen. England took second with 44 points. To add to the disappointment, Moran was leading the Danes during the last race when his engine slowed, and another Danish 1-2 followed. Sam and Kelly both scored 18 points each to attain the bronze medal.

The 1987 American Final featured five riders in a race, as the FIM said that they had to include Canadians in the field. Harry Oxley increased the field to twenty and introduced five-rider races because he didn't agree that the Canadians should be included. He felt that they should have to qualify through the British Commonwealth rounds.

This made little difference to an in-form Ermolenko, who won his first American Final by dropping his only point to Kelly Moran. But he came in for some criticism because he locked up in front of Shawn Moran, and 'Shooey' fell. Although disappointed, Shooey did not blame him for the fall, but there were some Sheffield fans that did. However, Sam illustrated how deserving he was of his place in the next round of the World Championship by storming to an 18-point maximum around Sheffield, and left the Morans in his wake.

He travelled to Bradford to defend the Overseas title and found himself getting off to an uncharacteristic start by trailing home in last place behind Jeremy Doncaster, Simon Cross and Andrew Silver. This, however, was a temporary blip, as he qualified comfortably with 10 points. He tied with Kelly Moran for third, but the elder of the Moran brothers won the race, while New Zealand's Mitch Shirra won the meeting.

A solid, if unspectacular, performance in the Inter-Continental Final saw Sam qualify for his third World Final with 9 points. Gundersen retained the title, and it very much looked like a three-way battle between the Danes and 'Sudden' Sam. As if to underline his intentions, Sam saw off the challenge of Nielsen to win the Olympique at Wolverhampton, which was a notable triumph – especially when you consider that Nielsen was a former Wolf himself, and he knew his way around Monmore Green.

Sam was fined £50 in an odd incident at Coventry. After a heavy fall, the American was dazed and he didn't leave the track straight-away. However, referee Ronnie Allen, believed that the American deliberately failed to leave the track to get the race stopped. Therefore, he imposed a fine and there was also the possibility of a suspension. Sam protested his innocence and refused to pay the fine, and insisted that he was dazed from the accident. The referee looked at the crash on video again, and he dropped the original fine and chose to issue an official warning instead. But this would prove to be a precursor to another over-the-top reaction from the sport's officials that threatened his livelihood.

I was living at John Cook's place in Milton Keynes, and my mechanic at this time was a man called Jeff Collard. He was the person who told me how to go about putting proposals together to obtain sponsorship like I did in 1985. He knew how to do this because he was a salesman for three motor products in America. One morning he was cleaning the bikes on the drive-way, and I had just got up after a night's racing. He was wearing shorts and had Wellington boots on. He looked a bit like the main character from the movie Young Einstein *when he came storming into kitchen.*

'Sam, quick, come and have a look at this.'

'What?'

'The brushes are moving in the bucket.'

I was still waking up, and I said: 'What? What are you talking about?'

'The brushes are moving in the bucket, come and have a look.'

'What's the matter with you?'

'Come and see for yourself, the brushes are moving of their own accord in the bucket.'

I went outside and he had the bikes on the driveway, and I looked down at the bucket that had the brushes inside. 'What?' I said.

Jeff was stood over the bucket, with his knees bent and with a stick he gave the brush a nudge and sure enough it moved! It wasn't, however, a paranormal experience like Jeff thought it was. I tipped over the bucket and a hedgehog came running out!

During a journey to Poland we had to pass through the notorious Checkpoint Charlie in Berlin, because this was the time of the old Soviet Union and the East and West divide. Jeff was really worried about having to go to an Eastern Bloc country. He had heard all the stories from people like Dennis Sigalos and Bruce Penhall. As a Westerner, it was normal practice to give the soldiers a souvenir when you go through a checkpoint to avoid having problems.

We passed through Berlin with no problems, but Jeff was not happy about seeing all the soldiers with their machine guns. They would search your vehicle and check your passports, and all this only seemed to make Jeff worse. We came to another checkpoint, and it was dark. The lights from our vehicle picked out the white barrier and the sentry who was standing outside the hut waiting for us. Our lights glinted off his machine-gun barrel, and Jeff was getting very concerned. I told him to relax and not to worry, but he didn't take a lot of notice.

When we stopped, the sentry guard tapped on Jeff's window. Well, Jeff was scared shitless as he opened the window, no doubt he thought that all the horror stories he had been told were about to come true. The soldier was only about seventeen with a cigarette in his mouth and a machine gun on his shoulder. He nodded his head at Jeff, and he scrambled around in the dashboard trying to find a souvenir. Jeff picked up a handful of stuff and eagerly gave him a postcard or something of Sam Ermolenko. But the soldier looked at it with a confused and quizzical expression.

'Calm down, Jeff, he wants a light.' I observed. 'Give him a light – that's all he wants.'

The soldier made a cigarette lighter gesture with his fingers, and Jeff eagerly produced a lighter. The sentry lit his cigarette, but Jeff was so scared that he told him that he could keep it. The sentry made a signal to his colleague in the hut and they lifted the barrier, and we continued our journey. But Jeff was a bundle of nerves throughout the trip. It was all I could do to keep him calm! He took all the stories he had heard from books and the movies to heart.

The British League welcomed Hackney back into the top flight in 1987. The track at Waterden Road certainly wasn't a favourite among the Americans. In 1982, Denny Pyeatt was killed there, and the Moran brothers both suffered serious injuries at the venue. Furthermore, Bobby Schwartz walked out of a meeting at the stadium, claiming that the track was unsafe. Imagine then how they must have felt when the Second Test between England and the USA was scheduled to take place there. It seemed obvious that it wasn't going to be plain sailing, and once again the venue proved unlucky in more ways than one for the US riders.

America narrowly lost the First Test at Ipswich 55-52. Shawn Moran had taken over as captain following Schwartz's decision to retire from British racing. Moran put in a captain's performance by scoring an 18-point maximum, and he received good support from Ermolenko and Miller, who both scored 11 points. The result was even more remarkable when you consider that they could only field six fully fit riders.

A large crowd gathered at Hackney to see these two nations engage in an on-track battle. This time, they had the luxury of being able to track two reserves. But to describe the meeting as 'incident-packed' would be a major understatement.

The Morans began the match with an opening heat 5-1. Sam followed this with a win in heat 2, after the race had had to be re-run twice because of falls for England's Kelvin Tatum and America's Ronnie Correy. Rick Miller was the next to take a heavy tumble, and then Kelly Moran had to be extracted from the Hackney safety fence following a fall in heat 4. Miller was in the wars again when he was hit from behind by Simon Wigg in a collision that resulted in the Englishman's exclusion. Grumbles began to come from the pits – mostly on the American side – about the state of the surface.

Heat 7 saw England's Jeremy Doncaster lose control and he also bit the dust, but Shawn Moran laid down his machine to avoid the Englishman, only to find himself backing into the fence. He didn't emerge for the re-run, and when his brother was excluded after another fall, the Americans had had enough. Skipper Shawn told the US team manager, John Scott, that he was pulling out of the meeting as the track was too dangerous. He had full support from his team-mates and it seemed that they were set to walk out.

The track was patchy – slick in most places, but grippy in others – and nine riders had fallen in seven races. Referee Frank Ebdon came down from his box to discuss the situation, and ordered the track to be re-graded, while Shawn made his feelings known. Some English riders were in agreement with the Americans, but the crowd obviously saw the Yanks as the villains of the piece, and they hurled abuse at the fun-loving Californians. As light rain began to fall, slow hand-claps echoed around the stadium as the arguments continued.

Eventually, after a long delay, the racing was resumed but the rain was now adding to the already tricky surface. Twelve heats were completed before the match was abandoned, with America leading 36-34. Ebdon fined both Moran and manager Scott £50 each for threatening to walk out, but the drama was not over just yet.

I met a photographer called Wayne who lived in the neighbourhood, and he came with me because he wanted to take photographs. He was surprised that I was working on my bikes – he thought that I would have a team of mechanics with me. Jeff Collard had to go home to America because his mother was sick. So Wayne said that he would like to help me, and I agreed. He didn't know enough to be able help seriously, but it was an extra pair of hands.

At Hackney, when you arrive in the pits, it has a small area to park your vans, and there is only one way in and out. So the last one in, is the first one out. I had a Citroën estate car at the time, and to be able to transport my bikes, we had to remove the front wheel to be able to get the bikes in.

There was a lot of trouble over the state of the track, and Kelly and Shawn were concerned because they had just returned from injuries so they didn't want to get hurt again. Wayne meant well, but I had to keep an eye on him because he was inexperienced, and while all this was going on, it started to rain. I wanted to get the bikes in from the wet and Wayne was asking me what he should do. We were going to race again, so I was putting my helmet on while I was telling Wayne what I wanted him to do when this official thrust a clipboard in front of me and said: 'Sam, sign this.'

'What? Not now, I'm in the middle of something here.'

'No you've got to sign; it's for a drugs test.'

'Drug test? Ask me later.'

'No you don't understand, you've been drawn for a random test.'

Wayne was helping by getting the bike in, so I grabbed the board and signed it. Now I could get on with what we were doing. They called the meeting off and everyone was packing away. I didn't want Wayne to load the bikes up because he wasn't experienced enough to remove the front wheel and then put the bikes in the back. I was afraid that he would damage the interior lining of the car as I had only recently acquired it. I told Wayne to wait while I went to take the drugs test.

As well as myself, Jeremy Doncaster and Kelly Moran were there too. We had to supply a urine sample for the test, but none of us could go. Jeremy decided he was going to go and shower and get changed. Kelly did the same, and after twenty minutes or so I decided to follow them. A fellow mechanic helped Wayne and they had loaded up everything. Simon Cross wanted to get out, so he came into the dressing room and asked me to move my car. I said 'yes, hold on a sec' and followed him out. Wayne was making his way to the dressing room soaked by the rain, I told him to get changed and I would move the car. As I was moving the car, I got a tap on the window from Robert Pfetzing.

'Hey, Sam, how do I get out of London?'

I told Rob how to do it, but then I decided it would be better for him to follow me. I was moving out of the way and then Wayne returned from the changing room. By now it was pouring down with rain and, before I knew it, Wayne was sat beside me and said: 'Okay, let's go.' Rob was waiting for me, so off we went.

There was a tremendous and spectacular electrical storm as we joined the M25 from the M11. The flashes of lightening were impressive, and then I realised I had forgotten to take the drugs test. 'Shit, shit, shit,' I said.

'What's wrong?' Wayne asked.

'I've forgotten to take the drugs test.'

'Surely you don't have to do that now? After all the meeting was abandoned.'

'Well,' I replied thoughtfully, 'I don't know – maybe I should go back.'

'Do you think they'll still be there? It's pretty late.'

The meeting had overrun because of all of the controversy with the track and so on. So he convinced me that I should leave it until the morning. I decided that I would call Chris Van Straaten in the morning to tell him that I had forgotten to take the test. I had nothing to hide, and I was sure that there was a test I could do in the morning somewhere to clear up any confusion or suspicions.

The next morning, Shelley came in and said that she had seen a property advertised that she thought we should take a look at. I said that I had to get things ready to race at Belle Vue and I had to call Chris, but she said that it wasn't far. So we went to have a look at this property, which was derelict and not really what we were looking for.

I prepared the bikes and I took Wayne with me to the match at Belle Vue. I was fooling around on the way up there, showing him the different suspension settings on the car when the bike became dislodged from the rack on the back. We had to pull over to secure it, and this made us late for the meeting. I just drove the rest of the way passing everything, and Wayne turned to me and said: 'You know, since I have been travelling with you, Sam, I've never seen anything pass you.' We arrived with about a half an hour to go before the meeting started. I was on my way into the dressing room when Chris stopped me and said:

'I hear you had a problem last night at Hackney, and you didn't take the drug test.'

'Oh yeah, I meant to talk to you about that.'

'It's pretty serious, Sam, you will probably receive a ban.'

'What? No way ...'

I did the meeting at Belle Vue and I couldn't believe that I would face a ban. But, sure enough, by Monday morning I was suspended from all British League meetings. I could only race in international and World Championship meetings. I would lose the bulk of my earnings as I wasn't permitted to ride for Wolverhampton until the tribunal – which was set for later in the season.

Sam was suspended by the Speedway Control Board from domestic racing until an inquiry was held, which was scheduled for 14 September. He was suspended for 'failing to take a drugs test', but it must be pointed out that he had taken no drugs. He had just forgotten about it throughout all the confusion and hustle and bustle of the evening. He told the SCB manager, Dick Bracher, that he was willing to take a test at a hospital to clear his name, even a brain scan at this time would show if he had drugs in his system. But the rules were the rules, and he was offered no leeway.

Edbon is quoted in *Speedway Mail* as saying that he told the riders before the start that he would be carrying out tests, and he chose the first three heat-winners of the night. He said that Sam couldn't produce a sample and he went to get showered and changed, but he never came back. In truth, because of the wet weather and the other demands, Sam decided to wait in his car until he was able to 'go' – but he had forgotten about it altogether with having to move his car twice, and also having an inexperienced helper to deal with.

Fortunately, he was able to race for the USA in the second round of the World Team Championship at Coventry, which the Americans won. Sam took the opportunity to try out a new ignition system, which proved to be the key to some of his problems. He took Erik Gundersen from the back in heat 12 to win the race, as America won the round by 6 points from the Danes – with England a further 10 points adrift in third.

Alex and I were working very closely together to get the bikes going for the World Final, but we found that we had a problem with the ignition. It took us a while to find this because everything we were doing wasn't working. We were doing all sorts of things like building camshafts and so on, but it just wasn't working.

We needed to know what revs we were running, so we fitted a tachometer to the bike to see what was happening. This way we could see what rpms we were running, and where we were having the problems. But when I was on the track, the tachometer was running all over the place, and then it wasn't working sometimes. I thought that the tachometer wasn't working properly, so I called the company and told them. But they said that they were working fine. They said that my ignition couldn't have been strong enough, because what you did was wrap the lead from the tachometer around the HT lead, and then it would pick up the signal and run the tachometer. The man from the company said: 'You can't be getting enough power going through the spark plug, so our tachometer wasn't picking it up.' Therefore, I thought, well, after we've done all these different things to get the engines going, if the tachometer isn't picking it up, then maybe my ignition wasn't strong enough for the developments that we were doing.

I changed from a PJS ignition system to an Interspan. It was Carl Blomfeldt who actually loaned me an interspan system at the Test match at Hackney, as Randy Green – who he normally worked with – was reserve for that meeting. It was then that I discovered the problem, because it instantly woke the bike up. From the moment that I dropped the clutch in that meeting, the bike was going better than it had done all season.

In spite of the ban, Sam arrived for the two-day World Final in Amsterdam in a confident frame of mind. He had already won the Dutch Golden Helmet at the track earlier in the season, and he had confidence in his engines. After one of the longest parades in the history of the World Final, the meeting got underway. Sam won his first race, but then dropped 2 points to the Danes Hans Nielsen and Jan O. Pedersen. But for the rest of the day he was unbeaten, and he joined Gundersen at the top of the score chart with 13 points, while defending Champion Nielsen looked out of sorts with 12 points.

The Ermolenko family, clockwise from left: Sam, Charlotte, Nicholas and Charles.

Flying high in the deserts, Sam shows his skills on board his motocross bike in this family snap.

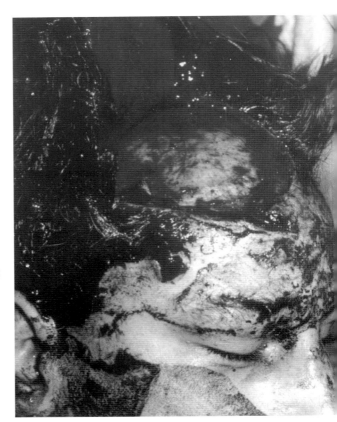

'To his horror, the helmet rolled and a pool of blood spilled forth from inside the helmet and out onto the ground.' This horrifying picture was taken shortly after Sam's arrival at the hospital following his road accident in 1976. It was this image that his mother was subjected to, even though she wasn't supposed to have been in the emergency ward.

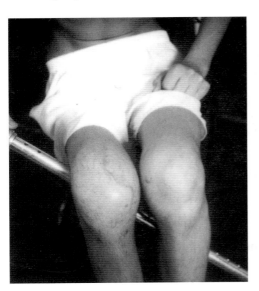

Sam lost a lot of weight in hospital following his accident in 1976, as is illustrated by this photograph as his knees are clearly bigger than his legs.

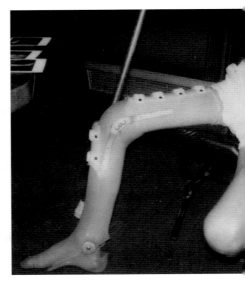

This special plastic brace was made for him so that he could begin to recuperate and become mobile again.

Wheelie King: 'I was known for being able to pull wheelies on any type of machine. This wasn't a problem for me as I had a lot of confidence in my ability to do this. It didn't matter to me what the speed was, whether it was 30mph or 90mph.'

This is a rare photograph of Sam riding his Jawa speedway bike for just the second time in the Indian Dunes.

Sam pictured wearing his 'Pick Your Part' leathers in 1985. Their sponsorship and also that of PCL, which can be seen on his left leg, were instrumental in his success that year.

'Niemi squeezed me a little bit, and at that point I thought that I could be a bit vulnerable so I backed off ... but that was the moment that cost me the World Championship.' The 1985 World Final at Bradford: Sam challenges Finland's Kai Niemi in heat 14.

'I agreed to join Wolverhampton and pursue what I thought were good odds of becoming World Champion.' Sam Ermolenko in a Wolverhampton Wolves race jacket in 1986.

1986 Overseas Champion at Coventry. He went on to win the title a further three times – no other rider has equalled that record.

Above, from left to right: Mike Faria, Shawn Moran, Bobby Schwartz and Sam in the pits at Coventry before the 1988 Overseas Final.

Opposite above: Sam displays his long-tracking style at an event at Scheesel, Germany in 1988.

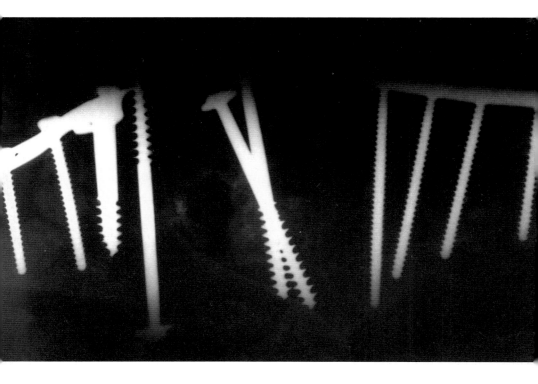

Below: 'I had broken my leg in over 12 places, and there were multiple fractures from the middle of my femur down to the middle of my shin. It wasn't a pretty sight.' An X-ray of Sam's shattered right leg following his horrific long-track crash at Herxhiem in 1989. This shows just some of the 27 screws that were used to fix his leg.

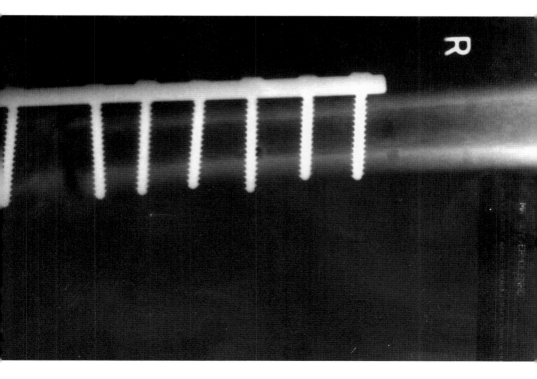

Team Ermolenko in 1989: Carl Blomfeldt (left) and Danny Gollagher flank Sam in this publicity photograph taken at the Veterans Stadium, Long Beach, USA.

The podium for the 1989 American Final, from left to right: Ronnie Correy (3rd), Sam (1st), Shawn Moran (2nd) and Lance King (4th). This was the third successive year that Sam won the American Championship and he went on to win the title a total of four times.

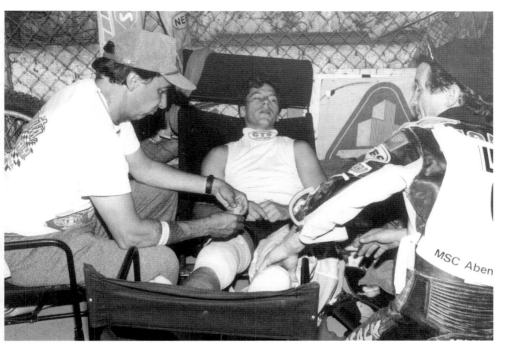

The World Championship semi-final, Abensberg, Germany, 1991: Sam's knee is strapped up in between races by Albert Rock, while fellow countryman Kelly Moran seems to be considering some massage.

Sam Ermolenko 1991 Division One Riders' Champion. This was the first of the three riders' titles that he won in Britain.

Heat 19 of the 1991 Division One Riders' Championship at Belle Vue: Sam takes control on the inside of Hans Nielsen in a race that he won to clinch the title.

Above left: Sam and his brother, Charles, in Wolves race jackets at Berwick in 1991.
Above right: 'Ronnie and I were the dudes around Wolverhampton; it was highly unlikely that anyone else would be picked for a last-heat decider and most of the time we would come out on top.' Ronnie Correy (left) and Sam.

Above: 'It wasn't until later on, because of my status as a champion, that I did more for the team and rose to the occasion.' Sam is congratulated by Ronnie Correy (left) and Bobby Ott after his second place clinched the 1992 World Team Cup for America. James Easter looks on in the background.

Below: The smooth, colourful and spectacular style of Sam Ermolenko. This was the orange colour scheme that he made famous. Note the brand name 'King' on the silencer. It was this make of silencer which was so popular in the British League and caused noise problems at the 1991 World Final for most of the competitors.

Right: 'We had to have guards to be able to get out of the pits, and when the match was over the fans would jump over the fence. It was quite an overwhelming experience in a lot of different ways.' Sam takes a celebratory tractor ride after another victory for Bydgoszcz in Poland. To his right is Tomasz Gollob; on his left in the jacket is Papa Gollob. Roman Matousek is sat beside Sam.

Below: Joe Screen leads Sam and Gert Handberg at Cradley in 1993. Note that Sam's footrest is scraping the kickboard of the fence – British League racing is very competitive!

Opposite: Sam was always an entertainer and his wheelies, lik this one at Belle Vue in 1992, thrilled the crowds and came t epitomise his showmanship and were characteristic of his racing

'The fact of it is that I went down because he knocked me down. I stayed down because I didn't deserve to be excluded because it wasn't my fault.' 1993 World Final: Sam leads Hans Nielsen, Billy Hamill and Andy Smith through the first bend during the notorious heat 15.

Above left: 'Look Sam, your name is on that trophy and you won it, no one can take that away from yo Sam Ermolenko, 1993 World Speedway Champion – the sport's ultimate prize.

Above right: 'When we got together as a team, we knew what it was all about. We were self motivated; we didn't need anyone to motivate us to do well because we always had a good level of team spirit.' The victorious 1993 USA team that won the World Team Cup at Coventry, from left to right, back row: Josh Larsen, Sam and Billy Hamill. Front row: Greg Hancock, John Scott (team manager) and Bobby Ott.

Above left: This publicity shot was arranged to promote the annual ice meeting at Telford in 1994. A fun boxing match with giant gloves was staged at the event to settle the World Final dispute. It ended in a draw.

Above right: From left to right: Sam, Henrik Envolsen ('Shut up, asshole!'), Alex Schroek and Danny Gollagher – Sam's long-track team for 1988.

The gate was shut and I had my front wheel in between the two gates. I had to rev up the bike and ride through the gates to get out!' Grand Prix Challenge, Prague, Czech Republic in 1996: Sam is pictured here remonstrating with the official. To the left in the Silkolene race wear is Sam's mechanic for that meeting, Steve Langdon.

America's first three World Champions. From left to right: Bruce Penhall (1981 and 1982), Sam Ermolenko (1993) and Jack Milne (1937).

Mo Baker was able to sort out a motor home that we borrowed from a friend of his that was a motocross rider. We were caught out at that Final because I didn't have the experience. Now I do, but I didn't then, and we just missed out. That was the difference between myself, Erik and Hans. The first day my motor was perfect, and I passed Gundersen and Per Jonsson by going round the boards. I was the first rider to do that successfully that night, and I also did that in a race with Jeremy Doncaster too. I knew that was the place to be, as I thought about it and I was thinking all the time about my strategy. So I was pretty happy after the first day.

But overnight Hans Nielsen sorted out the problems that had hampered his performance during the first day, and he defeated the American in their second race. He also dropped points to Gundersen and the Swede Jimmy Nilsen, and his advantage slipped away. He faced Gundersen in a run-off for second and third, as Nielsen's unbeaten performance on the second day meant that he had retained the title of world number one.

When the second day came, the bike that I was using the day before had lost its edge. On the first day the track was very slick, but the promoter said that it was going to be a lot grippier on the second day because they hadn't had the time to lay the track the way they wanted to for the first day. It would definitely be better the next day, 'definitely', he said.

Knowing that the engine I rode was perfect for the first day, I decided that I would use my second engine for the next day. It was a really good engine that Otto Lattenhammer had prepared for me. But when I went out there and dumped the clutch, it was spinning too much. So I jumped on the other one and won the race and then got a second, but the engine was slow and it was losing its edge. So I had to resort to the other engine, which was already spinning too much, and I was losing out because of this. I got caught out because I wasn't experienced enough at that level. When I was in the run-off with Erik, he just trapped on me and left me because my engine was too strong.

Sam appeared in the World Final revenge meeting, but crashed with Tommy Knudsen and sustained a broken wrist and ankle – his first major injury since taking up speedway racing. Battered and bruised from his injuries, he attended the SCB tribunal in a wheel chair and was accompanied by Ivan Henry. He was shocked to receive a 15-month ban for failing to undergo a drugs test, that was due to expire on 31 December 1988. He was also ordered to pay £400 towards the cost of the hearing, and he wouldn't be able to race in Britain until 1989. Furthermore, the SCB planned to make a recommendation to the FIM that the ban should be extended to international events as well. Even then, it seemed that his chances of racing in 1989 depended on whether the Board would rubber-stamp his licence, as he would have to re-apply.

He immediately announced that he would be appealing against the decision in order to clear his name; otherwise his speedway career was over. He received a lot of support from the fans and his fellow riders. US captain Shawn Moran spoke out about the decision in *Speedway Mail* and said:

'The fact of the matter is that Sammy hasn't actually *done* anything wrong. People have got to remember that what he did was fail to take the test. He didn't fail the test and he hasn't been accused or convicted of taking drugs. Taking away his living for over a year is out of line. A heavy fine was the most anyone expected from this case. Look what happened at the meeting – it was chaos and we all had something on our minds. If Sam didn't need to go, they could have been there until 6 a.m.!'

Chris Van Straaten agreed and said that they were optimistic that they would win an appeal. However, he warned that if Sam was not successful then he would have to reconsider Wolverhampton's future. He added: 'I don't know what the sport is coming to when we get verdicts like this. In my opinion, the Control Board's decision has been totally unfair, and I think the majority of people will agree with me.'

After the tribunal, I found myself in the lift with Frank Ebdon. I had told them that I planned to appeal, and he turned to me in the lift and said:

'You know, Sam; I'm really surprised you are contesting this. What are

you appealing this for? Why don't you just take your punishment and ride it out.'

I couldn't believe he said that to me. I was furious with what he said, and I felt like punching him out there and then. Even though I was all plastered up from the accident, I really felt like smacking him. Ivan Henry was with us and he was stood in between us, and it was all he could do to hold his tongue. He could see how angry I was, and I replied:

'Because I'm not guilty.'

When we got out of the lift, Ivan chuckled a bit and said that he thought I was going to hit him. He agreed that he had no right saying that to me. It was unbelievable.

The appeal was heard on Friday 6 November 1987, and it was successfully upheld. Sam was represented by John Matthews QC, an experienced barrister who had the original sentence thrown out on technicalities. *Speedway Mail* reported that his appeal was based on two grounds: 'First against conviction on technical grounds. Second against sentence, presumably in case the first grounds of appeal did not succeed.' In *Speedway Star*, Bracher admitted that he was cleared because his 'suspension was an unsound decision. The regulations governing these offences are badly worded,' he said. But while Bracher admitted that the SCB had got it wrong, and that it was handled absurdly, Control Board chairman Michael Limb was having none of it. No doubt embarrassed by their blunder, he was venomously quoted as saying that the American had come out of the situation with no credit at all. This is something that still annoys Sam to this day.

Technically I was charged on two different accounts for the same thing. My QC wanted to know which one I was being charged with so that he could argue the case. 'Is it this rule, or is it that rule?' They had it all messed up, the procedure was wrong and my QC had them tied up in knots.

I left there with all the charges dropped, but I earned no credibility out of it. To this day, no one knows what really went on. I have never been cleared of taking drugs. It cost me a lot financially to make my appeal, it was around £10,000 to £15,000. It messed up my 1987 season and it also ruined 1988 as well, because I had to concentrate on clearing off my debts from the appeal before I could plough any money back into winning the World Championship.

Sam returned to the USA and took his place in the US Long-Track Championship, winning the meeting. Hans Nielsen and Britain's Phil Collins were also in the line-up, but neither made it to the semi-finals, and that made his victory all the more sweeter. He defeated Randy Green, Schwartz, Pfetzing, Faria and Lance King in the final.

He returned to Wolverhampton for his third season in 1988, and he moved from Milton Keynes and rented a place in Coventry. It was a largely an unchanged team, except that Andy Grahame was recalled from his loan period with Oxford – it seemed that Wolves were also consolidating their financial position following the problems experienced by the club during 1986.

I had no money and just a couple of bikes, and that was it. The only way I could rebuild my programme was to get some more money behind me. It was very hard to get sponsorship in England, not like it was back home when after six weeks I had acquired financial sponsorship. I did get some product sponsorship, which was a help, but I never did get monetary sponsorship.

My children were going through school, so that was a priority, so I planned 1988 to be a year when I just wanted to get through the season and put as much money by for 1989 as I could. I met up with a man called Danny Gollagher, who used to be Andrew Silver's mechanic. Andy was having some difficulties, and Danny worked for me on occasions and he expressed a desire to work with me in 1989, and I agreed. It was also during this season that I met up with Carl Blomfeldt, who worked for Randy Green, but Green got hurt in 1988 doing long-track.

All the Americans that race speedway come from the same area in California. Randy was different: he came from Texas and he was a flat-track rider. When he came over, the word was that Hackney had signed a new American. But no one knew who he was. So I made a phone call, and chased him down and I discovered that he was a flat-track rider. Carl knew an air steward from Denmark called Yogi, and they all used live in the same area, and he always used to tell Randy to give up flat-track and go speedway racing. He told him all about the sport and gave him the phone number for Dave Pavitt, the Hackney promoter, and they bought two brand new Godden machines and started practising at Hackney. He was given a work permit, and they did all that on their own. We invited them to Cookie's house and we had a barbecue, and that's when I first met Carl. I actually lent Randy one of my GM engines because the Goddens were hard to ride round Hackney. Then he started to score points and Carl never forgot that. When I started racing in long-track we would meet at the tracks, and Randy got injured in a crash that I was involved in with Steve Schofield. He picked up the aftermath of the accident and hurt his shoulder.

Nevertheless, Sam was still unquestionably the number one rider at Wolverhampton, and he once again qualified for the World Final. He retained the American Championship on his way to the Final with an unbeaten score. And, once more, he was America's only representative.

However, he finished in fourth place with 12 points, but after two rides he was unbeaten. But as he was not really able to invest in his equipment at this point, he was prevented from making the impression he had hoped for on the dominant Danes, Gundersen and Nielsen. On this occasion, it was Gundersen who defeated his arch-rival in a run-off for first place. The Danes took a clean sweep, with Jan O. Pedersen taking third place on the rostrum.

Sam won the Coalite Classic at his one of his favourite tracks, Bradford, and he teamed up with Shawn Moran to ride in the 1988 World Pairs Final, which was also scheduled for Bradford's Odsal Stadium. Shooey also had a good a record around the Odsal bowl, so they were expected to be in with a good chance of getting in amongst the medals. But third place overall was the best they could do in another meeting where the gold medals went to Denmark.

The World Team Cup reverted to its original one-off final format for 1988, and it was widely believed that this was the only way in which America would consider staging the event. After the success of the 1985 final, it was hoped that the USA's flag would fly at the top this time. Sam was joined in the team by the Moran brothers, Lance King and Rick Miller.

But Denmark was even more powerful than before, and America had to settle for a very distant second place. Sam led the scores with 13 points, but his only worthy support came from Shawn Moran, who scored 8. He went on record to question some of his team-mates' less-than-professional approach, and said that things had to change if America were to seriously challenge Denmark.

As the 1988 season drew to a close, and as he had qualified for his first World Long-Track Final earlier in the season, he was planning an assault on both world titles in 1989. He had spent a quiet season by re-building and re-organising his racing programme, and then he was 'ready to play again'.

Randy Green retired at the end of the 1988 season, but Carl wanted to stick around. He called me and asked if I needed any help. At that time I had a full-time mechanic working for me and that was Danny. But he was keen to be involved, and he suggested that maybe he could help with the engines. Carl had a place to live near Manchester, so we agreed that I would keep him on a retainer of £50 a week. Therefore, we made arrangements for 1989.

It was around this time that Ivan Henry put me together with Don Godden. I struck up a deal with him that I would ride Goddens, but I would only ride his engines if they were going well. If they weren't going well, I reserved the right to go back to my GMs because they were really flying at the time. He agreed that I could ride PJ frames and Godden engines; but this went against the grain, because he thought that I should ride all of his equipment.

This arrangement was made over a dinner with Don and his wife, Ivan and his wife, and Shelley and me. The deal was that we would develop the engines with him, and Carl would also be a part of it. The beauty of it all was that Carl already knew Don because Randy used to ride Goddens, and Carl also knew Alex McFazdean. But Carl was going to concentrate on this, because Alex was getting busier with his own business.

I had a little shop of my own at the back of my house, and I could see that Carl knew what he was doing, so I had confidence in him. What I would do was send Carl down to Goddens to get the bits and pieces and bring them back, and Gary – who worked at Goddens – would work with Carl, and they would bring me an engine. Then we would work on them at my place: some were already assembled and some needed to have work done on them before they could be put together. We used to have four or five engines there sometimes, and I still had my GMs. In 1989, I rode both GMs and Goddens.

Sam was joined in the Wolverhampton team by Robert Pfetzing – with whom he had won the California Best Pairs Championship in 1983 – and there were more changes made to the team: in came the battling Neil Collins from Sheffield, and Graham Jones was signed from National League Stoke. Ronnie Correy, Jan Staechman and Andy Phillips were retained with Sam for the new campaign. But, significantly, the experienced Peter Adams returned to the Wolves side to take up the role of team manager. From all angles, it looked as though 1989 was going to be a year to remember.

But Wolves got off to a slow start in the Gold Cup, and lost home meetings to Belle Vue and Cradley Heath. Sam was also experiencing a few early-season difficulties, which were illustrated when he scored only 6 points in their defeat at Cradley. When they suffered another defeat at home to Coventry, this provoked the Wolves into a major backlash that the rest of the league would feel.

Sam had already begun to recover his form with a paid maximum against Bradford, and this was followed by a captain's performance in a notable victory at Belle Vue. Another paid maximum followed in the demolition of King's Lynn, before title rivals Oxford brought them briefly down to earth at Cowley with a 60-30 defeat at the home of Hans Nielsen. But Wolves then went ten successive matches without a defeat, and they were looking like potential Champions. The side was solid right the way through, and Sam was such an inspiration to his team-mates, and this, combined with Adams' experience at managerial duties, meant it looked as though

Wolverhampton's long wait for silverware was going to come to an end at last.

Sam won the American Final of the World Championship for the third successive season – proving beyond doubt that he was America's best hope for the world title – and then he won the Overseas Final for the second time at Coventry. Critics will say that he was fortunate to win that round, as England's Kelvin Tatum was denied the title by an engine failure.

Kelvin was having a good meeting, but he was riding with an illegal exhaust. A few of us were aware of it, but when it came to the last race I told him that if he won the meeting I would lodge an official protest. I don't think he knew that the exhaust was illegal at FIM meetings, as the rules were different for FIM events than they were for the British League – but they are the rules. So he deliberately retired from the last race, and I won the meeting.

Sam followed that success by retaining the Coalite Classic at Bradford, and he was also in inspired form for the USA in the opening two Test matches against England. As the season was progressing, he was getting stronger and stronger, and yet it was clear that he hadn't peaked yet. He was unquestionably one of the British League's top performers.

Everything was going really well. My long-track bikes were flying, the Goddens were going really well and that was why I pursued that competition because I knew I had the right set-up. The Goddens didn't go that well on the smaller tracks, but on the bigger tracks, they were awesome.

Sam qualified from the first qualifying round of the World Long-Track Championship at Korskro, Denmark, with an impressive 38 points, and he finished in second place behind Hans Nielsen. His next round was the semi-final at Herxheim, and he had to finish inside the top eight to qualify for his second World Long-Track Final. He was confident of making it through, as not only was he on good engines, but he had won a long-track meeting there earlier in the season.

The only hiccup in Sam's build-up to the semi-final was a report in the press stating that Ermolenko had turned down the chance to ride for his country in the World Pairs Championship. He was quoted as saying at the time that he had far too many riding commitments and because of an extra meeting – which he didn't expect – he felt that he wouldn't be sufficiently prepared to be able to give his best for his country. An injury to Kelly Moran, and the international ban imposed on Shawn by the AMA for failing an alcohol test, meant that Sam was the obvious candidate. His position on this was not helped when America failed to make the final for the first time since 1980.

Ever the professional, Sam put all this behind him and produced a spectacular performance for his country at Belle Vue, as he scored 13 plus 2 bonus points as the Americans narrowly defeated England 54-53. But Ronnie Correy crashed out in the opening race and broke his wrist. This was a blow to the USA team, but an even bigger one to Wolverhampton, who were just one point behind Oxford in the league title race, and they were on a roll. But more problems were to follow.

After an encouraging performance at Belle Vue, Sam left Kirkmanshulme Lane and flew to Germany in a confident frame of mind for the semi-final at Herxheim. His arrival was greeted by sunshine and blue skies and, furthermore, he knew that he could count on a lot of support in Germany.

The meeting attracted the attention of the television cameras and, because of their presence, the track was watered to keep the dust at bay. As Sam prepared for his third race, he had already scored 12 points and he was in a comfortable position to qualify. He turned on his fuel taps and was pushed off for his third ride of the afternoon; he emerged onto the track for a race that would define his speedway career.

Less than a minute later, Sam's world stopped turning; his brain blanked out all the memory he had of a crash that many seasoned race fans described as one of the worst they had ever seen. It was the sound of the air ambulance that first greeted him as he slowly emerged from an unconscious state, and he was whisked away for emergency treatment.

Meanwhile, Chris Van Straaten was taking a short break in Wales after checking on the progress of his other injured American, Ronnie Correy. He couldn't get a signal on his car phone until he came close to Shrewsbury. He knew his number one rider was racing in Germany, so he decided to take advantage of being stuck in a traffic jam and call Sam's wife to see how he got along.

'I was on the outskirts of Shrewsbury sitting in a jam when I rang up Sam's wife, Shelley, to see if there was any news. There was; and it was all bad – he was very, very seriously hurt. The club was devastated.'

Charles Ermolenko was also making his first slides as a speedway rider in the USA, and he later admitted in *Speedway Star* that it made him think about what he was doing on a race track.

'I got a telephone call about Sam's long-track crash, and you really feel it yourself. That was pretty bad for me; it made me think about what I was doing. I got to see the other side of the page, and it wasn't a comfortable picture.'

He had suffered multiple fractures to his right leg and the early indications were that his career could be over. With his season in tatters, so began another rehabilitation programme for the American to rebuild his fitness – and his career.

Five

GLORY DAYS

Sam Ermolenko saw many doctors during his recovery from his multiple leg injuries sustained in that long-track crash in Germany in 1989, but if their opinions differed about the necessary treatment required for his broken bones, they all agreed on one thing: warm sunshine was the best healer in the world. Therefore, after a successful operation in Australia, Sam remained Down Under as a welcome guest of speedway promoter, Trevor Harding. Harding had done much to improve the flagging fortunes of solo racing in Australia. He was well known around the speedway scene because of his involvement with a host of top international stars such as Billy Sanders, Phil Crump, Mick Poole and others. The invitation he extended to Sam was a big boost for the American, who had struck up a good friendship with Harding – who was instantly recognisable outside of Australia for his company's name, Kwiksnax, which appeared on riders' leathers.

Sam had spent the early part of the 1989 close season racing in Australia in some meetings that were promoted by Harding. He made an immediate impression by winning the Pepsi International Challenge Open at Liverpool. However, in a highly successful spell in Australia, he caught the headlines when he won the prestigious King of Claremont meeting in Perth.

Trevor Harding lived in Queensland in a place called Sanctuary Cove and it was a million dollar property. His house would back on to the harbour while the houses across the street would back onto a golf course. We lived in a flat which was about ten minutes from his place, and we could go along there and water-ski or jet-ski. I couldn't water-ski because of the injury to my leg, but I could get on a jet-ski.

It was a new development and the harbour had no real harbour patrol at this point because it was so new. So we were able to launch off the back of his house on a jet-ski and have a good time. The jet-ski was perfect for me because I could balance on my leg without putting any stress on it, and this helped build up the muscle. And this was what I needed to build up my fitness so that I could ride in the 1990 Overseas Final. That was my goal.

During the month and a half that I was out there, I used to go out on the jet-ski regularly, and I was getting a lot of muscle building up in my leg. My wife used to say to me: 'Yeah, go out there, but be careful – don't hurt yourself.'

'Hurt myself? Come on, it's a jet-ski – if you fall you land on water,' I replied. 'It's not like motorcycles where you fall off and hit the ground.'

We had a couple of jet-skis, and sometimes up to four of us would go out on the river together. We would chase the big yachts because they would leave a bit of a wake, and we would hit the wake and get a jump out of it and have a good time. I was feeling pretty confident about doing this as my leg was feeling stronger every day. But on one occasion there was this boat that had half a dozen people aboard, and I was out by myself for one of the last rides on the ski. I had a go at this nice wake coming off this yacht, so lined it up and went for it and they gave me a clap and a cheer.

I'm a competitor, so I went back for more to show off. I went up and took the wake, but I lost the control and I landed wrong – and it was no soft landing. I was in the water holding onto the ski with one hand, and I put my other hand up to say that I was all right. It was quite an impact and I was a bit worried because I knew I had overdone it. I climbed back up on the ski and idled back to the house which was about a mile away. I had composed myself by this time and managed to get up the steps and into the house. My oh my, with two days to go before I was due to leave for California, I had twisted my knee. I told Shelley that I had hurt my knee, but I didn't say how. But she had already figured it out, and said: 'Oh you can't hurt yourself, ha!'

The next day it was all swollen up, so I had to go and see the local doctor. He took a look at it and said that I had damaged it. It was bleeding inside, so he drained my knee and blood was drawn off. But that relieved the pain a lot. Therefore, I was comfortable enough to be able to travel. The next day I left for America, and then I saw Dr Almquist and it was good by then. I just had to take easy for a couple of weeks. I saw Dr Almquist and he had to drain it again.

Looking back at it now, by being aggressive and pushing the knee and leg to the limit, it helped the healing process. I felt that I had to do that before it would get better. I think exercising it in that way helped the knee to heal, and it built up the strength more quickly. When I went back to California, there was a river trail that led to the beach. I just rode my bicycle back and forth as many times as I could in a week. I continued my rehabilitation, and by this time I was feeling pretty fit and posting some record times. Even though the bones hadn't healed completely yet, I was feeling pretty good. I was working really hard to get myself as fit as I could for the Overseas Final, and it was while I was at home that I developed the orange bikes that I was famous for.

Wolverhampton stuck by their number one rider and left a place open for him in their team. The British Speedway Promoters' Association (BSPA) granted Wolves a guest facility to cover for his absence during the opening weeks of the season, as he was expected to be back in the saddle during the 1990 season.

While he received support from his club, family, friends, sponsors and his many fans, not everyone felt that they were able to support him for commercial reasons. Don Godden, whose engines had already powered Hans Nielsen to three world speedway titles; and also struck gold at long-track level with Shawn Moran and Simon Wigg, decided to pull out of the agreement that he had with the American Champion.

When I got hurt, Don pulled out of the whole thing. He was a funny guy, and on one occasion he called me and said that he thought that we didn't know what we were doing. He said that we shouldn't have been doing what we were, and then later I discovered that he was producing the same thing that we were doing with his engines. There was no doubt that his long-track engines were fast, but after the accident I went back to riding GMs again. GMs are still a leading speedway engine, but where are the Goddens? You don't see them in the Grand Prix.

In the sport's press, it was announced that he intended to make a comeback for Wolves in May, and it was clear that he was serious about getting fit to race. He was cycling a lot to build up his muscles, and Chris Van Straaten revealed in one article that he cycled 25 miles to meet him so that he could practice after a meeting at Wolves. Doctors had said that he could ride, but he was not ready to race alongside anyone else.

Wolves had covered for their captain's absence by using guests, but there was no real substitute for their inspirational skipper. In the Gold Cup, the season's opening competition; Wolves finished in third place and were eliminated from the tournament. Despite his hard work, Sam admitted defeat and told his boss that he wouldn't be fit enough to return in early May, and they signed former World Finalist, Bo Petersen, as a short-term replacement. Petersen wasn't nearly as consistent as Ermolenko, and they lost three matches in succession and ended the run with a hard-earned draw against Reading. But defeats in excess of 20 points away at Cradley, Coventry and Swindon, proved to the Wolves fans that Ermolenko's return couldn't come quickly enough. Therefore, June was pencilled in as a new return date.

No doubt Chris was getting some criticism over his decision to stick by his captain, but he continued to support him. He remained loyal to his rider, just as Sam had been loyal to the team during the turbulent 1986 campaign. It was one gentleman returning a favour to another.

The American Motorcycle Association (AMA) has a poor record when it comes to speedway racing. The first piece of real evidence that the AMA didn't take the sport seriously can be traced back to the American Final in 1978. To begin with, this qualifying round of the World Championship took place in December 1978, even though the prize that the field was racing for was two places in 1979 World Championship! If that wasn't bad enough, Scott Autrey, who finished third in the 1978 World Final at Wembley, England, was so angry with the lack of organisation of the whole event that he sacrificed his own World Championship dreams and withdrew from the meeting in protest.

The AMA looked upon speedway racing as a minority interest because its following was largely based in California. Consequently, they took the view that as it wasn't a form of motor sport that was recognised on a national scale, it didn't require the same kind of support and attention that other forms of motorcycle racing enjoyed. Even when the Americans won every competition in sight in 1982, and staged the World Final, the AMA offered little support to the riders or the promoters that put US speedway on the map. For many years, a lot of the organisation was left to Costa Mesa promoter, Harry Oxley. But when the FIM began laying down their requirements so that Oxley's company could stage events like the World Team Cup, he received very little support from his own federation.

The man who was in charge of speedway racing within the AMA corridors of power at that time was Bill Boyce. Boyce never really understood speedway and the way it worked, as he was more interested in road racing. He probably thought that speedway was a pain in the backside when compared with other forms of high-profile bike racing, and as it was such a small concern, it didn't warrant too much fuss. That's not to say that he wouldn't help, he always did, but

Breaking the Limits – The Sam Ermolenko Story

it was his lack of understanding that let down many riders and promoters. Sam Ermolenko would be another one of US speedway's
top stars to be let down by his own federation.

His doctor had already informed Sam that a femur break like the
one he had sustained at Herxheim in 1989 took a year to heal
properly. Therefore, he worked really hard to get himself fit to ride
in the 1990 Overseas Final on 24 June. He was confident that he
would be fit enough to be able to ride in that round, but before
that he was scheduled to appear in the American Final at Long
Beach on 2 June. It was a tall order to be fit enough to race and
qualify for this round, as there were only four qualifying places
available; whereas at the Overseas Final there were nine, and it was
nearly three weeks later. Those three weeks would make all the difference to his fitness levels.

Subsequently, as Sam was the closest any American had come to
winning the World Championship since 1982, he was hopeful that
his federation would seed him direct to the Overseas Final at
Coventry, England. Furthermore, he had qualified for every World
Final since 1985, and he had been their only representative in two
of them. As the reigning World Champion, Bruce Penhall was
seeded to the Overseas round in 1982 – so it had been done
before. Having suffered such bad injuries representing his country,
Sam had worked very hard to be fit enough to be able to compete
in 1990 World Championship; surely they would look favourably
on his request?

*Bill Boyce was the representative of the AMA that was dealing with speed-
way. He wasn't really a fan of speedway, but he was the administrator for the
AMA. He also represented the AMA and American speedway at the
FIM meetings.*

*If you take into consideration my World Championship record at that
point: I had a third in 1985, I didn't back it up in 1986, but I was on the
podium again in 1987; I didn't have the best of Championships in 1988,
but come 1989 – if it wasn't for the injury, who was to say how well I could
have done. The AMA were not fans; they didn't know the reasons why I*

performed well one year and not the other. But when you think about it, who else was there who was still consistently performing at the top level that had experienced such a rocky road? If you put everything into perspective: I went to race at Poole, but they had their financial problems, so I came home. But I returned to the international scene while I was racing in California and had a lot of success. Then, in 1986, my World Championship result was affected by Peter Adams' problems with the promotion, and, in 1987, the ban restricted my result. In 1988, knowing that I would be just cruising to get my programme back on track, I still finished in fourth place – despite the rain.

Consequently, I had all that experience and I was about to put it all together in 1989 and really go for it. I believe that I probably would have won it in 1989, and because Bill Boyce and the AMA were not fans of speedway, they had no idea. I was always led to believe by the people who had dealt with the AMA that they thought speedway was pain in the ass. No doubt the episode with Scott Autrey didn't help their attitude, but I thought I had a chance of getting seeded because I had such a good record in the Championship.

I had worked really hard on getting myself into a position where I was fit enough to be able to have a chance of winning the World Championship. Furthermore, the 1990 World Final was scheduled for Bradford, which was where I nearly won the title in 1985. I was so eager, and I knew that it was a track where you could really race. If you had the right set-up there, then you could make it work for you.

That was how I saw it; and I felt that it had to happen. All I wanted was for the AMA to wake up and see this opportunity. I had a good record at Odsal, as I had also won the Coalite Classic meeting there in 1988 and 1989. I asked Bill Boyce if he would at least consider it.

'No, I'm sorry. We can't do it', he replied. And this was from the word go, they put up a brick wall straightaway.

'Think about it,' I urged him. 'Put your best man forward, come on, it's gotta be worth it.'

'No, I'm sorry,' he repeated.

They didn't care about speedway; having a World Speedway Champion didn't mean anything to them. I had no support, and they just thought that

I wanted special treatment. I didn't dwell on it – that was the way it was. I couldn't change anything; they were not going to help me, so I just had to get on with it. But it was so disappointing, not only for me, but also for my team, Carl Blomfeldt, my wife, everyone was really disappointed because I deserved to be helped – but not in their eyes, as they knew nothing about the sport.

As he now had to compete in the American Final, Sam suddenly found that he had a shorter timescale to get back on a bike and be competitive. He put in eight laps at Ascot in preparation for the meeting at Long Beach, and while it wasn't perfect, he could get by.

Anyone who had studied the American's style before his crash couldn't have failed to notice the changes that Sam had to make to his technique so that he could continue to race. Before he was a natural racer, and he was very loose and would throw the bike into the corners. Now, however, he was more precise; he was still a spectacular rider, but he was more deliberate in his racing than he appeared before the crash in Germany.

Still disappointed and annoyed by AMA's decision not to seed him to the Overseas Final, he mentioned it to Harry Oxley, as he held a lot of influence in American speedway. He said that he would discuss it with the other riders, but it was reported that they were all against Sam being seeded because that would have meant just three qualifying places instead of four. You could see their point as every rider wants a chance to succeed in the World Championship. But Sam's record was not considered in this at all.

Therefore, he would have to make his return to the track in the highly pressured environment of the American Final.

CTI Brace made me an awesome brace to go on my leg which helped me to ride, so I knew if I had a fall, I had some support. I went there with a positive attitude, even though I knew that the odds were not in my favour. We had five riders in a race at that time, and in my first race I got a third. Then in my second race, I was leading it when my engine blew. So having a third and then a last; that meant I had no chance of qualifying and I withdrew from the meeting.

The fact of the matter was that I was just not strong enough to compete. In one race I came hard under my brother, Charles, and I stuffed him into the fence. I didn't mean to, I just didn't have the confidence to hold on to it. I didn't have the strength in my muscles to race — it was brave of me to ride, but I was not fit enough.

I made a return to ride in the Olympique at Wolverhampton, and although I was gaining in strength all the time, I only scored 2 points. But then I rode for Wolverhampton at Cradley the day before the Overseas Final, and I top-scored with 12 points. This proved to the AMA that they had made a mistake and I would have been fit enough to ride in the Overseas Final. I put my mind to it and I met the target that I had set myself. I was about 90 per cent fit now, whereas at the time of the American Final I was just about 50 per cent fit, because I had to cut down on my training and get my entire equipment ready to race at Long Beach. If I was seeded to the Overseas, then I wouldn't have had to take this time out from my fitness programme, and I could have continued to make progress. But it was all denied to me and what looked like a golden opportunity had gone.

On 23 July, Sam proved that he was definitely back with a paid maximum in Wolves' 53-36 win over Belle Vue. This performance earned him a call-up to ride for the USA in the World Team Cup qualifying round. America were eliminated from their automatic place in the final by their last place in the 1989 event at Bradford, which meant that they had to qualify through two meetings to make the 1990 final. In these rounds they met Sweden, Australia and West Germany. They finished second to Sweden in the first meeting at Olching, trailing the Swedes by just one point — Sam scored 7 points. In the second round at Mariestad, Sweden, they won by 44 points to Sweden's 40 to make the final — Australia and Germany were never in the hunt. Shawn Moran returned to form to score a 15-point maximum, and he received solid support from Sam, who dropped just one point in his 14-point total.

Following his unhappy exit from the world title chase, Sam was spending the rest of the season getting back to full fitness and racing for Wolverhampton. Then, suddenly, he was in the World Team Cup Final. He was joined in the team by the Moran brothers, Rick Miller and Billy Hamill. They faced the hosts, Czechoslovakia, the defending Champions England, and a weakened Danish team, who were without the injured Erik Gundersen and Jan O. Pedersen.

It was a closely fought contest between the three Western nations on the large Pardubice track, but the Czechs were also making their presence felt by taking some important points off of the top three at vital times. America kept in touch at the top, with Kelly and Shawn Moran in inspired form, and they were receiving solid support from Sam and, to a lesser extent, Hamill.

In heat 12, it was Ermolenko who put America ahead with a race win over Bohumil Brhel, John Jorgensen and Simon Wigg. He celebrated this win with a characteristic wheelie down the back straight, and he punched the air as he greeted his team-mates in the pits – America were ahead for the first time.

Denmark's challenge began to falter as the meeting neared its climax, and by the final four races, it was between the USA and England. Wigg defeated Shawn Moran to put the two countries level with two races to go. Kelly Moran, who was heralded as the hero of the day with four impressive race wins, gave his country the lead by winning heat 19. With England's Jeremy Doncaster back in third, it meant that it all depended on the last race.

Inspired and psyched up by the renewed team spirit in the Americans' pits, and with the promise of a gold medal, Sam rolled out onto the track to face Hans Nielsen, Kelvin Tatum and Zdenek Tesar. He lined up in gate two and was sandwiched by Tatum on his inside and Nielsen in gate three. It was Tatum who was the danger man. As the tapes rose, Nielsen and Sam were away, but Tatum was left trailing as they sped into the first bend. Nielsen was eager to keep the Danish flag flying in some way, and he pulled away. But Sam slotted into second and he knew that he had to hold station to clinch a memorable victory. Everyone in the American camp was hoping that nothing would go wrong, and the celebrations began as Sam crossed the finishing line in that vital second spot.

This was America's first speedway gold medal since Bobby Schwartz and Dennis Sigalos swept all before them in the 1982 World Pairs Final in Australia. No doubt Sam took some satisfaction – and pride, as it was his first gold medal – from clinching the gold for his country after all the controversy over the seeding episode. This victory marked the first rays of a new dawn that was about to rise for American speedway, and Sudden Sam Ermolenko would be at its heart.

I was disappointed that we didn't do better in the Final at Long Beach in 1988, because we were up for it then. Kelly was on form at Pardubice, but it was a team effort and we came through to win. I remember in heat 8, I passed Tommy Knudsen coming out of turn two and I clipped him as I went by, and that was a pretty good race. That was quite an accomplishment because there wasn't much passing on the slick surface. But I just rode the season out that year as I was regaining my fitness, so there weren't too many heroics.

Nonetheless, Sam made his first appearance in the British League Riders' Championship since 1984. The final usually clashed with the Nationals in America, but this time he rode at Belle Vue and finished in fifth place with 11 points. It was another indication that he was getting back to his best, and all the signs were that 1991 would see the return of the real Sam Ermolenko. For Wolverhampton, meanwhile, it was a season that ended with no major silverware, despite finishing runners-up for the second successive year to Champions Reading. One thing was clear from those two seasons of being 'so close and yet so far', if Sam had been able to finish both seasons, they would have probably won back-to-back league titles. Would it be third time lucky?

Van Straaten's team for 1991 had a familiar look about it. Sam was back with fellow American Ronnie Correy, who would spearhead their challenge. But they were joined by a third American – Sam's younger brother, Charles, or 'Dukie' as he was known. Graham Jones, Wayne Carter, Andy Phillips and Denmark's Lars Munkedal completed the septet. With the astute Peter Adams once again in the team manager's role, Wolves entered the new campaign feeling very confident about their prospects. Changes were made to the structure of the league with promotion and relegation between the two leagues that were now called Division One and Division Two.

But Sam faced an early challenge in the World Championship. The American Final was brought forward to 2 March 1991, as the Veterans Stadium at Long Beach was due to be closed. Therefore, it was the last time that one of the world's best tracks would stage a speedway meeting. Sam had been racing successfully in Australia, so he didn't go into the meeting cold like some of his rivals.

The victory went to Rick Miller, who won his first American Final with a 15-point maximum. Ermolenko took the runners–up spot as he dropped his only point to Miller in the opening heat. His Wolves team–mate Ronnie Correy was third, and the two remaining qualifying places were grabbed by Kelly Moran and Billy Hamill – their allocation had been increased from four to five following the 1990 World Final, when three Americans made the last sixteen.

It seemed to be something of a tradition that Wolves would start poorly in the Gold Cup, and the 1991 season commenced in much the same way. After completing half of the fixtures, Wolves had only one victory and that didn't come at home, but away, at arch-rivals Cradley Heath. Sam scored a paid maximum, and along with his fellow countryman, Correy, they clinched a memorable win. The Ermolenko-Correy partnership was beginning to blossom into one of the most potent spearheads in the British League. It was early days, but the potential of the side was illustrated to the Monmore Green faithful when they demolished Bradford 63-27 with another paid maximum for their skipper, and then they completed the double over the Yorkshire side with 46-44 win at Odsal – where Ermolenko and Correy won a last-heat decider. Things were starting to turn around at Wolverhampton, and suddenly they were top of the Northern Section of the Gold Cup. Andy Phillips revealed that the team spirit in the side was better than ever.

'We have team meetings every other week,' he said, 'and that helps tremendously. The track is a lot better too.'

But their slow start to the season meant that they were edged off the top of the group by the ambitious Berwick team. Belle Vue put them out of the Knock-Out Cup which left them free to concentrate on their own particular golden goose – the League Championship. And they underlined that they meant business when they won their first nine matches, but the sequence came to an end at Cradley. They strengthened their cause by signing Australian Scott Norman from Peterborough, as a replacement for Carter who was struggling for form. It was also in 1991 that Sam replaced Shawn Moran as captain of the USA team.

When I first came over to England, Bobby Schwartz was the captain of the team. The normal routine for the squad in those days was to meet at a central place and discuss the forthcoming season. The most central place to meet was Rick Miller's house, and we would just talk about what we were going to do and how we were going to do it. It was probably at one of these meetings that a decision was made that I should be the captain – although we would still make all the decisions as a team. Basically the captain was the rider who our team manager at the time, John Scott, used to talk to and share ideas with. Then it would be down to me to make sure that this was communicated to rest of the team – but John would do a lot of that.

I never thought that I did such a good job as Bobby did. Bobby would make sure that everything was right and he would fight our cause. In comparison, though, my job was quite easy because Ronnie and I raced together at Wolverhampton, and Rick and I raced in Poland together. Shawn, Kelly and Lance King were very experienced at international level, so the job took care of itself. It wasn't until later on, because of my status as a champion, that I did more for the team and rose to the occasion.

I always used to make sure that we got together at the beginning of the season, at a mutual time and place, and talk about the international racing ahead of us. As I possessed some mechanical ability, my workshop took the responsibility of helping out the riders with their engines. The likes of Ronnie Correy, Rick Miller, and Billy Hamill – when they first came on the scene – benefited from Blomfeldt & Associates. Ronnie and Rick probably got more out of it at that time, although Billy did later when he won his World Championship.

When we got together as a team, we knew what it was all about. We were self-motivated; we didn't need anyone to motivate us to do well because we always had a good level of team spirit. When we were all there together, we just had a good time and that was how we did it. It didn't really matter what competition we were in, if it was against the English riders we would have a laugh with them and have a good time. We were serious about racing, but we enjoyed ourselves too. For instance, if there were any problems, like the wheelie ban of 1986, we would all pull together and we'd deal with it.

At the time when I came over to Britain to race in 1984, we needed a Bobby Schwartz as captain because there was a lot to organise. There were funds that needed to be raised to support the team for Test matches, because the AMA wasn't interested in speedway. So if we needed race jackets, team jackets or hats, anything to make us look like a team, we had to find the money ourselves. What we had to do was negotiate an agreement with the AMA and the BSPA, so that if we had any Test matches, the promoters of the tests, or the BSPA, would have to put some money into a fund. This fund would be used for race jackets, hats and sometimes a bike, if one of the riders didn't have a machine to ride.

Those were the jobs that the captain had to do at that time, so he had to be an administrator as well as work alongside the team manager. Bobby had already been through all the battles to organise everything, but when I was made captain of the team, it was difficult to hold on to those things. This was because of the fact that there weren't many Test matches anymore, so we didn't have to demand these things. Most of the times they didn't run the series was when we had lost, so that we wouldn't get the opportunity to regain it the following year and instead they would do something with one of the other nations. Unlike in the 1980s, when I took over, it was never a consistent series that was staged every year.

I only had to be captain in world events and World Championship qualifying rounds, and I would do what I could to help the other riders as their national captain. When the likes of Kelly and Shawn were riding, they were so easy-going. But as a team there was never one rider who was selfish about something, or wanted something done for him. If there was something on the day that we didn't think was fair, we would tell John Scott, and he would raise our objections. John was a jolly type of guy, but if our objections were rejected, it would be 'Oh jolly good – thank you.' He wouldn't always come forward and force the point that something wasn't right and it should be done differently. It was only when Bobby was the captain that he would fight our corner and get things done. But the fights and the arguments were over by the time I was made captain of the national team. I got the blue USA jacket for John that he always used to wear, and he really was a nice man and he had the respect of all the Americans. Even though he was the perfect English gentleman, we adopted him as one of our own and he always did his best for us.

Meanwhile, Sam finished second in the Overseas Final at Bradford, with England's Kelvin Tatum lifting the title. It was a good final for America, with only Miller failing to make the semi-finals – Billy Hamill took third place on the podium. There was no doubting that Sam was on form, as he was top of the averages in Britain and looking better than ever. He had formed a brilliant partnership with Correy at Wolverhampton, which led to them representing their country in the revamped World Pairs Championship. But they were eliminated at the semi-finals at Pocking, with Correy scoring 12 points and Sam just 7. It was a surprise defeat for the Danes at the hands of Germany's Gerd Riss that knocked the Americans out of the Championship.

We had been struggling, but it was just coming together for us, and we were in with a chance of qualifying. The Danes, Hans Nielsen and Tommy Knudsen, were just flying: they were jumping out of the start and beating everybody. I could see that if the Danes won their last race against the Germans then we would qualify. But if they went out there and let the Germans win it – then we were out.

Erik Gundersen was the Danish team manager at this time, and I said to him: 'Erik, you guys are not going to throw the race or anything, are you?'

'*No way, we would never do that – the boys are here to win.*'

But they lied to me. They went out there and threw the race, and we got knocked out. I was afraid that would happen, and I never forgot the way they played that – the way they lied to me. If I was them, I would have told them we would rather race against the Germans, than race against you. I would have said the truth. We watched that and we were so disheartened, and I knew that I would never forget it.

Ronnie Correy was doing really well that year, and his average was right up there with me – he was easily inside the top 10 averages in the British League. Ronnie and I were the dudes around Wolverhampton; it was highly unlikely that anyone else would be picked for a last-heat decider, and most of the time we would come out on top.

Peter Adams was very clever with the way he would construct and manage the team. Prior to the event, especially if it was an away match, Peter would always call me or whisper in my ear what he was thinking about the match ahead. We would all walk the track together before the meeting as a team. I remember when we were at Bradford, there were always these little rocks or pebbles on the track, and Ronnie would move his foot over the surface and push these rocks around and say: 'I know where we're at now – it's Bradford.' We would check the condition of the track and this sort of banter would be going on as we strolled around; so, as a team, there was always something good that someone had to say.

At this point, Peter would begin orchestrating how we would approach the match. If he could predict what he expected would happen, as I was the captain of the team, he would pull me aside and say: 'Look, Sam, it's pretty important if we win the toss for starting positions that Ronnie gets the inside gate.' This was especially so if it was heat 15. Ronnie was superb from the inside gate. If he was on the outside gates, he would race. But if he didn't get the best of starts from one of the other positions, then he would back off and take what he had. I was more creative with my first turns than Ronnie was, so Pete recognised this straightaway. Therefore, when it came to heat 15, and we flipped the coin to decide the gate positions, Pete would whisper in my ear: 'You know, Sam, this is pretty important for us – you know where Ronnie's got to be, don't you?' I would reply that that I knew and to leave it with me.

I would go up to Ronnie and say, 'OK, Ronnie, what are we going to do here?' And I knew for a fact that he wouldn't take any other gate except the inside, and 90 per cent of the time he was always excited about having the inside. Therefore, I would say to him, 'Ronnie? Same again, you take the inside and I'll take the outside?' And his face would just glow, and he'd reply: 'Yeah, I'll take the inside.' That would help us to win as a team, and Ronnie would go full gas because that's the way he would make the start and ride.

I remember, on many occasions, he would be going flat out because he had the best gate, and when I finally got alongside of him, I would want him to slow up just a little bit. But he was going so fast that I would have to ride full gas to keep up with him. It was good, and we always left the opposition for dead, and sometimes we would finish half a lap ahead of them.

However, when we went to Ipswich, we had only lost one match in the league, so the pressure was on the team. They had to delay the start so that everyone could get into the stadium. In the last heat, Ronnie was on the inside and Peter Adams' instructions to us were to make sure that we had the right gates. I said to Ronnie, 'OK, you make the start and just have a look for me, and if I'm there, I'm there, if not – just go!' I was on the outside gates and Ronnie had his favoured inside. I took care of Shane Parker on the first corner, but Ronnie pulled out of turn two in front. I was coming around the outside, but to cover the ground, I had to cut back to the inside of Ronnie. His instructions were to look for me, and as he looked over his right shoulder, he could see that I wasn't there, but he heard that someone was on his inside. As I'm supposed to be coming around the outside, he was probably wondering who was on his inside, so he moved over to the left – just a little bit – and just as I was getting the drive to get by David Norris, Ronnie cut in front of me. My front tyre clipped Ronnie's back wheel and my handlebars flipped to the left, and it threw me over the right side of the bike alongside my teammate. I was sent cartwheeling down the track, and I hit my knee really hard and damaged it.

At the time, I had a guest from Canada with us, one of Carl Blomfeldt's friends. The plan was that as soon as the meeting at Ipswich was over, we were going to get into the van and catch the ferry for Germany.

This crash happened just four days before I was due to ride in Abensberg for the World Championship semi-final. This was the first year when they scrapped the Inter-Continental and Continental Finals, and they replaced them with two semi-finals. So they mixed up the 32 riders and we were split by ballot into two semi-finals: one was in Russia, and I was scheduled to race in Germany.

I was being looked after in the ambulance room at Ipswich and I had to make a decision about what I was going to do. The knee was all swollen up and it hurt like hell, but it was pretty obvious that it had fluid in it. I decided to make the planned trip to Abensberg as I didn't want to pull out of the semi-final – I had to get through this round. I decided to leave for Abensberg and I hoped that the knee would be better in the morning.

We started driving through Belgium, but when I woke up my knee wasn't feeling too good. I decided that it needed to be drained, so we peeled off the road and found a town. We asked for a doctor and found one and went to his house where he had a little clinic. He looked at me and drove a needle into my knee and drained it, and there was blood in it. So I had definitely done something, but by draining it I had relieved the pressure. We ice-packed my knee and drove on to Abensberg, and met up with some fans there who catered for my needs.

I went to the practice and after I strapped it up – well, Carl's friend Albert from Canada strapped it up – I did a couple of laps, but because the strapping was so tight, it was putting a lot of pressure on my knee. I removed the bandages, put an ice pack on it, then strapped it up again and did another practice. I felt pretty confident because the bikes were going really well, and I knew I only had to score a certain number of points to get through to the World Final. That night, after I had done the practice, and as the meeting was scheduled for the following day, I decided to go to the hospital and have it looked at.

I told them the situation and they took an X-ray, and it revealed that I had fractured my knee cap – that was the problem. I asked them if there was anything they could give me to get me through the race, and he told me to come back in the morning and they would see what they could do. So I went back, and they injected something into my vein. Well, it scared me because it made me feel a little bit woozy. At that point, I thought that they had injected something into me that was illegal, but when I told them about the code that I had to follow, they said that it was no problem. It turned out to be nothing more than paracetamol, or aspirin, and it took the edge off the pain.

By the time I got to the event, we had worked out what we were going to do by strapping it up. I raced and qualified by finishing in fourth place with 11 points. I went back to the hospital and they put my knee in plaster. The plaster was removed the day before the World Final practice, which was being held that year at Gothenburg in Sweden.

Therefore, by doing what I did best, which was team-riding with Ronnie, I just misjudged what I was doing and he misjudged it as well, and I clipped his back wheel and broke my knee cap. That meant that I wasn't able to ride until the day before the World Final practice.

When it came to the World Final, there was a lot of controversy about the exhausts. This was the FIM flexing their muscles again and screwing everything up. It put us [the riders] under pressure; it put everyone under pressure, and I tried to exclude myself from all that by going back to my hotel and staying out of it. My wife was there and my mother came over for the final, and I tried to keep away from it all. I had my bicycle with me, so I rode it from the hotel to the track, knowing that the only way I could succeed in this meeting was not to put too much pressure on myself.

My second race – heat 8 - was re-started twice, but I defeated Per Jonsson and Armando Castagna at the third time of asking. I had 5 points from two rides, but then I was out again in heat 9 and I lost to Tony Rickardsson, which left me with 7 points. By the time my fourth race came round, and after I had heat 8 re-started three times, plus the back-to-back races; in my eyes, I had done five races and I was knackered. I was in too much pain and I couldn't handle it anymore and had to pull out. You have to remember that I only had the plaster removed two days before the final. I struggled to hold on, but no one could touch Jan O. Pedersen that day – he was flying and was in a class of his own. I was determined to have a good result, and if you take Jan out of the equation, I probably would have done well because I defeated some of the top riders that evening. It was just that my knee had had enough by my fourth race; otherwise, I think I would have got on to the podium again.

The exhaust controversy arose because the majority of the riders had exhausts fitted to their machines that exceeded the noise level. This caused a flurry of problems as the riders had to find exhausts that conformed to the noise limit. Twenty-six machines failed the tests that were carried out during the practice, and the field struggled to reach the 102 decibels limit. Most of the riders were using King silencers, which were widely used in Britain, but then they had to rush out and purchase Tolba exhausts.

It was a ridiculous situation that led to the riders protesting against each other, claiming that their rivals were using illegal exhausts. Defending World Champion, Per Jonsson, protested about Sam's silencer, and then the American lodged a protest about Tony Rickardsson. Paul Thorp protested about Hans Nielsen's and so on.

Billy Hamill was so desperate to reach the necessary decibel limit that he had to borrow an exhaust from one of the vintage display bikes to be able to take his place in the final! The whole thing was a farce, and the situation descended into an absurd scenario.

Despite his discomfort, Sam continued to ride and he top-scored with 9 points for the USA, as the nation relinquished the World Team title to Denmark – who regained the trophy on their own track at Vojens. The American team finished in third behind the Danes and the rapidly rising Swedes. His injury also meant that he missed the last two Tests against England, and the Americans lost the series 3-0, despite the valiant efforts of their new riders on the international scene: Hamill, Greg Hancock, Bobby Ott and Dukie.

Back in Britain, and Wolverhampton continued to set pace at the top, with only one defeat at Berwick since losing at Ipswich. On 12 October, Bradford defeated Cradley Heath and the Championship was Wolverhampton's at last. It was their first Championship success since they won the Provincial League Championship in 1963. Van Straaten was elated and said: 'I am delighted for everyone connected with Wolverhampton Speedway. It was a real team effort, from the riders, the mechanics, the management and, especially, the supporters.'

Sometimes Ronnie was the captain of the team, and that was Peter Adams'
way of boosting the team. With me stepping aside, it gave Ronnie a boost
and he would rise to the occasion. It was a case of whatever it took to get the
team to win, that was the approach that Peter and Chris took. We talked
about everything at Wolverhampton, which Peter probably still does with the
Karlsson brothers.

That is how Peter Adams works; he is an in-depth manager and he
always had a good idea about how he wanted to do things, and he had a
plan behind it. We had a wonderful spirit in the team, and winning the
league was really nice after coming so close in previous years.

There was one meeting left for 1991 that carried a lot of prestige,
and that was what was now called the Division One Riders'
Championship. Sam was riding high at the top of the average table,
and it was only Hans Nielsen who had an average in excess of 10
points a match as the meeting arrived.

After both riders had completed four races, they were both
unbeaten with 12 points each, as they lined up against each other in
heat 19. It was simple: Sam had to finish ahead of Nielsen to win
the title – or vice versa. Kelvin Tatum and Shane Parker were the
other two riders who lined up at the start line, and Tatum was hoping for a good result as he still had a chance of a podium finish.

It was clear that the American had arrived at Belle Vue determined to win. From the inside gate, Sam arrived in the first bend
with Nielsen alongside. But the American took control on the
inside and ensured that he had nowhere to go on the back straight,
and streaked away for the race win and the title. After all of his heroics for Wolves, that also saw him top the table for the highest number of maximums with 17, his personal glory was well deserved. But
that World Championship still eluded the Californian.

Following their success in 1991, Wolves boss Van Straaten had to
make changes to comply with the points limit. He retained the
three Americans and Graham Jones, and brought in a promising
rider from Sweden, Peter Karlsson. Wayne Carter kept his place,
after he returned to replace Munkedal late in 1991, as they pushed

for the title, and they also brought in a promising newcomer, Stephen Morris.

The team started off the new season as they had left 1991, by winning their first 17 official matches – 18, if you include their season opener against Swedish side, Kumla. This run was brought to an end by Coventry, who pulled off a surprise win at Monmore Green on a very wet evening. But when they won the Gold Cup by defeating Reading, it appeared that it would be the first of many trophies.

However, the injury jinx struck again. Not Sam this time, but first Wayne Carter broke his leg in an off-track accident on a motorcycle, and then Graham Jones was sidelined when he broke his wrist. It proved to be enough for the team to lose momentum, despite the signings of veteran Gordon Kennett, Richard Musson and Nigel Leaver, they slipped down the table and, eventually, out of contention.

For Sam, if anything, he was riding even better than he did in 1991. Early in the season, he raced in four meetings for Wolves and dropped just one point. In fact, throughout the year, he only dropped below double figures on three occasions. Surely 1992 would be his year?

The American Final was cancelled as they were unable to find a suitable venue, and Sam was seeded to the Overseas Final, along with Greg Hancock, Billy Hamill, Ronnie Correy and Bobby Ott. But once again, the AMA's embarrassing lack of knowledge of the sport saw them reverse their decision and remove Hancock and Ott, and replace them with Rick Miller and Mike Faria!

Nonetheless, they all started off from zero for the Overseas Final, but it was a difficult afternoon for Sam. After two races he had 4 points, but then he thrilled the crowd at Coventry by surging through from fourth to second in exciting style. He took second by inches over Correy at the chequered flag that put him on 6 points at the interval stage. Then, in his fourth ride, he was pegged back into third place by the British duo of Kelvin Tatum and Andy Smith. With just 7 points, he was hovering around the cut-off point of qualification or failure. He had to wait until the final race to make sure of his place in the semi-finals when he lined up for what, on paper at least, was his easiest race of the afternoon. He made no mistake; and defeated Shane Parker, Mark Thorpe and Martin Dugard, to finish in a very respectable fourth place with 10 points.

But the big story over the weekend of World Championship action was the elimination from the Nordic Final of the triple World Champion, Hans Nielsen. The man they dubbed 'The Main Dane' scored just 6 points, and would be absent from the sport's big night for the first time since 1979.

There were no such worries for Sam, however, as he was never troubled as he qualified from the semi-final in Wiener Neustadt, Austria, with 14 points. He dropped his only point to the winner, Gert Handberg.

The World Final was being held at Wroclaw, Poland, and this time it looked as though the title was Sam's for the taking. His two biggest rivals were already out of contention: the reigning World Champion, Jan O. Pedersen, was not able to defend his title due to a serious back injury sustained earlier in the season, and Nielsen, always one of the favourites, had been eliminated in the early rounds. Therefore, it was Per Jonsson, the 1990 World Champion, who was looked upon as his biggest rival for the crown. Once again, Sam was top of the averages in Britain and he was in equally impressive form in the Swedish and Polish Leagues. When compared with 1991, his form may have been just as impressive, but this time he wasn't carrying an injury and he entered the final fully fit. Surely his long-awaited moment of glory had come?

They had all the riders staying in one of the old-style hotels which had a casino, a bar and a lot of traffic in the street. My preparation for that final was quite good, and I thought that it wasn't a good idea to stay there as I wanted a good night's sleep. Knowing that the heat was going to be a big problem, I didn't want to get dehydrated, so I drank a lot of water to make sure that I was feeling good. But when I went to bed that night, I couldn't stop peeing – I constantly had to get up and go to the bathroom! I guess I overdid it by thinking that I was being clever. I had a really good practice and my bikes felt really strong, and I was confident that I was going to have a good meeting.

It was a long drawn out parade, as they usually are in Poland, and all the riders were standing there on the start/finish line. We were looking at the grandstand, and behind the stand there were these big, dark clouds that looked very threatening and they were creeping toward the stadium. When you looked the other way, the skies were not clear but it wasn't threatening. It was a super hot day, and there were thunderstorms around and you could see the lightning flashes in the distance.

I was in heat 3 for my first race, and I was starting from gate three. I gave this race a lot of thought, and I had Jimmy Nilsen on my outside and I felt really confident about getting to the first corner. I watched the first race from the pits, and I was certain that my bikes were set up just right. As the second race started, it began to drizzle as the clouds were getting closer, and when it finished, the rain started to come down really hard. I said to my mechanic, Danny Gollagher: 'I think we should be ready for a change here, as it was raining in heat 2. I think we should watch to see what happens as I think we may have to make a change.'

We all thought that the referee would let the storm pass before he started heat 3, because by now it was hammering down with rain. There were some doubts about what was going to happen, whether they would run the next race or not, and I was beginning to wonder whether to put my helmet on or not. But the track staff were telling the mechanics to get the bikes ready, but I was still having doubts. Then I looked around, and I realised that if we were going to go out, we had to make some changes to the bike because the track was different now. My mechanic, Danny Gollagher, was looking at me and asking me what changes I wanted to make, as I was looking over the bike.

At that point, Carl Blomfeldt came up to me and said, 'What are you doing, Sam?'

'Well, I'm thinking about making a change here as it's starting to rain and I need to set it up a little bit different.'

'Why do you want to change?'

'Well, because I normally do.'

'Look down the pits; do you see anybody else changing?'

'No, I guess not.'

'Then just go out there and win the thing.'

I thought that maybe he was right, and Danny was waiting for a decision from me and I told him to leave like it was. He asked if I was sure, as
Danny was always with me in the pits, and I said I was. As he wheeled my
bike out and I was strapping my helmet on, it was really pouring down with
rain. I thought there was no way that we were going to race in this, but they
ordered us up to the start line. As soon as I dropped the clutch, I just span,
and I did that all the way to the first corner. I was lying third or fourth going
into the corner, and Jimmy just hit the dirt line and he was away. I ended
up in third place, and I was sure before that race that I would win it because
the bike was set up so well in practice.

Then I won my second race and then another third, before I was excluded from my fourth race after a clash with Per Jonsson — and that was my
World Championship over with for another year. It was a disaster when the
rain came, and I made the wrong decision for the first race. Gary Havelock
won the meeting, but the rain ruined it for a lot of us.

That was the first time that Carl Blomfeldt was in the pits and advised
me on something. Usually it was left between Danny and me, but Danny
was not happy that I overlooked our arrangement and listened to Carl. Later
in the season he raised his objections with me during a journey back from
another meeting.

'Look Sam, every time we go to the race track, it's me and you. We do all
the races in England together, the internationals, everywhere, and you always
make the right decisions and you always ask me what I think. Then I'll
remind you about what we did before and the changes we made, and I would
tell you that we made that change and it worked in a similar situation.

'We always did that in those circumstances, and I was waiting on your
instructions during the World Final. Then you and Carl talked, and you
came back and said leave it alone. That's not what we do. But I didn't say
anything because you ride the bike and I figured you knew what you were
doing and you made the decision. But I'm questioning you now about that.
Why did you listen to him, when he's never in the pits as a norm? He's
only here for these big meetings, and he comes in and you listen to him.'

I saw his point. Therefore we made an agreement, because he was very upset about the fact that we didn't make the changes we should have done at that point. So Danny said:

'From now on, Sam, whenever we are at the Championships, we make the decisions.' I agreed, as he was my main mechanic, and there was a lot of truth in what he said.

Nonetheless, Sam and Correy won the World Pairs semi-final and qualified for the final. In the final, they were joined by a determined Hancock, who was reserve. Ronnie Correy was struggling and Hancock replaced him for his country's third programmed ride. Eager to prove that the American selectors were wrong to drop him from the World Individual Championship, he turned in a stunning display with Sam as his partner, and the USA's flag was flying high. After the races were completed, the USA and England had tied for the gold with 23 points. A run-off was required and Hancock faced England's Gary Havelock, and he sped to victory to bring the gold home for America.

Following the World Team Cup success of 1990, a lot was expected of the nation the following year, but it seemed that it was a false dawn, as America failed to build on that triumph. But 1992 was a different story.

With the success in the World Pairs, they then held a 2-0 lead over England in the Test series, with one Test remaining at Swindon. Skipper Sam had scored a paid maximum in the second Test at Wolverhampton and then they travelled to Kumla in Sweden to take part in the World Team Cup Final. Sweden were the favourites on their home track, but the Americans suffered an indifferent start. There were concerns over the surface of the track, which was very grippy to begin with, and this caught out the home nation and their Scandinavian rivals, Denmark. America were also not exactly comfortable with it, but the English team were enjoying the conditions. But the events of heat 8 changed the face of the competition.

I had a big crash in heat 8 with Denmark's Gert Handberg, or Handbag as we called him. The track was pretty hard to ride, as it had a little bit of grip on it and a lot of the guys couldn't handle it. Gert always had a style where he rode on the back of the bike, and the bike would lift and he would drift wide a lot of the time.

I was on the outside of Gert on the first turn, and he hooked up and just speared me as we came off the corner. My bike and I just did somersaults down the track, and my bike climbed the fence. I went down big time and it was pretty painful. It took a long time for me to get up from that crash because it was a big, big crash. My mechanics were sorting the bike out during this time, but the organisers decided to grade the track because the Danes were complaining about it.

The English liked it; they had no problems with it. We had a problem with the surface, but we didn't think that there was anything we could do about it − we just go on with it. But following the crash, we thought that maybe we should try and do something about it. Gert was excluded from the re-run, and I got a third, but I was still pretty shook up from the crash.

At that point, only Greg Hancock had won any races for America and he had two wins. But his Cradley team-mate, Billy Hamill, then won heat 10, and the boys from California began to get to grips with the meeting. Sam then won heat 12, but Ronnie Correy was struggling and his place was taken by Bobby Ott. Ermolenko defeated Hans Nielsen in a thrilling heat 16, when the Dane found his every move blocked by the US captain.

Then it was decided to reinstate Correy for heat 17, because he was drawn from the inside gate, and he was known for his awesome ability from that starting position. England, Sweden and the USA were locked in a battle for the gold medals, while Nielsen fought a lone battle for the disappointing and demoralised Danes. Correy made the start and had England's Tatum on his shoulder, but the American refused to give ground and Tatum was forced to shut off, or the fence was waiting to collect him. This enabled Sweden's Tony Rickardsson to slip by for second, but there was no stopping 'Rocket' Ronnie, who raced to a vital victory.

Hamill then passed the recently-crowned World Champion, Gary Havelock, and they were on the verge of winning their third World Team Championship. Enter Sam Ermolenko, who once again shouldered the responsibility of clinching the gold for his country. Just as it was at Pardubice, second place was sufficient to clinch overall victory. He did it in a typically spectacular and exciting style, by blasting his way from fourth to the important second, and with England's Mark Loram at the back, the American camp were assembled at the pit gate to begin their celebrations.

Also helping out in the pits was John Cook. 'Cowboy' Cookie was racing regularly in Sweden, and just a fortnight before the Cup Final, he had won the Swedish Championship at Kumla with a 15-point maximum. He was on hand throughout the contest to advice his fellow countrymen about the track, and how conditions usually changed.

America then travelled to Swindon for the final Test against England. As they had already sealed overall victory in the series, Sam was released to ride in Poland. However, his plane was experiencing mechanical difficulties and his flight was delayed. When he realised that he wouldn't be able to make the league match in Poland, he made his way to Swindon. He was then put in the team at reserve as a replacement for the injured Donny Odom. This move infuriated the English management, as he could be used at any point during the match. Sam's brother, Charlie, crashed heavily in the opening heat, and withdrew from the rest of the meeting, and was replaced by his elder brother. Teaming up with Correy, he scored 11 points as America defeated England 58-50, using tactics that England were far from happy with. 'Ermolenko should have been in the American team from day one,' protested England's co-manager, Colin Pratt. 'If he or any other rider want to earn their living in Poland, then let them go and live there. It is not sour grapes because we lost. We protested before the meeting, and we weren't even notified in the morning that Ermolenko would be riding.'

It had been another storming season from Sam Ermolenko, but he experienced a dismal meeting at Bradford when he defended the

Division One Riders' Championship. He was well off the pace on a bleak night, and scored just 5 points. That apart, and the obvious World Final disappointment, it was a good year for him, as he finished top of the British and Swedish League averages.

There were changes to the formula for the British League in 1993. The number of races was increased from 13 to 18, and the number of riders in the team was also increased from seven to eight. But the most controversial change was a rigid pay structure that was put in place in an attempt to reduce costs for the promoters.

Wolverhampton's season got off to a disastrous start when Ronnie Correy sustained an ankle injury while racing for his Polish club after just one appearance for Wolves. Neil Evitts and Phil Ashcroft were the new faces in the side, and the team looked as though it had great promise once Correy was fit to race. When he made his return, Wolves began their climb up the league table.

It was business as usual as far as Sam was concerned, as he was in scintillating form and was riding high at the top of the averages with a figure in excess of 11 points. Everywhere he went he was just flowing. He won the Trasborg Silver Plate in Slangerup, Denmark, and followed that by winning the World Pairs semi-final with Correy.

Once again there was no American Final, and the five riders that were selected were chosen from the squad that won the World Team Cup in Sweden in 1992. This seemed fair when compared with all the controversy that greeted the indecisive decisions of the AMA the previous year.

The Overseas Final was again another worrying round for Sam. He was excluded from his first race and then won his second. But then he took an uncharacteristic fall in his third race to leave him with just 3 points at the interval stage – and staring elimination in the face. He was forced to draw on all of his experience to win his final two races, and the Coventry crowd jeered Sam's last win as they sensed team orders were at play. He was followed by his fellow countryman, Hamill – who was also in need of points to progress – and Correy took third, as he had already made sure of his place in the semi-finals. As a result, Britain's David Norris was pinned at the back, and his hopes of further involvement in the Championship came to an end. Therefore, you could see why the patriotic Brandon crowd were less than impressed by the Americans' suspected team riding.

Before the semi-final at Vetlanda, America were due to defend their World Pairs title at Vojens. Sweden emerged from the meeting as the winners through a clever use of tactics employed by their three riders Per Jonsson, Henka Gustafsson and Tony Rickardsson. America took second, with Ronnie scoring 14 and Sam 9, but they didn't call upon their reserve, Greg Hancock. The following weekend and Sam overcame a second race mechanical breakdown to safely qualify for the World Final with 11 points. The Final was staged at Pocking, Germany, and it was scheduled to be the last one-off World Final, as the FIM were bringing in a Grand Prix system from 1994.

Following the disappointment of the 1992 World Final and the very valid comments from Danny, I didn't invite Carl Blomfeldt to the Final in Pocking. I took Morgan Andersen and Danny as my mechanics, and Mo Baker and Richard Childs as drivers and minders. Morgan was my mechanic in Sweden.

I remember at the semi-final in Vetlanda, I had a really good engine and it blew up. I was sat in the stands by the pits where the riders watch the races, and Erik Gundersen was there. He wasn't riding as this was after the bad crash he had at Bradford in 1989. We were talking and he said, 'Sam, you looked really good before the engine blew up.' I agreed and, as he had won three World Championships, I asked him, 'How do you do it at the World Championships; how do you become better?'

'You've got to rise to the occasion, Sam – just soak up the atmosphere and rise to it.'

I thought that was interesting, so my build-up for the 1993 World Final was different. The Final was the same day as my son's birthday. So I decided that I wouldn't stay with all the other riders and have to do all the FIM dinners and events. I thought I would go against the grain, and I decided that I would take my family with me for a holiday and relax. We stayed at a golf resort, which was away from Pocking, and we swam in the pools, and I cooked my own meals because I was on a strict diet at the time.

After the 1992 Final, I took into consideration a number of facts. I had worked really hard to come back from injury in 1990, and then, in 1991, I was injured just before the final in Gothenburg. Then, in 1992, I was really going well and everything was perfect, when the referee made us ride in the rain in my first race when he should have let the rain pass. I didn't make the change I should have, and the whole meeting was a disaster. I blamed the referee more than I blamed Carl, because he didn't give us the time he should have. Therefore, I decided that this time we would run with what we normally use every day. I wasn't going to make a big fuss about it like I had done previously, I was just going to go there and do it. I didn't really give two sticks about the occasion, we were just going to run with what we always ran, and try to win it like that.

Danny and I went to the practice, and the track was as slick as it could possibly be. We realised that the bikes were too strong for this type of track, so we wondered what we were going to do. Carl wasn't there, and I decided that I was going to lower the compression and take the engine apart, like I did in the early days. I knew what I was doing and I could remember all that sort of thing.

The practice was on Friday, Saturday was a day off and the Final was on the Sunday. I went to a shop which I used to use when I raced for Landshut. We went there and removed the cylinder head and put a gasket in it and lowered the compression. I had to go to Otto Lattenhammer's place to get a gasket, which was quite a journey from Pocking. It was only 65 pence, and on the way back we dropped in at Landshut and watched some of the Golden Greats racing that was taking place there.

Danny and I did all the work ourselves, and the kids stayed with my wife at the resort and enjoyed themselves. It rained all day on Saturday, and Danny and I decided that we would drive to the stadium and have a look at the track. When we got there the stadium was closed, so we jumped the fence and we couldn't believe what we saw. They never touched the track from the practice. You could still see all the tyre marks where everyone had been riding, and there were puddles of water everywhere. This was a World Final, *the last of the one-off World Championships, and they hadn't prepared the track! They had plenty of time after the practice, but I suppose they were all off catering to the FIM parties, which I didn't want to be a part of. And here was the track, still unprepared.*

When we arrived for the meeting, they had to prepare the track and they got a grader and made a real mess of the surface – it was absolutely torn up. All they did was wheel-pack it, and it was a mess. It was totally different to practice; you could never use the same set-up as you used at practice. I looked at it all and I thought after all the effort we put it in to change the bike and now look at it. I exchanged looks with Danny, and he was waiting for my instructions, and I said: 'You know, Danny, who cares? I know how to ride my bike and I'm just going to race it.'

I had my own personal stereo with me and plugged it in, and listened to some music in between the races. I sat in the pits and did my own thing. We had a game plan and we stuck to it. I did my own thing and concentrated on what I had to do.

Hans Nielsen, Sam Ermolenko, Per Jonsson and defending Champion Gary Havelock were the pre-meeting favourites. Nielsen was riding a lay-down engine, which is now commonplace among the riders, but at the time it was a new innovation. Carl Blomfeldt may not have been at Pocking, but he had absolute faith in his rider, and was quoted in *Speedway Star* as saying: 'If Sam finishes five races, I believe he will be Champion.' This was a view that was shared by a member of the public, who jumped over the fence during the pre-meeting parade and gave the American a congratulatory slap on the back, and then returned from where he had come from!

Sam may have taken a more relaxed approach to this final, but he did invest in a set of special lightweight leathers for the event. The manufacturer, GTS products, made a special suit that weighed less than 935 grams – less than a packet of sugar. Gerald Smitherman of GTS said of the suit:

'When Sam tried out the first set of leathers I made him, they were too heavy. He wanted to use Kevlar, which is artificial leather, but they would have been far too expensive for speedway. In the end we used glove leather, and they were even lighter than the pair I made for Jan O. Pedersen for the 1991 Final.'

In his first race, Sam defeated Per Jonsson and looked to be in sparkling form. He returned to the pits and put on his headphones and listened to music by Gary Moore. This was a routine that would continue to good effect throughout the meeting. There was no stopping him in his second race either, as he made a good start from gate three and was away into the distance.

However, when it came to his third ride in heat 10, he didn't get such a good start and drove inside Poland's Tomasz Gollob, and the Pole baled out and brought down Armando Castagna. The race was stopped, and the referee, Frank Ebdon, ordered all four riders back for the re-run. Castagna took the lead in the re-run, but Sam rode a determined race to blast around the outside of the Italian on turn four and, despite a clash of elbows, he sealed his third race win.

Crucially, as it turned out, Nielsen dropped his first point to Peter Karlsson in heat 12 – the last race before the interval – and Sam was in the driving seat. At this stage, the field had all completed three rides, and it was only the American who was unbeaten with 9 points; Nielsen was close behind with 8, Gary Havelock had 7 points, and then Gollob and Chris Louis followed, with 6 points each.

Heat 15 was the showdown, as Sam would meet his nearest challenger, Nielsen. They were joined by Andy Smith and Billy Hamill in what turned out to be the most dramatic race of the final. Sam was on the outside gate, with Hans in gate three alongside him. It was the American who led as they exited the second bend, and he was hotly pursued by Nielsen. As they raced into the third bend, Sam was in command but he drifted a little coming off the fourth bend, and Nielsen stormed into a supposed gap. But instead of making a clean pass, his rear wheel clattered into the American's front wheel and dumped him in the Pocking dirt.

Understandably, Sam didn't leave the track, as he was leading the race when the Danish rider brought him down. He stood up and looked up at the referee's box and, with outstretched arms, he asked:

'What chance did I have?' For once the referee agreed with him, and he put on the white exclusion light that signalled that Nielsen was excluded. The Dane didn't believe it, and he carried on preparing for the re-run. He cruised round to the tapes, but was turned away. He refused to go and no matter how much he protested, the referee, Ebdon, would not reverse his decision. It was almost a carbon copy of what Nielsen did to Tommy Knudsen during the 1986 World Final – only this time he wasn't going to get away with it.

While all this was going on, Sam was having problems of his own as his bike was damaged in the clash with the Dane, and he had to swap to his second machine.

When Hans and I had that collision, I had a problem with my first bike. I couldn't use it because it was damaged from the crash, so I jumped on my other machine. There was a lot of confusion in the pits with Hans and his team. His manager was on the phone, protesting that he shouldn't be excluded, and the press were there taking photos while we were trying to get my second bike going. But when I was pushed off and dropped down the hill to go down to the track, I knew straightaway that there was something wrong with my bike – it was too loose at the back. The other two riders were already at the start, and I knew that if I turned back, Ebdon would exclude me – those were his rules. The riders were already on two minutes, so I didn't have the time to go back to the pits and get it adjusted. But it wasn't my fault that I had this problem, so I looked up at Frank Ebdon in his referee's box, perched high up on the stands, to try and get a little bit of extra time. At the very least, I thought he could cancel the two minutes and start another one. I made it obvious to him that I had a problem, as I signalled to my mechanics to come and tighten the chain, but as I looked up, he just shrugged his shoulders.

I took up my starting position and just hoped for the best. As I left the start and got to the first corner, Billy and I clashed and the chain came off, just as Billy crashed into the back of me. I knew I had a problem before the race, it's just that it happened as we touched going into the corner. The race was stopped and Ebdon made the call that all three of us were back in the re-run. I went straight back into the pits, and my mechanics got to work. It was the perfect opportunity and I admit that I was lucky, but after all that I had been through, I believe I deserved that bit of luck.

Ebdon's decision angered the Danish fans on the back straight, who jumped over the fence and staged a sit-in protest. They were not happy about the fact that he didn't exclude the American, as he wasn't under power at the time that the race was stopped. This gave the Ermolenko camp a little bit more time to sort out their problems. The meeting was delayed by fifteen minutes while the supporters carried out their protest, and the track staff made several fruitless attempts to persuade the fans to return to their seats. The riders were left waiting for them to be cleared so that they could race in the re-run, but eventually the German police arrived and they restored order.

None of this unsettled Ermolenko, who retained a calm exterior, made a perfect start and won the race. His victory did not please some sections of the 18,000 crowd, and he received a mixed reception on his slow-down lap. Indeed, his rival in the race, Andy Smith, let him know in no uncertain terms how unhappy he was with the verdict, as he sprayed Sam in shale on the slow-down lap as he passed by! But for once, Lady Luck had smiled on Sam Ermolenko.

Poland's Tomasz Gollob was the only rider who could deny Sam the title, but he had to win heat 16 to keep his slim hopes alive. He was beaten by Henka Gustafsson, who passed him on the inside. Sam didn't have to win his last race to win the title, and he was World Champion at last with 12 points.

Someone came up to me after Gollob had failed to win that race and he told me that I was World Champion, but I was still pumped up to win my last race. We fixed the bike that had the chain problem, but in my last race there were noises coming from the engine. I made the start, but I could hear noises, so I didn't attack the track. I didn't go where I wanted to go on the track, I just stayed out of the way, because I didn't want it to let go in front everyone and cause a crash. Knowing that I was already the winner, I let Rickardsson, Henka and Havelock go, and I was last. But it didn't matter and I started celebrating in my helmet, and I pulled a wheelie as I was the Champion at last.

The officials collected us and paraded us around the track and we did the podium stuff, and then they took us into the press room. On the way around the track to the press conference, Hans Nielsen asked me why I didn't get up from the crash. I said: 'It wasn't my fault, Hans. Sure I stayed down – I wanted the race to be stopped.'

'Oh right, so you could have got up,' he said.

'Of course I could have got up, I could have got up in a second, but you took me down.'

Then I read the reports and his opinions in his book, The Main Dane, saying that I went down and stayed down. The fact of it is that I went down because he knocked me down. I stayed down because I didn't deserve to be excluded because it wasn't my fault. If I didn't stay down and got up and got out of the way, perhaps the referee wouldn't have stopped the race. But the fact was that it wasn't my fault, and the ref. called it in my favour.

Hans was a God in his home country, and the press would follow him around wherever we went in Denmark – and he was a great rider. But he would speak in Danish to them and he could tell the story how he wanted to tell the story. There were many occasions when my Danish mechanic would tell me that Hans had said this, and Hans had said that in the press, which was at odds with what he would say in the English press. I don't have the facts about what he said exactly, but a lot of what he said would favour him. He was such a superstar in Denmark that he could say whatever he wanted to the Danish press, and they would believe him.

Frank Ebdon wasn't Nielsen's favourite referee, and he made that clear to the English press and he was short-changed because of that. Let's face it, how many times has Hans Nielsen taken other riders out? He is a hard racer, and he will take what he can, and he pushed me off. He pushed me off far enough that I went down. I remember he took Kelvin Tatum out in the World Final in 1990 and he went from a first to a last, and we all saw what he did to Tommy Knudsen in the Final in Poland in 1986. If you give it out, then you have to be prepared to take it.

Ebdon was the person who spoiled the Final for the riders. He is a very intimidating sort of man and he likes to bring all the riders together to tell them 'Don't move around at the start line, and don't delay the start, or I will exclude you. And I can exclude and I will exclude you.' That is what he normally preaches to everybody.

I remember when Wolverhampton were racing at Oxford, and Adam Skornicki was in the team. Adam was not in the dressing room, or was not available when Ebdon was around. He spoke to all the riders and told them his usual stuff, 'be still at the start and don't move around, or you will be excluded and I can fine you and I will fine you.' He says that everywhere he goes, just so that he can demonstrate his authority and let us know that he can do it. Adam was late getting there for traffic reasons or whatever, and he was in the dressing room when Frank Ebdon went back there just as we were getting changed for the racing. He had already given us his speech, and he came in asking where Adam was. Adam made it known that he was there and asked him what he wanted. He is Polish and although he understood English, he didn't speak it that well.

'Adam, do you understand English?' Ebdon asked him.

He confirmed that he did, and he said to him: 'Right, I want to make it clear to you now: no moving at the start, no mucking around at the start, come straight to the start and don't turn around or delay it or I will fine you – and I can do that.' Then he walked out.

Poor Adam was left wondering what he had done wrong, and he was looking at me, asking me what he had done wrong. This referee has a style that isn't stylish, why would you do something like that? This is the kind of atmosphere he generates at riders' meetings, he doesn't get them in there and say something like, 'This is a great event guys, go out there and enjoy yourself and perform. Be safe, don't get hurt, don't break any rules and we will have a clean meeting today and someone will come out a winner. Good luck.' That's what a good referee does, you hardly know they are there – but that's not Frank. He is constantly calling you and telling you if you have done something, and he will make his presence known. He makes a lot of people feel uneasy.

After the Final, I decided to drive home with Danny while my family went back with Mo Baker. We went back to the hotel where all the riders were staying as Morgan had stayed there, and I used his phone to tell my mom the result and she was pretty excited about it. When we went up in *the elevator, I held the door open for some fans from Coventry – which was Hans Nielsen's team – and they said: 'Oh no, we don't want to get in there with you.' They said that the referee was unfair to their rider and so on, and they gave me a hard time and told me that I was lucky. I was polite to them because nothing was going to bring me down, but it did chew on me.*

When Jan O. Pedersen won, he smoked everyone. But I had won a disputed World Final. I accept that I was lucky, mechanically as well, but I was the Champion and no one could take that away from me.

I was travelling back to England and I pulled in at the services and Ivan Mauger was behind us. He came up to me and congratulated me, but I admitted to him that it felt a bit sour because of the protest and the confusion. But he said: 'Look, Sam, your name is on that trophy and you won it, no one can take that away from you.' So that was nice, and it gave me a lift. I wasn't feeling that down, but after all the trials and tribulations I went through to win it, it was a shame that I had to deal with all those problems.

Sam faced some tough questions in the press conference, and the situation was debated in the sport's press. Ronnie Correy was the reserve for the meeting, and he said of Sam's victory: 'Sam has been trying very hard and put a lot of effort in over the years, and I think he will be a good Champion.'

Kelvin Tatum said that Sam was fortunate, but went on: 'The referee ruled in favour of Sam, but you would have to say that Hans has been in those situations before and got away with it.'

'Sam's record this year has proved how good he is,' said Van Straaten, 'and I think it's fully deserved.'

And Barry Briggs, who first met Sam on the training tracks in California, also offered his congratulations, and said: 'Sam has put so much into speedway, and you cannot argue with a rider who is top of the averages and has his sort of record. But no doubt he would have liked to have won without all the controversy.'

Sam travelled to Vojens and won the World Final revenge, but Nielsen defeated the American when they met in heat 17. Nonetheless, in the final analysis, it was Ermolenko who stood on the top step.

He received a hero's welcome on his return to Wolverhampton, but his 12 points couldn't prevent Cradley from trying to spoil the party by winning the Dudley-Wolves trophy with a 62-46 win. But somehow it didn't matter, as Wolverhampton's adopted son was World Champion at last.

The World Final controversy continued to be dissected in the sport's press, but no one denied that he was a worthy Champion. As it went on, however, the question was whether Ebdon was a referee worthy of a World Final.

But Sam had the perfect opportunity to put the record straight, once and for all. America was due to defend the World Team Cup against England, Denmark and Sweden at Coventry, Hans Nielsen's home track. As the meeting progressed, the finale couldn't have been scripted any better, and it became the footnote for the whole Pocking controversy – the aftermath of which still lingered in the air, as the riders from the four nations gathered at Brandon to do battle.

America entered the final without the services of Ronnie Correy, who had sustained a serious injury in a league match for his Swedish club, Bysarna. His place in the team was taken by Josh Larsen. It was scheduled to be the last of the five-man, four-team tournament-style finals, as the FIM were planning a big shake-up of international speedway.

If the crowd were waiting for the showdown between Ermolenko and Nielsen, they didn't have to wait too long, as they met for the first time in the opening heat. Sweden's Tony Rickardsson and Joe Screen were also in the race. However, as the tapes rose, Rickardsson was squeezed out in a tight first bend and he hit the deck. Sam was left with nowhere to go, and he catapulted over the top of the fallen Swede. Happily, after treatment, both of the riders were back on their feet and were able to take their place in the re-run, as all four were ordered back. This time Nielsen made a clean start, and he streaked away to win the race. He was followed by Screen and a shaken Ermolenko, who was third.

After five races had been completed, the USA had just 6 points and had yet to win a race, while Denmark were leading the way with 13; Sweden and England were both on 5 points apiece. It seemed that the Danes were going to run away with it, as they had dropped just one point in heat 5 to Sweden, courtesy of the fast-emerging Rickardsson.

But then enter Sudden Sam Ermolenko. The new World Champion and American captain led the revival of the defending Champions with an emphatic victory over Tommy Knudsen. Billy Hamill then kept the momentum going with another win in heat 7, before Denmark restored the balance with a victory from Nielsen. Rickardsson won again for Sweden, and then the next three races were shared between the three nations: Nielsen won heat 10, Ermolenko won heat 11, and then Per Jonsson won heat 12. At this stage, the talk around the Brandon terraces was not of the three-way battle at the top, but the dismal display of the host nation, who had mustered just 8 points.

As the meeting progressed, the USA and Denmark began to shrug off the challenge from the inconsistent Swedes, and when Larsen – in for Ott – won heat 17, with Denmark's Brian Karger at the back, that put the Americans level with the Danes for the first time. Gary Havelock provided England's only race winner in the next race, but with Hancock second, and Denmark's John Jorgensen at the back, America were in the lead. Tommy Knudsen won heat 19, but Hamill was unable to find a way past Chris Louis for second and, with one race to go, the scoreline was USA 37 and Denmark 37.

This set up the much-anticipated showdown between Sam Ermolenko and Hans Nielsen. This race would decide the destiny of the World Team Cup, and settle the arguments that were still going on after Pocking. It was Sam's *High Noon*, the white-leathered American versus the man in black from Denmark. It wasn't quite good versus evil, but as they arrived at the tapes for the final race, the crowd were witnessing a contest between the two fastest guns in Western speedway racing. There could only be one winner – it was speedway's equivalent of *The Gunfight at the OK Corral*.

Sam was in gate three with Nielsen in gate one, and he gave the Dane a brief steely glance of determination before he settled down for the start. The tapes rose, and Sam was away and he was in front at the first bend. But Nielsen had very little time to line up an attack as Rickardsson slipped by the Dane on the back straight, and he blocked an expected reply. The World Champion briefly glanced over his left shoulder for his rivals as he exited turn four, and then he raced on to a sweet victory and another gold medal. There was no celebratory wheelie over the finish line, just a determined nod of the head that said it all: 'What say you now, critics?'

I was in Hans Nielsen's backyard, Coventry was his home track. It was between me and Hans, and he had the best gate and I had gate three – which isn't the best gate at Coventry. He hadn't dropped a point all night and it was down to me to do it. It was the perfect time to shut up all the critics and, as it said in Speedway Star *in its report, I had the last laugh.*

Those two Coventry fans who were in the elevator with me must have witnessed the fact that Sam Ermolenko had beaten Hans on his home track. I did it when everything was in his favour: he had gate one, he was on his home track and he would have expected to have a good start from that gate – and I beat him. This was not a disputed World Championship, it was won fair and square, and it was all down to me winning that last race. I'm quite proud of that, and I got a lot of personal satisfaction out of it – I did it in style.

Despite all that was said in the press, Hans was still dignified in defeat – and he always was good like that. Hans was a great rider, and to beat him was always an accomplishment when you raced against him, but I didn't need to rub his face in it – I had the gold medal. He knew what the ups and downs were all about, and it was my up and his down.

There was no stopping Sam as he led America to a 3-0 series victory over England, and was never beaten by an English rider during the three Test matches – including an 18-point maximum around the super fast Sheffield track that usually favoured the English. Then he flew to America where he rode in the US National Championship and blew away the opposition to win with an unbeaten score. It was his first National title, and he easily saw off the challenge of the defending Champion, Chris Manchester.

When I went back to Costa Mesa to ride in the Nationals, everyone was pretty excited about my World Championship win. When I got third in 1985, that was pretty special, but this was the big one. Cypress is my home town, and I had a big party at the golf course where Tiger Woods grew up and played, and it was a brand new facility and they rebuilt the hall at Los Alomitos. They held a party there for me, and among the guests were the mayor of my home town, America's other World Champions, Jack Milne and Bruce Penhall, all my family and friends, and all the promoters. It was really special, and the mayor made a speech and it was great.

Fortune has not always been on Sam's side, and Wolverhampton were suffering a spate of injuries and their stranglehold at the top of the league was coming under threat from a resurgent Belle Vue. Wolves' Correy was sidelined with a back injury, Charles Ermolenko had a broken arm, and Graham Jones was also suffering from a back injury. It would be fair to say that as the season was reaching its climax, Wolves were in the middle of an injury crisis.

But the icing on the cake for Sam's year would be to lead Wolverhampton to the Division One League Championship again. As they faced Bradford in a crucial meeting at their home track, Wolverhampton's Championship hopes took a tremendous blow when Sam crashed in the opening race and broke his left leg – not again!

It was a cold, frosty evening, and I faced Kelvin Tatum and Sean Wilson from Bradford, and my partner in the race was Gordon Kennett. Tatum made the start on me, but he made it known that he didn't like Wolverhampton that much, so I thought that it was just a matter of time before he would make a mistake and I would be able to pass him. The track produced moisture from the frosty atmosphere that was descending.

I went into turn three really deep, and also in turn one really deep too, as I was trying to get closer to him. I caught up with him, and then going down the back straight, I was running up to his back wheel. He put his wheel in the right place and shut me out. As he dived into the corner on turn three, I drove in really deep too, but as I was going through the apex of the corner,

I realised that I was going in too hot. At that point, the momentum was pulling me away from the inside, and I knew that if I turned too much, it would have locked up on me and I would have gone into the fence backwards. Then, all of a sudden, I saw the fence coming, so I laid it down nice and easy, but as I did so, I clipped a pole and I broke my left leg.

I felt the crunch in my leg and I thought, 'Oh no.' I had broken my tibia, fibia and femur – they were all broken. I was rushed to hospital, but there were some complications. I also had a back injury, but they didn't know how bad it was, so they didn't want to move me about too much. They did a full CAT scan and found that it was stable, so they didn't think that they would have a problem with the surgery. But this delayed the operation for twenty-four hours. They set my leg in a position so that I could spend the night there, and I was scheduled for surgery the next day.

I went into the surgery, and it was a procedure that I had experienced all too often. They put an IV in me, but I wasn't feeling too good. I was feeling sick in my stomach. I told the nurse as they were getting ready to put me under: 'I'm not feeling too good, I've never felt like this before.'

So they put this little gadget on the end of my finger and it probed the oxygen levels in my blood, and they realised that my level was low and they put me on oxygen straightaway. This relieved the nausea I was feeling, and they explained to me that when you break a major bone like a femur, the bone marrow gets into your blood system. When it went through my lungs and brought the oxygen to me, the marrow was clogging up the little fingers that were in my lungs that soak up the oxygen and bring the air into me. It was common when you break a bone and, because of that, my body wasn't getting enough oxygen. The delay had allowed the bone marrow to get into my system.

They were concerned about it, but they put me under for the operation. They completed the operation, but they had to keep me pumped up with oxygen. Therefore, when they pulled me out of surgery, they put me into intensive care.

The bizarre thing about it was that I was in the intensive care unit inside an oxygen tent, which was pumping oxygen into me. I was lying in this room with this bag around me, and there were two rooms next to us which were divided by glass. The nurse was there, watching over everything, and a *doctor came in and he obviously saw that my oxygen count was still low. He was furious; and I saw him walk out of the room and then he was screaming at the nurse. I was in no condition to react to this, but I wondered what was going on. Then, in what seemed like only a couple of minutes, four men came in and they put an emergency stretcher underneath me, strapped me in and put me on another trolley and they pulled me out.*

World Finalist, and a former team-mate of Sam's, Jan Staechmann, had arrived with his mother and father to visit Sam. As he arrived, he saw Sam being wheeled out of the hospital to a waiting ambulance.

'Hey Sam, where are you going?' he asked.

They put him into the ambulance and drove him to another hospital. But as he had a back injury, they had to transport him to a hospital which had a better intensive care facility. The other hospital was only five miles away, but according to Staechmann, who followed Sam, they never went faster than four or five miles an hour. They couldn't go any faster in case they hit a bump, and they couldn't take the risk of causing further damage to his back. The journey took them around twenty minutes to complete. Sam was cared for twenty-four hours a day in the new ICU for three days, until his oxygen levels returned to normal.

He had to wear a body cast and he faced another winter of recuperation. But he took the opportunity to keep tabs on the progress of Wolves' showdown with Belle Vue. It was another winner-takes-all meeting, and a weakened Wolves team faced an Aces side who had hit a rich vein of form. Every couple of heats, Sam would receive a phone call, and it seemed that they were going to win the league. But it came down to the very last race, and Belle Vue's Bobby Ott won a dramatic race that clinched the League Championship for the Manchester club.

Once I was in the body cast, I had to prove that I could get around on my own with the aid of crutches so that they could release me. I had to go up and down the stairs and the physiotherapy department were there to help.

The press came along to see how I was doing. I had to come down the steps to greet them, and I had this woman from physio. with me, and I let go of the crutches for dramatic effect. I sort of threw them away and it made a great photo opportunity, but the physio. woman was not happy. But I didn't care as I felt strong, and I knew I was going to get out of there. I got out in time to go to the Wolves dinner and dance. But one of my ambitions that year was to win the league, and we were very unlucky — but that was how my year ended.

The AMA had their awards night on the Queen Mary at Long Beach, and because we won the World Team Cup, the rest of the boys were there. I went up to collect my medal on my crutches, and I was also nominated for Rider of the Year. But a flat-track racer called Ricky Graham won it. Then I went to the FIM awards, and Scott Russell also picked up a medal for his win in the World Superbikes, and I got to meet those riders and that was cool.

Sam's Championship year may have ended with a bit of a setback, but he again finished the season at the top of the British League averages. He was the last rider to finish at the top of the averages with a figure over 11 points a match. This achievement is all the more impressive when you take into consideration the fact that the format that year meant that he was programmed to have at least six rides. Therefore, he had more opportunities to drop points, and this underlined the fact that he was, without question, the best rider in the world in 1993.

Six

A NEW ERA

In February 1994, it was announced that Sam Ermolenko had been granted a testimonial for his services to British speedway and, in particular, the Wolverhampton Wolves. He was only the third American to be granted a testimonial, and the first from this nation as a reigning World Champion. Plans for his big day began in earnest, and the date was set for Sunday July 31. Sam is a very professional person in everything he does, and he applied this quality to organising his testimonial meeting.

The meeting was set to be a four-team tournament, and the contest was scheduled to be between Wolves, Cradley Heath, Poole and a young guns team. Bobby Schwartz agreed to make the trip over to England, and so too did another former Cradley rider, Phil Collins. Phil, the third of the famous Collins brothers, retired from British racing at the end of the 1986 season, but continued to slide his machine around the Californian circuits instead. Ole Olsen, Peter Collins, Phil Crump and Jiri Stancl were all scheduled to be very special team managers.

Sam's aim for the day was entertainment, and among the many attractions on display was The Kangaroo Kid – real name Matt Coulter – who performed many spectacular stunts on a quad bike, as well as Damon Hill's Renault Formula One car, live bands, and much more. Local television and radio stations were also there to cover his big day.

It was billed as Sudden Sam's Summer Spectacular, but the weather was anything but summer. On an emotional day for the popular rider, a heavy downpour eventually forced them to postpone the event. All the riders were willing to give it a go on the wet track, but Sam was mindful of the fact that many of them had very important meetings ahead and he didn't want to see any of them sustain an injury during his meeting.

The meeting was rearranged for 4 August, and the format was changed to an individual contest. Schwartz, Billy Hamill and Greg Hancock were unable to ride in the rearranged meeting, but it was no less competitive for their absence. As befitting a rider who was the reigning World Champion, Sam won his own testimonial and a GM bike he had put up as first prize. The Grand Final was a unique one-lap dash event held over five heats and it wasn't until the final dash that he was beaten – but by then he had done enough to clinch overall victory.

He told the supporters: 'I won't be keeping it. Maybe we can auction the bike and raise some money for charity.'

His testimonial programme offered an interesting insight from his brother, Charles, who said of him: 'He's definitely a constant thinker. Every time you talk to him, he's got something on his mind, whether it's bettering himself or his situation, that kind of thing. He's always got an eye on the future, thinking how he can make himself better.'

Charlie's observation about having his eye on the future was very accurate, as he had a special suit made by GTS. It was race wear made from Kevlar, which was similar to the suits worn by Formula One drivers. He was ahead of his time, and it wasn't long before all the top riders were wearing the new suit.

The other big event of 1994 was his defence of the World Championship. The much-debated Grand Prix did not commence in 1994 after all, and its start was delayed until 1995. The Final was set for Vojens, Denmark; which caused grumbles from Britain, but it was a track that Sam had performed well on during his previous visits.

He began his season at Wolves in sparkling form, with two 15-point maximums in the opening meetings against Cradley in the Clubcall Trophy. He followed that with an 18-point maximum at Ipswich, and the presenters at Wolves were getting all excited about his unbeaten run, but it was ended in the home match against Bradford, when Gary Havelock defeated him in the opening race.

Sam once again led a Wolves team that had a familiar look to the one that finished in 1993: Peter and Mikael Karlsson, Charlie Ermolenko, Gordon Kennett, Wayne Carter, and the newcomer was Tony Atkin – Ronnie Correy was still recovering from his back injury, sustained at the end of 1993. Furthermore, Sam was also feeling the effects of his broken leg too, although sixteen races without a defeat didn't suggest it was a major problem.

However, his impressive start to the new season was curtailed by a heavy crash that ruled him out of action. Initially, the fears were that he had injured his left leg again, but, thankfully, the injuries were no more serious than bruising and muscular injuries - the latter, though, proved to be more troublesome than was first thought. Happily, the status of being World Champion meant that the AMA seeded him to the Overseas Final.

This was the year when British speedway brought dirt deflectors into the sport for the first time – or rather rushed them in. It was a controversial move, as the riders claimed that they were dangerous and not enough testing had been carried out. It certainly slowed down the racing; and a spate of crashes and injuries seemed to support the riders' view that they made their bikes unsafe. When Sam crashed in early 1994, he put some of the blame on the dirt deflector, and said that it was like 'wheeling a trolley behind you'. As is often the case in speedway racing at all levels, it takes a high profile accident before the officials take the riders' opinions seriously, and it wasn't long after the American's crash that the deflectors were suspended from racing – too late now, I suspect Sam thought.

The final was once again held at Coventry, and Sam won the title for a third time with 14 points. He dropped his only point of the afternoon to his fellow countryman, Josh Larsen, in his final race.

I could have won that meeting with a maximum, but Josh needed the points to qualify for the semi-finals. So being a team-man, and national captain, I put my country first – I settled for second behind him. I had a camera on the back of my bike for that meeting, and the TV had some cool shots.

Sam qualified comfortably for what was the last one-off World Final in the history of the sport. There had been much debate about the last final being held at Vojens, Denmark. It was Ole Olsen's track, and he was looked upon as one of the main players behind the introduction of the Grand Prix. Furthermore, at one point it looked as though Wembley – the spiritual home of the World Final – would be able to stage the last-ever Final, but Olsen was blamed for the final not going ahead at Wembley and standing in the way of what would have been the last speedway meeting to take place at the famous Twin Towers.

All this was of little consequence to Sam, who was eager to defend the title in what was proving to be a hard season. Unfortunately, Danny Gollagher – who was such an important part of Sam's team – had retired after the 1993 season, and his experience was greatly missed. He got off to the worst possible start when, after a coming together with Mark Loram, he fell and was excluded from his first race.

We made the most stupid mistake. I span in my first race and Jason Crump beat me to the first turn, but I just couldn't hook the bike up. I had Carl Blomfeldt with me but he didn't have the answer, and Morgan Hughes was my new mechanic, and I couldn't expect him to have the answers as he was young and learning the trade. They had brought in these new silencers in the British League, and they were non-megaphone silencers. The megaphone gave you another 700 rpm, and you have to set up the engine a bit differently. I went to Vojens and I had the megaphone on, and I shouldn't have had it on.

Afterwards, I was speaking to Danny, and he asked how I got on. I told him that I couldn't get the bike to hook up, and he asked me what muffler I had used. When I told him, he said, 'What did you have the megaphone on for? You don't use the megaphone there.' And then I remembered — I should have had the British League muffler on. But it was only afterwards that I found out why I couldn't get the bike to hook up. No one could tell me what I had to do, so, once again, I lost out because I didn't have the right people around me.

Then I went back to Vojens for the World Final revenge, with the same bike but with the BL muffler on, and I won it. I had a bad, bad Final and I had the wrong set-up, the wrong bike and my team didn't have an answer for it.

It was Sam's worst World Final performance that saw him score just 6 points. The world title was won for the first time by Sweden's Tony Rickardsson in a dramatic run-off with Hans Nielsen and Australian Craig Boyce. The Swede passed Nielsen on the inside in exciting style to win the race and announce to the international world that a new Champion was crowned. As it was the last World Final, Tony got to keep the World Championship trophy. The 1993 Final should have been the last one, and when Sam won the title, he thought that it would be the last Final. Unfortunately it wasn't, and he had to hand over the trophy for the 1994 competition.

But Sam was one of the seeded riders for the 1995 Speedway Grand Prix series, despite his disappointing performance in the Final at Vojens. Therefore, he could think about planning for a new series. He was also signed to ride in the Australian Series 500 competition, which was looked upon as a major boost to the flagging fortunes of Australian speedway racing.

The American returned to California and he retained the US National Championship. But the next big meeting on the calendar was the Division One Riders' Championship, which was being held at Swindon. Prior to the event, Sam had on-track altercations with both Rickardsson and Nielsen. He had been riding throughout the season with the metalwork still in the left leg he had broken at the end of 1993. Combined with muscular problems, it seemed that his opponents were taking advantage of his weakened physical condition, and he was being shoved around the track more than usual. His cause was not helped by the fact that he was the reigning World Champion and, as a consequence, his opponents would try that much harder to lower his colours.

Therefore, the Division One Riders' Championship was a meeting that he looked upon as one where he would like to prove a point. But his preparations for the biggest individual meeting of the British season did not go well, when he struggled at Coventry the previous evening on engines that were losing their power. Nielsen and Sam clashed elbows in their encounter, but as the night wore on, he realised that his engines didn't have edge he required for the fast Swindon track.

He overcame all the problems by burning the midnight oil – or I should say that it was Graham Jones who spent the time in the workshop – and arrived at Swindon in top form. Only Hans Nielsen, who was eager to win the meeting as it was his final British season, seemed to be in the same league that evening, and Swindon's biggest crowd for over a decade soon realised that the clash between Ermolenko and Nielsen in heat 15 would decide the winner.

Also involved in the race were Martin Dugard and Peter Karlsson. It was Dugard who made a lightning start from the inside berth, and led going into the first bend, with Nielsen tucked in behind. Sam, from gate four, had missed the start, but he produced a determined ride that had the crowd roaring with excitement. He rounded Nielsen on the back straight, and then dived under Dugard to take the lead. It was a breathtaking manoeuvre, which he achieved in the space of one lap. There was no stopping the American, and he won the meeting with a perfect 15-point maximum.

Winning that Championship was the sweetest of the three riders' titles that I won in Britain. Nielsen was in superb form and he was fired up to win it, but Dugard got the start on Hans, and I was able to pass them both.

I had problems with one of my engines the night before during a league match for Wolves. Graham Jones came over, but I had to sleep. He sorted out my engine for me, stripped it down and put it back together – thanks bro! And I went there and won.

Morgan Hughes's quote in *Speedway Star* revealed the effort that went into the engines that night so that Sam was able to win his second riders' title: 'We finished rebuilding at 7.30 in the morning – I've now been up for 48 hours straight!' he said.

The season ended with Sam scheduled to visit the hospital to have the metalwork removed from his left leg. It was the first time for three years that he hadn't finished top of the British League averages. Per Jonsson and Hans Nielsen finished ahead of him, although Per only completed a dozen official matches as he crashed in Poland and sustained serious back injuries that confined the quiet Swede to a wheel chair.

Fully fit once again, Sam began the 1995 season with Wolverhampton in an expanded league that saw the First and Second Divisions merge to form one big league.

All eyes were on the new six-round Grand Prix series: traditionalists were hoping it would fall flat on its face, while more forward-thinking people hoped that it would improve and enhance the sport's fallen image. As a rider, it was another competition that needed to be raced in and, preferably, won.

The format was the traditional 16-rider, 20-heat format, but those races were followed by four finals. The top four scorers went into the A-Final, where the winner of this race would win the Grand Prix, and this was where the big points were scored. The next four highest scorers would meet in the B-Final, and so on with the

C- and D-Finals. The problem with this format was that the races that mattered were the last four. The rest were essentially qualifying heats.

Sam struggled in the early rounds of the Championship, and it wasn't until the fourth Grand Prix at Vojens when he finally showed the form that made him a World Champion. He finished runner-up to Hans Nielsen, and then he was second again in the British Grand Prix at Hackney, behind Greg Hancock. He had picked up enough points during the series – with a sixth place in the opening Grand Prix in Poland his previous best – that suddenly he found himself in third place overall, and received his third individual bronze medal.

His World Championship form was at odds with his performances in the British Premier League for Wolverhampton, where he had an average of well over 10 points a match. Furthermore, he was also in splendid form for Vastervik in the Swedish Elite League, where he finished top of the averages.

It wasn't a good start to the new campaign, because Carl Blomfeldt was trying out new things and testing a lot of new ideas. As Carl was going in all sorts of different directions, I wasn't very happy because the feedback I was getting was inconsistent. I was travelling a lot, because I was racing in England, Poland, Sweden, Denmark, and Germany – I was riding everywhere, so I didn't know what was going on in the workshop. I was doing well in my league racing, but I was struggling in the Grand Prix because we were getting carburettor problems. I couldn't put my finger on what was going wrong.

In the end, I took everything I had to Sweden, and I spent three or four days practising there. During this time, I worked something out that was helping me, but nobody else could do it. Carl and the rest in the workshop couldn't work it out, so I did it myself. After being there and discovering the problem ourselves, I got everything going well again and I finished third in the Grand Prix series. The problem was that we just had too many choices.

1996 was even worse, because Carl was trying to get the business going. He was distracted because he was so busy in the workshop doing other peoples' stuff, but he always did what I asked him to do. But I found out afterwards that when we found something that was working well, because he had other peoples engines to do, he would take the parts out of mine and put them in someone else's. So when I asked him to put it back the way it was, he couldn't because he didn't have the parts to do it. Then he had to invent something else, and I was told by Steve Langdon that he wasn't doing it, so that was why I was getting inconsistent motors. He had become too big and he was looking after the business side of things more than me. I was so busy racing around the world that I wasn't able to keep tabs on it all. I wasn't being lied to, but I wasn't being told the truth either.

In 1996, Sam decided to forego racing in the British League and just concentrate on fulfilling his European commitments and the Grand Prix series. He took the decision that as Wolves raced on a Monday night, it made more sense – both financially and from a scheduling viewpoint – not to return to Wolverhampton. It was the end of an era.

My routine until 1996 was that I would fly to Poland on Saturday night – if I wasn't racing in England – stay the night, and then race in Poland on Sunday; back in the hotel on Sunday night, get on a plane in the morning to England, race at Wolverhampton on Monday night. Go home and sleep for four hours, get up and get on a plane and race in Sweden on Tuesday night. As soon as I finished racing in Sweden, I would get on a plane for Denmark, and race there on Wednesday evening and then come back to England on Thursday. I did this for two or three years in succession.

I had good mechanics in Poland, Sweden, Denmark and England. But if I didn't ride in England, I wouldn't need a full-time mechanic – who I had to pay – which I didn't have to have in the other countries because they were supplied as part of your contract. And I would always get picked up at the airport, I had a hotel, and I could leave my kit bag there and it would be washed and cleaned. I was free to do my travelling and life consisted of racing, shower, clothes, bag and off to the next meeting.

I thought that if I didn't ride for Wolverhampton in 1996, I wouldn't have to spend money on a mechanic, and the cost for them was climbing all the time. I wouldn't have to have a van and extra insurance, and I worked it out that with all the travelling, I wouldn't have been making enough money to make it viable. Furthermore, I would get a better quality of life by not racing in England, so I decided to take a break.

But just as it seemed that the American would not be racing in Britain, he responded to an offer from Neil Machin of Sheffield to ride for the Tigers on a short-term basis as a replacement for their Hungarian international, Zoltan Adorjan. Sheffield had one essential advantage over Wolves, and that was that their race night was on a Thursday – which meant no mad weekend dashes back to Britain. The deal was originally just for three months, as Adorjan could not race in the Premier League until June because of family commitments. Machin described the prospect of one of the world's most spectacular riders racing around the Owlerton bowl as 'mouthwatering'.

Sam made his debut for the Tigers in a challenge fixture at Hull on Wednesday March 27 and top-scored with 13 points, but his team went down 62-33. He made his home debut in the return fixture and top-scored again with 16+1, but the Tigers lost that fixture, 50-46. On 5 April, Sam scored his first 15-point maximum for the club as they defeated Middlesbrough, 55-41.

When Adorjan arrived to take his place in the side, Sam left to continue with his continental commitments. But when Adorjan crashed and was ruled out, he returned to race for the Tigers. Although Sheffield could hold their own around their home track, they didn't have the strength in depth to trouble the top clubs on their travels, and they finished next to bottom in the final league table. However, Sam was just what Sheffield needed to lead their struggling side and, to underline his supremacy around Sheffield's track, he won the Northern Riders' Championship with 14 points.

However, at international level, it was a different story. The FIM planned to introduce a new solid block tyre for the Grand Prix series and other World Championship events. GP riders refused to race in the series, as they believed that the tyre was dangerous, and a stand-off between the FIM and the riders took place. Other FIM events outside of the GP were expected to use the controversial tyres. The arguments raged all season, and it came to a head when the top Americans, Danes and English riders refused to ride in the World Team Cup because they didn't wish to ride on the unsafe solid block tyre. US manager, John Scott, withdrew America from the competition.

Sam's performances in the Grand Prix series were disappointing. In the second GP in Italy, he crashed in the D-Final and was taken to hospital with a cracked bone in his groin area and severe bruising. He was involved in another horror crash when he attempted to close down the Swedish duo of Henka Gustafsson and Peter Karlsson, when they bumped and he slid off. The two pursuing Swedes couldn't avoid the fallen American, and they ran over him.

While I was in the hospital, Renzo Giannini of the FIM came to visit me and he said: 'You see, Sam, the FIM are not so bad. We have given you a nice hospital and good doctors, you see we're not so bad, we're looking after you.'

'The FIM are shit for bringing in these solid block tyres!' I replied.

I was part of the Grand Prix Riders' Association with Hans, Chris Louis and Steve Brandon was our secretary, and we stuck together. They were dangerous, but the FIM pushed the tyres upon the riders and said that we had to use them. They wanted to use them at the highest level first, and then everyone was expected to follow. The idea was that they would slow the racing down and it would create more passing. Therefore, it would bring everyone down to a level playing field and it would look better on TV. The fact of the matter was that they were dangerous. They were unpredictable when you were riding – they could be fine in one condition, but not in another. It was in the rule book, so we had to use them.

But what they didn't realise was that if there was twenty-odd riders at an event and they didn't want to use them, with a strong association that was supporting them, they didn't use them. In the end, we compromised that we would test them in practice, but use our normal tyres for the second practice and the event. The result of the tests was that they were dangerous. I think the FIM became tired of all the arguments in the end.

There have not been any stupid changes like that in the last five years. I don't think there has been a muffler change or a tyre change, and there doesn't need to be – why fix it if it isn't broken?

This meant that Sam was relegated to reserve for the next GP, but an injury to Tommy Knudsen meant that he was reprieved and he raced in the German round after all. From then on, it was a battle to keep up with the front runners: Billy Hamill, Hans Nielsen and Greg Hancock. His best performance during a difficult campaign was a second place in the B-Final at the British round. But he travelled to Vojens, Denmark, for the final GP of the season looking at the possibility of having to make sure of his place in the 1997 series by racing in the Grand Prix Challenge. All the attention was focused at the top of the leader board, where Nielsen and Hamill were locked in a battle for the world title – but Sam would have a big say in its destiny.

It was not only a case of points mean prizes for Hamill and Nielsen, but also for Sam. He had to get into the A-Final to be in with a chance of automatically qualifying for the following year. He wasn't the only rider in this situation, but there was a matter of a World Championship to be resolved.

Hamill was unbeaten when he was due to race against Ermolenko in heat 20, and as Nielsen had just won his last race, the calculators came out. Britain's Mark Loram had to win heat 20, with Sam in second, to prevent Nielsen from making the A-Final, thus enabling Hamill the opportunity to clinch the title in the A-Final.

I remembered what the Danes did to America in the World Pairs semi-final in 1991 – I never forgot the way they lied to me and threw the race. I was having a decent run around Vojens that night, and I had Steve Brandon, who was the Grand Prix Riders' Association secretary, doing the mathematics for me. Throughout the evening, he was keeping me up to date with situation and how I was doing, while Carl was just soaking up the atmosphere.

I was watching what was going on around me, with the situation developing between Billy and Hans, and I thought that Billy could win it that day. I thought someone should go over and tell Craig Cummings, who was Billy's mechanic and manager. I spoke to Carl about it, but he just told me to go out there and win my races. Nonetheless, I went over to Craiger and said: 'Hey Craiger, you know what? Billy could win this if we do something right here today.'

So I told him what was needed, and I checked with Steve and asked him if it would affect me at all, and he said: 'No. You're all right.' Everyone around me said that I would be okay. Therefore, we went ahead and did it. I let Loram pass me around the outside and I stayed in second, with Billy in third behind me. And that's how it finished – Nielsen could only make the B-Final, while Billy and I, Greg Hancock and Loram, we were all in the A-Final. But Billy still had to win the race to win the Championship.

When it came to the Final, I got a big shove on the first corner and I was pushed wide, and I ended up last. I was in third, and Loram moved me and Greg right over, and he was into second. What I didn't realise was that Loram and Chris Louis, who were both in a similar situation to me, had their own little arrangement going. I got caught up in something that I didn't know about. Peter Adams wouldn't have let that go by without telling me. I missed the cut by two points, and Hans would have won it that night if it wasn't for me going over to Craiger. I was a team player; I was being patriotic, but I had to go to the challenge because they all stuffed me. All I got from Billy's camp was a can of beer – Craiger came over to me and brought me a beer to say thank you. I've only thrown three races in my career: that one, and I gave up my last race win in the 1994 Overseas Championship so that Josh Larsen – another American team-mate – could qualify for the next round; and I also let Andy Smith beat me in a league meeting for Wolverhampton. I had gone a lot of races without a defeat, and the Wolves announcer was coming up to me and saying stuff like, 'You've won your last twenty or so races, Sam, do you think you can continue winning tonight?' It was putting extra pressure on my team, so I let Andy win the first race of the meeting – not that he knew that at the time of course.

The Grand Prix Challenge was one of the toughest qualifying rounds. Only the top four would qualify for the 1997 Speedway Grand Prix. To make matters more difficult, it would be run using the controversial solid block tyres. The season-long dispute had not been resolved when it came to the meeting, and Ermolenko also had to make sure that his engines were running to his satisfaction for the meeting.

Things were not going right, and I made the decision that I wouldn't take Carl with me to the Grand Prix Challenge in Czechoslovakia, because I wasn't being told the correct things. When Steve told me about some of things he had to do, I realised that Carl was instructing the others to do the exact opposite of what I told him.

I walked into the business and said: 'Steve, Morgan, you're coming with me – the business can stay as it is for now.' We went there a week early, and I went to Poland and I did my league meeting. Jiri Stancl helped by providing a track for us so that we could test the solid back tyres. We tested all day long and we made some changes, and we got my engines back to where they should have been. But before that, I couldn't tell you what I was running, but now we had the engines running well. But I was the victim of t hose tyres.

Simon Wigg, because he was a Jawa works rider, had access to softer solid block tyres than the rest of us. Barum produced a softer compound tyre, but the rest of us couldn't get our hands on them. We ran lap after lap after lap on the solid block tyre, and they didn't even look worn because they were so hard. But Simon, because he had this softer compound, after he had done four laps, the tyres he was using were worn out. I tried to get my hands on these tyres, as other riders knew they existed and asked me about them, but because I wasn't a Jawa rider, I couldn't get them. I even went to a place where I was told they were stored, but I could only get the usual ones. It gave him an unfair advantage over the rest of us. I hold nothing against Simon at all, he was a good rider and I don't want to tarnish his memory, but he definitely had access to better tyres than most of us did.

In one of the hardest and toughest World Championship qualifying rounds in recent memory, the track at the Marketa Stadium in Prague – where the Czech GP is now held – produced some fast, furious and desperate racing from the 16 competitors. England's team manager at the time, John Louis, said that he had never seen Ermolenko ride like he had in the challenge before, commenting that he 'was halfway up the fence!' In heat 13, the American went outside Brian Karger, and then he swooped underneath Mikael Karlsson in spectacular fashion to take his first win of the meeting. In his final programmed ride, which he simply had to win, it was reported that he was almost bouncing off the fence as he pursued the fast outside line to race to victory. This win put him into a four-man run-off to determine the third and fourth places – which were the last two qualifying spots. His opponents were Karlsson, Andy Smith and Jason Crump.

In a dramatic run-off, Crump initially led, but he was elbowed aside by Karlsson, and was quickly followed by Sam and Smith. At one point, it looked as though Sam was in the lead, but Karlsson held on, and in all the positional changes that occurred in those four pulsating laps, it was Smith who managed to squeeze past Sam and qualify for the GP series – and knock Sam out of the 1997 World Championship.

I was getting ready to go out for the run-off, and I was rolling down from the pit lane to the track, when the official there closed the gate on me! He wouldn't let me through, and I was already on a two-minute time allowance. Frank Ebdon was the referee, so I knew what the score was with him. After my last programmed race, the marshal said that I had to put my bike into the parc ferme, which is what we have to do after World Championship meetings. I told him that I had to go out for the run-off, but he didn't understand because he was Czechoslovakian and he could only speak broken English. The gate was shut and I had my front wheel in between the two gates. I had to rev up the bike and ride through the gates to get out! Naturally, he wasn't very happy about it, but I had a race to ride in and I knew that Frank wouldn't give me any more time than was left on the clock.

We had a bit of a scuffle and an exchange of words, but there wasn't time to get into a heated debate. It wasn't the best way to prepare for an important run-off. I rode out of my skin that day and got nowhere, and it was purely because of those tyres.

The riders didn't stick together as a group at the Challenge, and when someone voiced their concerns, the FIM just flexed their muscles and said that if those riders didn't want to ride, then they would take the next guys in line. Tommy Knudsen had a crash in the first race, and as a result of that he wasn't interested in the GPs and retired at the end of 1997. That just goes to show how the system worked: it either worked for you or against you. And it didn't work for Tommy or me that day.

There was one major individual championship left for 1996, and that was the Premier League Riders' Championship. The new World Champion, Billy Hamill, was among the top-class field at Bradford, and he was also top of the averages in Britain and a pre-meeting favourite. Jason Crump led the qualifiers with an unbeaten 12 points, while Sam scraped through to the semi-finals with 7 points – an ailing engine in his last ride was almost enough to be eliminated.

However, he qualified from his semi-final and was through to the winner-takes-all Grand Final against Jason Crump, Chris Louis and Leigh Adams. It was Louis who made the start and was away, with Sam in second. But just as it seemed that the Ipswich rider would win the title, his engine seized, and the American slipped by to win his third senior riders' title.

Sam was lucky to win, but after consoling the disappointed Louis, he went on to celebrate in true Sam Ermolenko style by completing almost a full lap on one wheel. It was a good end to what was a difficult season, as he then had to face up to the fact that, for the first time since 1982, he would begin the 1997 campaign knowing that he didn't have a chance of winning the World Championship. What price patriotism now?

Seven

HERE TODAY, GONE TOMORROW

In 1990, Poland opened up its doors to allow foreign riders to compete in their league. Speedway racing in Poland is a national sport, and a top league match between two leading clubs can attract crowds of nearly 20,000 supporters. Therefore, racing in Poland can be both exciting and lucrative. Despite this impressive pedigree, Poland has only provided one World Individual Champion, Jerzy Szczakiel, in 1973. It was probably because of the fall of the old Soviet Union, combined with the fact that the nation had fallen from international grace, that they decided to open the doors to Western riders.

At this time, following his horrific long-track crash, Sam Ermolenko had decided not to continue racing in that particular competition. Hans Nielsen had also retired from the long-track scene, and he cited the eight-man race format as his reason, because he believed that it was too dangerous.

Sweden had already opened their doors to foreign riders. Denmark's Super League and the German Bundesliga had also decided to include foreign riders in their league programmes. This was the beginning of the nomadic international speedway rider as we know him today.

It was Nielsen who set the Polish wheel turning when he was the first of the big names to race in the Polish League – he was the reigning World Champion at the time. He appeared for Motor Lublin, and he was also joined by the Czechoslovakian World Finalist, Tony Kasper. Another Dane, Lars Jorgensen, also raced in ten matches for the team. But although Nielsen only rode in a handful of matches, the doors were now well and truly open for the flashy and stylish Western riders.

The following year, riders such as Martin Dugard, Rick Miller, Peter Karlsson, Kelvin Tatum, Marvyn Cox, Per Jonsson and even Tony Briggs, were seen crossing the Continent to race in front of big crowds for the extra income. It was inevitable that a rider of Sam Ermolenko's showmanship and professionalism would attract prospective Polish clubs. It was in 1992 that the American agreed to ride for Polonia Bydgoszcz, where he experienced at first hand the exhilarating atmosphere of league racing in front of big crowds – and also the politics that blighted the sport over there.

Carl Blomfeldt was the man who used to keep his ear to the ground, and he suggested that I should race there. I couldn't see the reason behind it because, in 1991, I was having a good season and I was making money. The idea behind racing in long-track was to fill in the gaps that were left by speedway, and to go abroad at the weekends and earn some extra money. But after I was hurt so badly, I didn't want to do it any more. There are trends in our sport, and at the time I was riding in long-track, it was the trend to win both the speedway and long-track World Championships.

Carl suggested that as I wasn't riding in long-track at the weekends, I should follow Nielsen and go to Poland. At the time, Shawn Moran was riding in the Swedish League too, so that was how it came about. Peter Collins took over a group of riders to ride in Poland at the end of the 1991 season. We had two meetings on a Saturday and Sunday, and I won both of them. The second meeting was at Bydgoszcz, and I went with Jeremy Doncaster and Mitch Shirra, as I was inexperienced in Poland.

It was after that meeting at Bydgoszcz, when I went into the office to collect my licence and prize money, that I met an interpreter there called Jovita. She told me that they were interested in me riding for them in 1992. Rick Miller was already riding in Poland at the time, and we were doing his engines, so we got to hear about it. Carl probably realised by speaking to Rick that there was some money to be made there. But it was only after I had done those two meetings, that I realised that there was an opportunity to make some money.

I negotiated my contract with them, but I had heard all these horror stories about leaving your bikes there. Most of the time, the club has practice sessions going on at the tracks on a regular basis. It was said that if you left your bikes there, and they had access to them, they would get on and ride them. When you went over to fulfil your commitments, you would find that your bike was bent, or it wasn't cleaned properly from where someone had been riding it. Therefore, your own performance could be affected. So I insisted that I had my own facilities, a mechanic and someone who I could train to keep the bikes in shape. They agreed to all this, but when I asked them if there was any place I could keep them under lock and key, Jovita looked at her father and he said that I could store them at his place. They agreed everything that I asked for too. During this tour, I was approached by three or four clubs, but I had a feeling that Bydgoszcz was the right place and I had a good deal.

They were eager to impress me with drinks and everything, but I had to go and catch a plane because I had to be in England the next day. I didn't want to appear rude, but I needed to go. The clock was ticking and I asked Jovita what was going on, and said that I couldn't stay much longer because I had to get to the airport. But she said: 'Don't worry they will get you there in plenty of time.' Then they asked me over to the window and there was this white limousine waiting, and its windows were blacked out and they said: 'That is for you to get to the airport. We look after our riders here.'

I had Rick with me because he was going to ride for them too, and we stepped inside the limo and made our way to the airport. But it was so cold in the car. We had some vodka to drink, and we were getting quite happy. However, eventually Rick tapped on the chauffeur's window and rubbed his hands up and down his arms and gestured to the chauffeur that we were cold. There was a switch inside our part of the car to increase the heat, and we didn't realise. When we pulled up at the airport, there were all these people walking by the car, and we could see them staring at the windows and wondering who the heck was inside such a big vehicle. We waited a little while before stepping out. We were only dressed casually and we were a little drunk. These people were probably expecting to see someone like a glamorous film star or a well-dressed businessman emerge, so you can imagine what there faces were like when they saw two slightly drunk, slightly scruffy-looking speedway riders, stumbling and staggering their way out of the vehicle!

Sam's time racing for Bydgoszcz saw him as a team-mate with the rapidly emerging Polish rider, Tomasz Gollob, and his brother, Jacek. This also brought him into contact with their famous father, Wladyslaw – who is known within the speedway scene as Papa Gollob. He soon discovered that Polish League racing was more like the club mentality that he expected to find in the British League in 1983/84. It was also at this time that Sam signed for the Swedish club, Skepparna (Vastervik). But his form for Bydgoszcz was always good, and his showmanship style was popular with the supporters. On one occasion, he was enjoying a victory parade after another win for the team, when he was swamped by supporters and he spent an hour signing autographs.

Speedway is very popular in Poland – it is as popular as football is over there. Most of the stadiums that are over there are speedway stadiums with purpose-built tracks that have been there for decades. In England we race in stadiums that have speedway tracks, but in the main they were not purposely built for speedway. This is not the case in Poland: they have pits, they have garages, they have a mechanic shop where they can do their engines, which I believe was the old communist way. They had mechanics at the club that worked on the bikes, and the riders rode and that was their job. There is evidence of this all over the country.

When I first went over there, because of the language barrier, the Polish riders worshipped the Western riders. When we used to roll up to the start line, we knew that we had them beat, because we had superior equipment. Riders like myself Hans Nielsen, Rick Miller, Mitch Shirra and Jeremy Doncaster, and the other Western riders; we were educating the Polish riders and the public. The bikes that they had in those days were just clapped-out old Jawas. They had new Jawas, but they used them so much. They rode them every day as they had practice sessions, and they were constantly riding them. The modern bikes of the time were the Antig-GM, and Hans' were the Goddens and, of course, there were the Jawas. All the development for speedway racing was in England, so when a good rider went over to Poland, he had an advantage straightaway because he had all the latest equipment.

It wasn't until three, or maybe four years into opening up their league to foreign riders, that they had access to the modern equipment. Now that they have access to that equipment, look how good they are. They have the grounds available to them so that they can train as much as they want to, and there are so many talented riders over there. They weren't against the Western riders when we first went over there – they were interested in seeing what we had to offer.

Their way of cleaning a bike compared with ours was two different things. We had soap and hot power-washers, and we had all the necessary cleaning equipment to not only get them clean in a short space of time, but also to have them looking like they were new. They used to clean their bikes with methanol and diesel, and a cold water pipe. The bikes would look pretty bad after they had done that a few times. As Westerners, we expected our bikes to look brand new every time because we had the equipment to do that. There was so many things that they didn't know about then, but they do now. The Polish youngster today has got it made when compared with when we first went over there.

Our van was kitted out with a bed and it had proper upholstery, and we had bikes racks fitted in the back. Even then, there were times when I would get to a race track, and because the bikes were transported in bulk, the fender would be broken or the grips on the handlebars were worn – it was silly things like that.

The way a Polish team would travel was with a big flat-bed truck that would have a canopy over it, and they would put all of the bikes in the back. They would put some used tyres in between the machines and strap them in place with a rope, and that was how they used to get to the different tracks. They all travelled together in a little minibus and they would sleep in a bed and breakfast. Or they would sleep over in an old army barracks because they were cheap — and there were sports clubs all over the country. They expected me to stay there as well. It wasn't because I was better than them, it was because I wasn't used to that, so I would always seek out a hotel to stay in where I could get some decent food.

The riders usually lived in the town of the club they raced for, and speedway was their job. They would have training regimes and they all practised together. Tomasz Gollob was a little different, but he had his time on the track. However, they probably had fifteen teenagers that were there for a job. So if they managed to get into the stadium they would have to do something such as cleaning bikes, cleaning leathers or whatever. I remember seeing Tomasz come off the track and he would take his helmet off, and someone would grab his helmet, someone would grab his bike, and he would walk off into his garage. Those same kids that were there that day are now working for Tony Rickardsson — they have come a long way.

When I rode for Bydgoszcz in 1992, we won the Polish Championship for the first time since 1971. Therefore, it was a major achievement for the club, and the crowds were huge. The stadium was always filled to capacity, and the fans would go nuts! We had to have guards to be able to get out of the pits, and when the match was over, the fans would jump over the fence. It was quite an overwhelming experience in a lot of different ways.

Jacek Gollob would practise his English with me when we were in the dressing room, but Tomasz wasn't keen to participate. His brother would tell me that he was a little embarrassed, which I could understand. He would talk a little bit, but Jacek was keen to learn.

Jacek would pull me aside and ask me to bring him stuff from England: clutch plates, chains, pistons, anything that I could bring over, because it was easier for me to do this than it was for them to search and pay for it. At the time, I was riding GMs in Antig frames, while in Poland they were riding Jawa frames and Jawa engines. Jacek pulled me aside one day and said:

'Hey, Sam, I want one of those Antig frames.'

'That's no problem; my sponsor can supply one for you.'

'Sssh, don't say anything,' he said, 'I don't want my father to know.'

I guess the reason was that his father didn't want his son to be seen to be spending money on equipment like that. After talking to him, he explained that Tomasz and Jacek would only get so much money from their deals and their father would take care of the rest. Through their broken English, I assumed that their father took the rest and banked it for them. I raced there for three years, and I came to realise that Papa Gollob was their manager, and he was receiving a commission for this role – and I believe it was a considerable sum.

The way it worked over there for individual meetings was when you arrived at the venue you had to hand in your licence, sign up for the meeting and then you could race. Then after you had showered, you had to go to an office and collect your licence. It was a case of first come, first served, as all the riders had to stand in a line; then you'd go in, sit down, collect your licence, travel expenses and prize money or whatever, then you could leave.

I remember that when the Gollobs were racing in one of these individual tournaments, whether it was in Poland or on the European Continent, all the riders were stood waiting to go into the office. We could wait for up to three hours sometimes, but all we wanted to do was get out of there and catch our planes to where we had to go. We were all joking around when Papa Gollob came along. No one took particular notice of him, but he walked straight in! And we wondered how it was that he could jump the queue? But what he was doing was collecting the money for Tomasz and Jacek, and this happened all the time: Papa would come in and then go.

After I won the 1993 World Final, I went back to race in Poland and everything seemed fine. The fans were cheering, and everyone who I could speak English to congratulated me on being the new World Champion. But later in the season, a journalist came up to me and asked if he could carry out an interview with me. I agreed, and we arranged to meet at a hotel in the city. He began the interview by asking me what I thought about what was going on. I didn't know what he was talking about, and then he told me that there had been stories in the press saying that there was a conspiracy at the 1993 World Final against Tomasz Gollob.

The journalist didn't want it known that he had told me this, but what he said was that Papa Gollob did the press releases for Tomasz, and he said that I engineered a conspiracy to prevent Tomasz from winning the World Final. It was in the press that I had the other riders gang up on him so that he couldn't win! I told him that was impossible.

But the journalist went on and said that in the press release, Papa was quoted as saying that how could Tomasz, a rider from an Eastern Bloc country, race and compete against the Western riders because he didn't have the money or the equipment that the Western riders have. They needed more money to be able to compete against the Western riders, and that was the reason why Tomasz didn't win.

I thought that was crap, because that wasn't how it was. When I had that incident with Tomasz in Pocking, it was a racing incident when he fell off. There was also Greg Hancock and Armando Castagna in the race, and it was Greg, who was on my inside, who made a good start. I was trying to get over the top of Greg as we were going into the first corner, and he was leading. Armando and Tomasz went down because I was trying to get over Greg and he was pushing me. He wasn't having a good meeting, and I didn't have such a good start, so when I tried to get over Greg and he moved me over and Tomasz was leaning on me, it was a domino effect – first bend bunching. There was no way that I was going after Tomasz, I was trying to beat all three guys and Greg had the advantage over me. And Tomasz used that by saying that I did it on purpose which was utter rubbish!

They were using these stories in the Polish press to make excuses for why Tomasz Gollob wasn't where he should be. I believe after Gollob failed to win the title, they had to come up with a reason why he didn't, and they said that it was because Sam Ermolenko had everyone gang up on him. Probably because of all the controversy, this played into their hands a little bit. This explained why there wasn't a big thing made out of the fact that I returned to Bydgoszcz as a World Champion like I had at Wolverhampton. Furthermore, Poland was the place where I expected it to be the loudest and the most colourful, because there were 15,000 people there on a regular basis – but it didn't happen.

I did some publicity with one of Gollob's sponsors, which was a Mercedes dealership, and his name was Tomasz as well. After I did a photo shoot for *them, he asked me up to his office above the showroom. I took a seat and he reached inside his drawer and pulled out an envelope and he handed it to me. I opened it up, and inside was an American $1,000 bill. I asked him what it was for, but he couldn't explain it because of the language barrier. We left there and we met a man called Tomek, who interpreted what he said that it was for.*

He said that when Tomasz, the Mercedes man, was a young boy, he had won a bicycle road-racing championship, and his father gave him this $1,000 bill for winning it, and he told him: 'This is for you, one day you will find someone who is deserving of that bill and you can give it to them.' I was very honoured, and I still have that $1,000 bill now.

A dinner was organised at a hotel in Warsaw, and I stayed overnight before I was due to fly back to England. Tomasz and Papa Gollob were part of the dinner party, and so was Tomasz from the Mercedes dealership. Tomasz Gaszynski was the interpreter, and he had lived and gone to school in San Francisco, but he had returned to Poland and was working for the club as a translator. He would later work with Tomasz Gollob as a translator.

During the meal, I had the opportunity to face Tomasz Gollob with my translator, and it was an ideal opportunity because we were away from the track. I put my translator in an awkward position because he was working for the club. But I said to him that I wanted him to help me to ask him these questions, and not to change the translation and to say exactly what I said to him. I made a point of making sure he would say it exactly how I said it because I wanted some answers, and he agreed.

I asked Tomasz Gollob: 'Look, Tomasz, there has been some stuff in the press saying that I ganged up on you in the World Final, and I got some of my compatriots to help make sure that I won and you didn't. Can you explain why you put this in the press, because I don't get it?'

By the time my interpreter had finished translating my question, all the eyes at the table were focused on us. Then they were waiting for Tomasz to answer it, but Papa Gollob answered it. He was rambling on about it all, and he was making gestures with his hands, but I didn't want to hear what he had to say about it – I wanted to hear what Tomasz had to say. My interpreter began translating Papa's words into English, but I stopped him and said: 'Wait a minute, hold on; Papa Gollob just said all that?'

'Yeah.'

'Can you ask Tomasz this question for me?'

'Yeah.'

'Does Papa Gollob wipe Tomasz's ass when he takes a shit?'

And he wasn't very sure about asking him that, but I told him to and he translated my question. When the translator finished translating what I said, the other diners' faces at the table lit up and they just burst out laughing. Tomasz looked up with a slight smirk on his face, but didn't say or do much. He did answer a couple of questions, but his father would come in and say his piece, and what it amounted to was that they didn't deny it, but they didn't admit to it either. But that was the end of the matter as far as I was concerned, because I had said my piece and we carried on with the dinner.

But after the dinner, Papa pulled me aside with my interpreter and it was translated to me that there were no hard feelings, but it wasn't easy to talk about it. But he made it known that he didn't have a problem with me, and that he hadn't anything against me. However, at the end of that 1994 season, Papa Gollob became one of the finance organisers of Bydgoszcz Speedway. I was getting ready to go over to race in Australia when I called Bydgoszcz to find out what was happening for the following year.

I got the cold shoulder from Bydgoszcz, and it didn't appear to be open for discussion. My interpreter said that they were saying that it was up to me: if I wanted to ride I could, if I didn't then that was fine. I thought that was peculiar, because I was on the ball and regularly scoring double figures. I said that if that was the way that they felt about it, then perhaps I should change clubs. The response was that I could do what I wanted. I believe that was Papa Gollob's influence, and I think that he must have been annoyed with me because I may have made him look bad in the press. I don't know for certain – I can only put two and two together.

Toward the end of 1994, I was approached by a man called Slawomir Walczak, who said that he was re-opening a track at Lodz, and that they wanted a top-line rider like me to spearhead their challenge to give the club some credibility. It seemed an interesting proposition, but as I was riding for Bydgoszcz, I told him that I didn't think it would happen. Nevertheless, he gave me his card and he said that if there were any problems then I should give him a call. Therefore, when I got the cold shoulder from Bydgoszcz, I *made the call and I signed for Lodz, who were in the Polish Second Division. It was Slawomir's dream to open up a speedway track at Lodz as he was a fan, and he also had a very successful business promoting the 'Holiday on Ice' shows. He had all the right people around him, and he gave up the ice shows and he became a speedway promoter.*

It was while he was racing at Lodz that Sam organised a benefit meeting to help a young Polish boy, David, who had been blind since he was born. He had suffered from cataracts since birth, and the family required $10,000 to be able to go to a specialist hospital in Russia to have the operation to restore his sight. The meeting was staged at Lodz, and Sam invited the newly-crowned World Champion, Billy Hamill, together with Tony Rickardsson, Greg Hancock, Tomasz Gollob and his brother Jacek, and a host of other Polish riders. It was Tomasz Gollob who won the meeting by defeating Hamill and the previously unbeaten Ermolenko and Rickardsson in the final heat. Sadly, David's sight had deteriorated to such an extent that the doctors in Moscow were not able to carry out a successful operation. But if it hadn't been for the kindness of Sam Ermolenko, the family would never have had the opportunity to go to Moscow.

I raced there for two seasons and the team did quite well. However, at the end of 1996, when I was knocked out of the Grand Prix, I was no longer the 'superstar' in the club's president's eyes. There was another man who was the co-promoter of Lodz who I had to deal with, and his name was Andrea of JAG. The team was known as JAG Speedway Lodz, so Andrea was not only a co-founder of the club, but he was also the club's main financial backer. He had a marketing business in Germany, and he owned the Lodz football team, and would also promote big boxing events. I believe that it was Andrea's financial backing that enabled Slawomir to realise his dream. Andrea had a very successful business, but his answer to any problems was usually to throw money at it – which doesn't solve everything. He would always be asking me how much equipment would cost, and if there was a problem he would only spend five or ten minutes at the track, sign a cheque and leave. This wasn't the answer, as Slawomir wanted to build the club step by step, which was the right way to go about it.

I had a problem negotiating a new contract with the club. We couldn't agree terms for the new deal — because I had been knocked out of the Grand Prix, they didn't want to pay me the money I needed to be able to ride for them. Andrea is Polish, but his business is based in Hanover, which is where the celebrated German engine tuner Hans Zierk is based. They believed that they could get Simon Wigg or Mark Loram to ride for them much cheaper than me, and both of these riders had agreements with Zierk — Wiggy was especially successful on his engines in the World Long-Track Championship. At the time, I thought that I was a better rider than those two guys, so I washed my hands of the club because if they preferred them to me, then good luck to them.

I then discovered that Papa Gollob was being employed by Lodz. Andrea was eager to get involved in the international scene because he thought that it would be good for his company — especially as Tomasz Gollob was the national speedway hero in the country. It was probably during the time that I organised the benefit meeting for David that Andrea met the Gollobs for the first time. I can imagine that as Papa Gollob was a very influential figure in Polish speedway at that point, the Lodz officials took particular notice of what he had to say — and why not, as Papa was very shrewd when it came to matters of business in speedway racing. No doubt he told them how important it was that the club was racing in the First Division if they wanted to be successful, and to make the kind of progress that they wanted. I imagine that as money wasn't a problem to Andrea, Papa could see that he could influence the club. This wasn't the plan — it wasn't Slawomir's vision to spend a lot of money early on. He brought me in to give the club a number one rider, and to train and help the young riders and just go along steady and build up the backbone of the team. But when Andrea began throwing his money around, and Papa Gollob's influence was very visible, I didn't want to be involved anymore. That wasn't the way to go about it, and Slawomir also had problems with them after I left, and he resigned. I brought the team to its highest point, and after that it has gone nowhere. The club still owes me a substantial amount of money, but I realise that I will never see it, because of all the problems that the club was having after I left them.

The PZM [Polish Speedway Federation] is made up of people who are top promoters and it is influenced by people with money. Andrea wanted to be a part of that, and with Papa Gollob's experience, it was likely that he would have got there. However, he disappeared from the speedway scene. If you're a top promoter, then it's likely that you will be on the PZM because you will have the financial clout to be able to influence decisions. There are two kinds of speedway clubs in Poland: rich and poor.

I continued to race in Poland and I won the Second Division Championship with Gdansk. But I was mindful of the problems that I had experienced at Lodz, so I set out certain conditions in my contract to avoid these situations arising again. Therefore, because I couldn't be influenced by all the politics that go on within the clubs, they didn't help me much.

Sam also raced for clubs in Sweden, Denmark and Germany. He finished top of the Swedish Elite Averages in 1992 and 1995, with Vastervik. Sam spent some very successful seasons at Vastervik (who were originally known as Skepparna until 1993). When Todd Wiltshire was injured in Australia in early 1992, this meant that Vastervik were looking for a rider of a similar calibre, and they signed Sam Ermolenko. The best finish that the club had during the time that Sam was with them was third.

Morgan Anderson was one of Sam's mechanics when he won the World Final, but he was also attached to the club and always worked on the American's bikes. Sam was able to get off the plane and climb straight onto some of the best bikes in speedway. It was an excellent combination.

I was happy there, but when they had an ex-rider take over as team manager, he revamped the contracts. To be honest, the contract they offered me to stay was such a major reduction from what I had been getting that it wasn't worth getting out of bed for! It was embarrassing. I knew that they had plans to review the pay structure because sometimes they couldn't afford to bring Craig Boyce over. It was frustrating, because when Craig was in the team, we usually won. I discovered that they had already agreed a deal to bring back Todd Wiltshire, and they were just tying up the loose ends with

Craig. I thought that if I challenged my deal, they would say that they couldn't agree terms with me and were going to sign Craig.

At this time, we had Mikael Karlsson – or Max, as he likes to be known now – using the facilities in my workshop. He was on the phone arranging a new contract with a Swedish club, Valsarna, for the coming season. Tony Rickardsson rode for Valsarna and they won the Championship that year, but as his local club, Marsarna, had been promoted to the Elite League – the top division – he was going back to them. As I was without a team, I said to him: 'Hey, ask them if they need another rider?'

He said: 'Oh, by the way, there's an American guy who is interested in riding for us. He's a pretty good rider; do you want to talk to him?' Then he handed the telephone to me and the guy on the other end said that his name was Anders. He began by saying that he understood that I was interested in riding for them this year, and he said that he would like to talk about it and he thought he could use me on the team. And then, all of a sudden, he asked: 'What is your name?'

'My name?'

'Yeah, what is your name?'

'Sam Ermolenko.'

'Sam Ermolenko!'

Mikael hadn't told them who I was, and he continued: 'Oh we would be so honoured, it would be great, do you really want to come and ride for us?'

'Yeah, I'd like to talk about it.'

We talked about it, and I agreed a deal to ride for Valsarna. I sent a letter to Vastervik, saying that I couldn't accept their offer. I never spoke to them.

When I went to Valsarna, they had won the league with Tony, but now he had gone the press were writing us off. Mikael and I both rode for the club, and Rune Holta – the Flying Flea – and we won the league again. To this day, in my contract, the door is open for me to go back there and manage the team when I retire. This is because they say that I transformed the club when I arrived. When Tony was racing for them, he still team-rode but he was a racer and he was there on his own mission.

Both Mikael and Rune Holta have left now, and we have signed Billy Janniro, Bo Brhel and Adam Skornicki. Speedway has been booming in Sweden, but it's at the point now where it costs a lot of money to have good *riders. So what we are doing is concentrating on building up the backbone of the team, and we're building workshop facilities, so that in the future Valsarna will be inviting top riders to race for them. The lifestyle of a Grand Prix rider is off a plane and on a plane. They don't want to worry about preparing the bikes because they want good mechanics that can do this for them, so that they can just turn up and ride. This is crucial for them to produce good results and also to experience carefree travel. If all that can be done, then the top riders will want to come to Valsarna, because they will know that this is all available to them.*

This was what I put together for them during the winter of 2002/03 – and they didn't think of that. Even people like Rickardsson had never come up with this, and I flew over there and we drew up these plans. They were all worried because they had lost a couple of good riders, so what I did was turn a negative into a positive. I came up with a scheme which was similar to the club scene in Poland – only it was Westernised. Now everyone is happy and enthusiastic. Both in Sweden and Poland, there is not an outright owner of the club like there is in England. But I have a lot of respect for Swedish speedway, more so than in Poland, where the sport is open to corruption.

Of course, Australia has long been a popular venue for Europe-based racers, as they run their season when the European one is closed. Sam had already raced there, and had a successful time during the 1988/89 season. He won 7 out of the 10 events that he rode in; as well as winning the aforementioned meeting in Claremont, he also won at the famous 'Ekka' at Brisbane too.

Ivan Mauger was the only person who was running any meaningful solo racing in Australia and New Zealand. Solo speedway, as they call it over there, was struggling. I called him one time and asked him why he never asked me to go over there to race, because Simon Wigg was consistently going there. He told me that he didn't want to embarrass me because he couldn't afford me. He explained that this was because I wanted to take my family over there, and he couldn't afford the accommodation for us all.

Then I received a call from Trevor Harding, explaining that he wanted me to go over there and race in some of the events that he was promoting. I explained to him that I wanted to take my family, and I also wanted to race in other meetings, not just the ones that he was promoting. And he agreed to all that, and I had a very successful tour there in 1988/89.

Trevor tried very hard to get speedway going over there, but he was having the same kind of problems with his federation that we get with the AMA in America. But he would put his money where his mouth was. Although he would go in there with his show, he would explain to the promoters about the best way to get the people in. His view was: what was the point in having 3,000 people in there watching good racing, when if you spent some money on advertising, you could get 13,000 people – speculate to accumulate. That was what he tried to get across to people, and quite often he would have to spend his own money, not only to make the event a success, but also to show the local promoters how to do it. He took Russian and Swedish teams over there to tour and he showcased them. And when I went over there to race after my accident in 1989, he would showcase all the overseas riders. This was because he knew that it would benefit the Australian boys later in their careers.

I have a lot of admiration for Trevor, and it was his phone call when I was in hospital in 1989 that inspired me. But the arguments and the disagreements burnt him out and he gave it up. He knew what he was doing, and that what he was doing was right, but he wasn't getting the support. He was responsible for bringing Phil Crump out of retirement with his Kwiksnax Company, and he helped a lot of the Aussie boys.

Perhaps one of the most successful tournaments to run during the 1990s was a whole series that was promoted by the charismatic David Tapp. Tapp put together a Grand Prix-style tournament that was called the Australian Series 500 Masters. It ran for the first time in 1994/95, and it was actually in operation before the FIM World Championship Grand Prix series. The FIM were not happy that he had stolen their thunder, and, to make matters worse, he adopted the same format that the FIM intended to use. Furthermore, the Masters tournament was scheduled to run over ten meetings, compared with the FIM's six.

Sam Ermolenko was joined in the series by the then reigning World Champion, Tony Rickardsson, and Simon Wigg. The majority of the field were Australians, and they included some of the best Aussies like Leigh Adams, Craig Boyce and Jason Crump. The series was a big success, and it attracted a lot of publicity and gave the sport a much-needed boost in the southern hemisphere. Rickardsson won the series, with Sam finishing third overall, and he won the final round at Brisbane.

During its initial staging, the Australian riders failed to win a single round. The following year, however, Craig Boyce emerged victorious, despite a lot pressure from the runner-up, Sam Ermolenko, who won three rounds. This series, and the events staged by Harding, provided the platform for the Australians to build on, and they are now World Champions.

Just like any other successful international rider, Sam has ridden all over the world. As late as 2002, he was still considered to be a name that was big enough to be invited to ride in a special event in the Stade de France in Paris. This was because the Speedway Grand Prix had been attracting good television audiences.

Speedway seems to be breaking new ground through the coverage of the GP series, but it would be hard to find a 'speedway' nation that Sam has not raced in. The traditional countries in Europe continue to be the sport's mainstays, and Sam's entertaining style and approachable showmanship ensured that America were represented by a slice of sideways Americana. Through all the race wins, the travelling, the rivalries and the disagreements, they can all say that Sam Ermolenko entertained and brightened up all the venues where he appeared – both on and off the track.

Eight

THE SKY'S THE LIMIT

Sam was on the move again in 1997. This time he signed for Belle Vue, and he was joined in the team by three other Americans: the reigning World Champion, Billy Hamill, former US National Champion, Chris Manchester, and a newcomer, Charlie Venagas. With the hard-riding Aussie Jason Lyons and Kiwi Nathan Murray included in the team, they entered the newly-formed British Elite League as one of the favourites. But the team underachieved, and they ended the season with no silverware. The team boss, John Perrin, made several changes throughout the season, by bringing in former Aces Paul Thorp and Paul Smith. But this didn't help the Aces, and they finished well behind the leading sides that year.

It seemed like a good team, and I couldn't understand why it wasn't successful. Nathan Murray crashed during practice, and that didn't get us off to a good start. Chris Manchester had a big crash in Australia during the off-season and it affected him psychologically. He didn't really get over it, and this accident affected his season with Belle Vue. I think he recovered some of his nerve by riding at home, but only time would tell for sure if he came over to England to race again. Charlie was doing OK — especially at Belle Vue — but they shuffled the team around and he was dropped.

For a rider who was as professional as Sam, it was important that he was in the Grand Prix. The series was growing in popularity, and Ermolenko was one of the leading names who were not racing in the series — the other top stars that were conspicuous by their absence were Joe Screen and former world number three Craig Boyce. The Grand Prix Challenge was held at Wiener Neustadt in Austria, but there was some confusion over what format the series was going take in 1998. On the day, however, the top two finishers were guaranteed a place in the series, while third and fourth would start as reserve.

But the meeting was a disaster for Sam, who scored just 7 points and struggled on the slick surface — the meeting was won by Poland's Piotr Protasiewicz. Sam couldn't find the right set-up, and he admitted that a winter of contemplation was on the cards.

The following season, he returned to Wolverhampton, and it seemed that he was back on the pace when he won the American Final for the fourth time with a 15-point maximum. The Grand Prix series had changed its format to a more cut-throat knockout system, and had also increased the number of riders from 16 to 24 — but he still wasn't included in the competition and was on stand-by as reserve. However, he was approached to ride in the German Grand Prix as a replacement for one of the injured regulars, but he had to decline the invitation because the date clashed with the American Final.

He raced his way into the challenge, which was staged at Pardubice, in the Czech Republic, but suffered disappointment again when he was eliminated in heat 20 — along with Britain's future World Champion, Mark Loram. Ermolenko was also joined on the 'eliminated' list by another ex–World Champion, Gary Havelock. The American's mechanical preparation had not been good, and in an interview he gave to *Speedway Star* before leaving, he admitted that his build–up to the meeting had been 'screwed up by mechanical problems'.

However, he wasn't without a gold medal that year, as he was a non–riding reserve in America's successful World Team Cup victory in Vojens. The competition had been revamped yet again – this time it was a pairs format – and it was Billy Hamill and Greg Hancock who brought the gold home on the track. Sam may have been reserve for the team, but he was always a team player and he helped out as much as he could in the pits and contributed to his country's victory. As a result of this success, the three victorious riders received a letter of congratulations from the US President of the time, Bill Clinton.

Hull had joined the Elite League where former Wolverhampton team–mate, Graham Jones, was installed as the team manager. Therefore, he approached the American about racing for the Vikings and Sam agreed. It was the fourth time he had changed British clubs in four years.

The death of the AMA representative Bill Boyce left the British League-based riders in some confusion. Sam returned to ride in the American Final, although he had expected to be seeded to the Overseas Final – but he hadn't. He didn't make a big effort, and scored just 7 points on machinery that he used in the US when he won the National Championship in the early 1990s. He still believed that he would ride in the next round, as he didn't expect the Americans who qualified to make the expensive trip over to England. But they did, and Sam's Grand Prix dream was over for another year.

Back at Wolverhampton for 2000, Sam was in good form for his club. It appeared that when he won the Overseas Final for the fourth time with a blistering 15–point maximum at Poole, he was back in the groove to make a return to the Grand Prix series. But just as injuries had punctuated his career at exactly wrong the time, so it would prove again when he was an innocent victim in a clash with Ipswich's Jason Bunyan during a league match for Wolves.

I was looking after my team-mate, Adam Skornicki, during the race, and I slowed up for him. He was with me coming down the back straight, and I was team-riding with him. I was coming off the corner, but Adam didn't have the speed, so I was getting on the power when Jason just came straight underneath me and took me down. He is a balls-out kind of rider and doesn't really care, and he made a mistake and took me out. I hit my head and broke my wrist. I was unconscious for five or so minutes from the impact.

Everything had come together; I would have got into the Grand Prix series for certain that year if it wasn't for that accident. The Inter-Continental Final – which was the next round – was held at Holsted, Denmark, and I loved that track. Despite my broken wrist, I raced in the event and I was leading in each of my first three races, but I had to pull out because of my wrist injury – I couldn't hold on. I was so ambitious then, but another crash – which wasn't my fault – ended my hopes of a Grand Prix place.

The following season, Sam qualified for the Grand Prix Challenge again, which was held at Krsko, Slovenia, but once more his challenge ended painfully. He had won his first two races, and had also safely raced through an eliminator when he faced another elimination race, against Lukas Dryml, Nicki Pedersen and Andreas Jonsson. He was attempting a pass on the young Dane, Pedersen, when he crashed and hit the fence with his back. He was able to walk away, but it was later diagnosed that he had fractured his vertebrae. Not only were his World Championship hopes over, but so, too, was his season with Wolves.

While Sam was not able to participate in the Grand Prix series as a racer, his experience, knowledge and his ability to convey his opinions in an eloquent manner led to the beginnings of a blossoming career as a guest panellist and commentator for Sky and Channel Four television. It was also during this time that he began looking seriously for a career away from racing, and he slowly begun to build up an engine-tuning business.

I did the BBC television programme A Question of Sport *when I was the World Champion, and I was on the same team as Ryan Giggs and the former England Rugby Union captain Bill Beaumont. I also did some television work for Wireless TV when I was the Champion as well.*

One day, I received a telephone call from Philip Rising, and he asked me if I was interested in doing some television work. Apparently, someone had asked him about me because I was not in the Grand Prix, but I had recently been in it. I said that I was interested, and a man by the name of John Nolan called me and explained that he had been hired to produce a programme for Channel Four. The first thing I did was a photo shoot, which was for a commercial for the show, and then they sent through a contract and that was it.

The very first show I did for Sky was at Coventry for their Elite League match against Wolves on 13 May 1999 — it was Sky's first live broadcast of a league match. I knew Sky television was going to cover the sport, and Steve Brandon was the person who tied me into this arrangement. It was also Jonathan Green's first speedway show, and it was in the outside studio.

I was due to be at Coventry for 5.30 p.m., but I left my house a bit late because there were things that I had to finish for my racing. I had to stop on the way to visit the bathroom which put me further behind, but as I pulled off the A46, I could see the airship over the Brandon Stadium and I thought that was pretty cool. I had called Steve to let him know that I was running late, but I told him not to worry because I would be there. As I walked through the pits, I saw Steve and he pointed to the studio which was where we were going to do this outside broadcast. He said: 'Coming into turn one is where you have to be, Sam.'

I didn't waste any time, I walked straight over there to see what was going on. I saw Jonathan Green there, and he was practising his dramatic commentary in preparation for the event. At the time, James Easter was stood nearby, and Green was introducing himself, and he looked up and said: 'Hello there, and welcome to Sky Sports and Coventry Speedway, and you can see me and I'm right here,' and he's waving up at the airship in the sky and he went on: 'This is the view from the airship,' and the airship was focusing down on him. 'Here we are on the first turn, and right next to me is 1993 World Champion, Sam Ermolenko.' But I wasn't there.

He was looking at the clipboard while I was just sitting there, because there wasn't anyone around to introduce me, and he had these headphones on. So he began practising again, but I knew where my cue was to come in. He went through the opening part, and just as he said: 'And right next to me is Sam Ermolenko.' I jumped onto the stage and went: 'D'dah!' He took off his headphones and he gave me a quizzical look and said, 'Yeah?'

'I'm Sam Ermolenko,' I said.

'Oh hi, how are you doing?'

So that was how I introduced myself to Jonathan, and I was able to watch him practise. Then they supplied me with a microphone, the radio was put on my belt and the headphones. Jonathan and the director explained to me what was planned, and then the fans began to come in and the atmosphere began to build up. When the riders began to come out of the dressing rooms, Jonathan went through the rehearsal again. But I thought it was live, because no one had told me in my headphones that it was a rehearsal.

'I'm Jonathan Green and welcome to Coventry Speedway,' said Green. 'It's a beautiful night, the sky is blue and here we are on the first turn …'

Then he introduced me with something like, 'What do you think is going to happen?'

I started talking, but I was getting all tense as I was talking about the meeting ahead of us, then Jonathan said, 'Thanks, Sam, we'll go over now for the line-up of the riders.' And then he stopped. I thought to myself, 'Well okay, I'll just stand here then.' Then, all of a sudden, he started talking to somebody saying: 'Oh right. Yep, right, okay'.' Then I realised it wasn't live. I thought it was live and I was getting all nervous. Then he did it again, and I thought this must be live, and I tried to calm down a bit. I wasn't that nervous – it was the anticipation of what was coming up. But this time, I was a bit better. Then he did it again! I looked over at James Easter, and I mouthed to him, 'James, are we live?' And he shook his head.

'Oh, we're not live?'

'No, not yet.'

But the third time we were live. However, as I had just practised it twice thinking it was live, I felt quite comfortable. So when we did it for real, I was comfortable, and the show went well. It was Jonathan's first time covering a speedway meeting, so it broke the whole thing in. I was very honoured to do it, and that's how my involvement started. I have been able to do commentary and I've also been a studio guest, and I have enjoyed it. I would like to be the reporter running around the pits interviewing the riders – I think I would do a good job. I think I could explain things well to the public, and the riders respect me when we're on the track, and I could get into the middle of the action. I did it once at Oxford when Suzi Perry hadn't arrived, but I didn't do it as well as I would have liked. I have more experience now, and I think I would be a lot better.

Sam Ermolenko has contributed more to the sport than just being a very successful speedway rider. He has tried to raise the level of professionalism for himself and the sport in general. In 1994, as the reigning World Champion, he made attempts to improve safety, but his efforts were severely hampered by the lack of finance that were available to many of the British League clubs. His views and his mechanical knowledge were also sought when the BSPA wanted to bring in parts in a bid to restrict the costs. However, his opinions were not always welcomed, especially if he didn't agree with what was being proposed.

He was the first rider to build a professional team around him to improve his chances on the track, and it is this team element that was pioneered by him, which is so prevalent in today's Grand Prix series. Incidentally, he already had plans in place for a Grand Prix team of his own, which would have involved both Billy Hamill and Greg Hancock. The initial plans were drawn up during the close season of 1995/96, and included all the elements that are now considered to be accepted practice at a Grand Prix meeting.

During the research for this book, I have seen the original drawings for the corporate hospitality tents and pit area, the motor home, and he also had some established people within the sport to carry out the project. Among them was Nigel Tubb, who was responsible for the STP campaign that ran so successfully with the Moran brothers during the 1980s. But Hamill and Hancock drew up their own plans and formed Team Exide. However, as an acknowledgement to the forward-thinking Ermolenko, Exide's Tony Summers thanked Sam for the inspiration in the folders that announced the company's proposals.

As Benfield has now taken over the marketing of the sport's flagship series, the Speedway Grand Prix, Sam – in his role as a television commentator and rider – has been privy to all the debates and arguments behind the scenes. Therefore, he is well placed to see where the sport is heading in the coming years.

I have seen all the different of levels of speedway racing during my career, from the domestic racing in the USA, to the league racing in the different European countries, and the World Championship. In America, being involved with the Gaston & Dillon sponsorship, I saw how the politics came to play with Harry Oxley. But when I came over to England to race for Poole, it was a whole new ball game. That was a breath of fresh air because of the team racing.

But when I became more successful, the door opened up on the political side of the sport, and I was involved when we had to form a riders' association. When we had new secretaries involved, we had rewrite the policies. When I rode for Vojens, Ole Olsen told me some stories, and then I was involved in the riders' association for the Grand Prix. I saw Trevor Harding try his heart out and he had all the fights with his federation, but he had some success as well. But I believe that everything that has happened has been done with good intentions, and I also think that a majority of it has been for the good of the sport. There was nothing out there which I can say was really bad and it shouldn't have happened. In some ways, the decisions affected me and made things a bit difficult. But you do get yourself into a position within the sport to be able to comment in a certain way. Now I appear to be in that position again.

I've always been in favour of the Grand Prix, because it gives the rider more opportunities to practise what we used to do once a year – which was the World Final. Having the World Championship spread over different events will give us a true World Champion. But what I don't like about it is the qualification. When I started as a speedway rider, after the Christmas festivities were out of the way, you then had the New Year to celebrate. When it came to 12 o'clock and everyone welcomed in the New Year, I could say that I was going to be World Champion this year. Wouldn't it be great if you could go to bed after celebrating the New Year and wake up the next morning, knowing that you could be World Champion? When I started as a speedway rider, that was all the motivation I needed, and I worked hard to try and get that title. If I didn't succeed, come 1 January I could try again. But you can't do that now. And that was the appeal that the old fans say was so magical about the one-off World Finals. But you can't wake up on New Year's Day saying that you are going to be World Champion unless you are already in the Grand Prix – where is the motivation for the young riders? There should be a qualification system in place, even if you only have a long shot, then at least it's still a chance.

I've seen the development of the Grand Prix, and the conflict that has arisen between that competition and the league racing in Britain. But I have yet to see everyone pull together in one direction and go forward for the good of the sport. It would be great if there was one governing body that looked after everything, from the internationals down to the leagues. But that won't happen overnight. It's a tough world to be able to go out there and get the backing at all levels of the sport. The GPs have to spin off into an entity of their own to be able to go forward. Benfield Sports International is building up the show, and the television is helping a lot. Hopefully, just the exposure itself will keep the ball rolling for the sport as a whole.

If the sport became really big on a national scale in America, you could kiss goodbye to all the financial worries that it has at present. The sponsorship would be beyond anything that the sport has seen in the past.

The cost at home in America is tremendous. Now that there is a new European community, you will find that all sports will change. When I was teenager in the USA, when I used to sit down and watch the TV, during the commercial break we would always get: 'Hi, my name's Mr Jones, and I slipped and fell on sidewalk when I was walking to work, and I'm suing the city for $200 million. And you can do it too, with help of Smith Associates.' Twenty years later, it is now happening here. In America, if a promoter wants to run an event, the biggest problem is insurance and liability. You can't get a young rider to come through the ranks in America because of this. The medical expenses are so high that if someone gets hurt, someone is responsible for it. The only riders that are racing now are *professionals who have good sponsors, riders who have a business and can afford to do it, or a young kid who is insured by their parents' work. This is not the only problem, but it is one of the biggest, and it is only a matter of time before it happens here.*

Sam had a difficult 2002 season with Belle Vue. Just as he began getting it together and scoring some points, he crashed and broke a bone in his hand. His average dropped, but although he was now classed as a veteran, he went to Poole and defeated Tony Rickardsson. That was no minor accomplishment, as Tony won his fifth world title in 2002, and he didn't drop many points at Poole. It was a result that proved that there was still some racing left in Sudden Sam, and as he said to me after a meeting at Oxford that year: 'Not bad for an old guy.'

At the time of writing, he had signed to ride for Wolverhampton again. He always wanted to return to Monmore Green as this was his spiritual home. Just as Sheffield was to Shawn Moran, Cradley was to Hamill and Hancock, and Ipswich to John Cook, so is Wolves to Sam Ermolenko.

I really cannot say if 2003 will be my last year. It all depends on how I feel. If I am fit enough and I am enjoying it, then I could do another year. There are a lot of opportunities opening up for me, but I enjoy racing – that's why I keep coming back.

There are very few riders who have managed to capitalise on our sport. Ivan Mauger did well and, although he paid his dues in his early days, he was in it when the sport was booming. When you look at my career, I came in just when the sport was going down from a prosperous period during the 1970s, and now I'm going out just when speedway is starting to make its presence felt again. I think Hans Nielsen did well, because speedway was booming in Denmark at that time, and he was able to capitalise on that. But I have spent the last few years building up a business to give me something to go into when I finally hang up my steel shoe. It is because of these plans that I lost my focus as a racer a little bit, but I'm determined to get myself back in shape and have a really good season this year.

In the early 1990s, when Sam was experiencing his best seasons, the Wolves fans would greet their hero's race wins with the chant: 'Sam-O, Sam-O, Sam-O!' It would appear that this familiar chant of admiration will not be lost around Europe's speedway tracks just yet. Sam Ermolenko is an exceptional speedway talent, but as the sun slowly sets on a remarkable track career, what will be the next phase of his fascinating story? Sam Ermolenko, the television star? Or Sam Ermolenko, the successful team manager? As he often said during the creation of this book: 'That's another whole story.' Therefore, I suspect that this is not quite the end ...

STATISTICS

Club Honours

British League Championship winner with Wolves in 1991

Gold Cup winner with Wolverhampton in 1992

Premiership winner with Wolves in 1992

British League Averages finished top in 1991, 1992 and 1993, while riding for Wolves

Swedish Elite League Championship winner with Valsarna in 1999

Swedish League Averages finished top in 1992 and 1995, while riding for Vastervik

Polish League Championship winner with Bydgoszcz in 1992

Appearances for the USA: 63

Major Honours

World Champion 1993, third in 1985, 1987 and 1995

World Team Champion 1990, 1992, 1993 and 1998, runner-up in 1985, 1986 and 1988, third in 1987, 1991, 1995, 1999 and 2000

World Pairs Champion 1992 (with Greg Hancock and Ronnie Correy), runner-up in 1986 (with Kelly Moran) and 1993 (with Ronnie Correy and Greg Hancock), third in 1987 (with Kelly Moran) and 1988 (with Shawn Moran)

British Grand Prix runner-up in 1995

Danish Grand Prix runner-up in 1995

Division One Riders' Champion 1991 and 1994

Premier League Riders' Champion 1996

US National Champion 1993 and 1994

California State Champion 1988

American Champion 1987, 1988, 1989 and 1998

US Long-Track Champion 1987 and 1988

Overseas Champion 1986, 1989, 1994 and 2000

Californian Best Pairs Champion 1983 (with Robert Pfetzing)

US Masters Champion 1985

Ascot Track Champion 1985

Australian 500 Masters Series Runner-up in 1995/96, third in 1994/95

British League Record

Year/club	Matches	Rides	1sts	2nds	3rds	Unplaced	Pts	Bonus Pts	Total Pts	CMA	Maximums	
											Full	Paid
1983 Poole	4	16	0	5	5	6	15	2	17	4.25	–	–
1984 Poole	40	177	34	63	40	40	268	29	297	6.71	–	–
1986 Wolverhampton	39	184	9	77	16	12	407	40	447	9.72	3	8
1987 Wolverhampton	27	127	62	49	8	8	292	21	313	9.86	2	2
1988 Wolverhampton	41	226	108	76	28	14	504	27	531	9.40	2	3
1989 Wolverhampton	16	80	37	29	10	4	179	18	197	9.85	1	3
1990 Wolverhampton	24	133	58	38	19	18	269	26	295	8.87	–	3
1991 Wolverhampton	27	143	103	25	5	10	364	20	384	10.74	5	8
1992 Wolverhampton	28	151	99	31	9	12	368	19	387	10.25	5	4
1993 Wolverhampton	43	237	170	55	7	5	627	32	659	11.12	8	9
1994 Wolverhampton	31	166	100	38	12	16	388	20	408	9.83	6	3
1995 Wolverhampton	40	236	121	87	13	15	550	65	615	10.42	–	13
1996 Sheffield	19	104	57	32	9	6	244	9	253	9.73	1	2
1997 Belle Vue	38	202	91	57	23	31	410	18	428	8.48	1	1
1998 Wolverhampton	44	243	74	56	63	50	397	54	451	7.42	–	2
1999 Hull	35	180	76	53	27	24	361	26	387	8.60	–	3
2000 Wolverhampton	27	129	43	42	21	23	234	22	256	7.94	–	–
2001 Wolverhampton	32	157	45	43	46	23	267	21	288	7.34	–	–
2002 Belle Vue	27	128	25	34	38	31	181	23	204	6.38	–	–
Career Total	582	3,019	1,382	890	399	348	6,325	492	6,817	9.03	34	64

The above averages cover all official league and cup matches only. CMA (Calculated Match Average) is the total points, divided by the number of rides and multiplied by four.

World Individual Championship Record

World Final:

1985	Bradford, England	13 points	3rd
1986	Katowice, Poland	9 points	7th
1987	Amsterdam, Holland	24 points	3rd (held over 2 days)
1988	Vojens, Denmark	12 points	4th
1991	Gothenburg, Sweden	9 points	7th
1992	Wroclaw, Poland	7 points	8th
1993	Pocking, Germany	12 points	1st
1994	Vojens, Denmark	6 points	13th

Speedway Grand Prix (series held over six rounds):

1995	83 points	3rd
1996	52 points	9th

BIBLIOGRAPHY

The following periodicals and books were of great use for research and reference material during the preparation of this book:

Speedway Star, Speedway Mail, Speedway Now, Speedway Magazine, The Champion, Sam Ermolenko Testimonial Year 1994 Souvenir Paper (PCP, 1994) *Speedway and Short Track Racing* by Dave Lanning (Hamlyn, 1973), *The Complete History of the British League* edited by Peter Oakes (Front Page Books, 1991) *Shale Trail (Speedway Mail,* 1986), *Shale Trail 2 (Speedway Mail,* 1987) *Speedway Yearbook, 1990, 1991, 1993* edited by Peter Oakes (Front Page Books) *Loader's Speedway Annual, 1990, 1991, 1992* edited by Tony Loader (privately published), *1986 Speedway Yearbook* edited by Peter Oakes and Philip Rising (Sportsdata, 1986), *California Speedway '97* by Gary Roberts (Sherbourne Publishing, 1997).

INDEX

F

Faria, Mike, 78, 90, 104, 132, 160

Foster, John, 54, 58

FIM (the Federation of International Motorcycling), 120, 130, 136, 143, 144, 157, 168, 177, 183, 193–4, 199, 215

G

Gaston, Al, 72-7, 224

Gdansk Speedway, 212

Godden, Don, 118-9, 134, 142

Gollagher, Danny, 132, 162, 164, 168–70, 175, 187

Gollob, Tomasz, 171, 173, 203, 205-8, 210, 211

Gollob, Papa (Wladyslaw), 203, 206–9, 211-2

Gollob, Jacek, 205

Gothenburg, Sweden, 156, 169, 232

Green, Jonathan, 221-2

Green, Randy, 128, 132, 134

Gundersen, Erik, 18, 24, 84, 86, 88, 93, 94, 97-8, 99, 100-3, 107, 111–2, 114, 117, 120-1, 127-8, 129, 133, 148, 153, 168

Gustafsson, Henka, 20-1, 168, 173, 194

H

Hackney Speedway, 24, 123-4, 126, 128, 132-3, 191

Hamill, Billy, 148, 150, 152-3, 158, 160, 165-7, 171, 178, 185, 195, 199, 210, 217, 219, 223, 226

Hancock, Greg, 24, 158, 160, 164-5, 168, 178, 185, 191, 195, 196, 207, 210, 219, 223, 226, 230

Handberg, Gert, 161, 165

Harding, Trevor, 7, 22, 25, 139-40, 214, 216, 224

Hartke, Bill, 65

Havelock, Gary, 163-4, 166, 170-1, 173, 178, 186, 219

Hedge, Chris, 63, 69-70

Henry, Ivan, 119, 130-1, 134

Heffernan, Paul, 78, 81, 104

Hughes, Morgan, 188, 190

Hull Speedway, 193, 219

I

Indian Dunes, the, 55, 61-2. 64, 69-70

Ipswich Speedway, 86, 103, 116, 119, 123, 155-6, 158, 186, 199, 220, 226

J

Jones, Graham, 135, 150, 159-60, 180, 189-90, 219

Jonsson, Per, 129, 157-8, 161, 163, 168, 170-1, 178, 190, 201, 220

K

Karger, Brian, 119, 178, 198

Karlsson, Mikael, 159, 186, 198, 213